BALANCING

JUVENILE

JUSTICE

BALANCING

JUVENILE

JUSTICE

Susan Guarino-Ghezzi

and

Edward J. Loughran

TRANSACTION PUBLISHERS
New Brunswick (U.S.A.) and London (U.K.)

First paperback edition 1998
Copyright © 1996 by Transaction Publishers,
New Brunswick, New Jersey 08903.

This book is printed on acid-free paper that meets the American National Standard for Permanence of Paper for Printed Library Materials.

Library of Congress Catalog Number: 95-18852
ISBN: 1-56000-213-1 (cloth); 0-7658-0453-0 (paper)
Printed in the United States of America

Library of Congress Cataloging-in-Publication Data

Guarino-Ghezzi, Susan.
  Balancing juvenile justice / Susan Guarino-Ghezzi and Edward L. Loughran.
    p. cm.
  Includes bibliographical references and index.
  ISBN 1-56000-213-1 (alk. paper)
  1. Juvenile justice, Administration of—United States. 2. Juvenile corrections—United States. I. Loughran, Edward L. II. Title.
HV9104.G83   1995
364.3'6'0973—dc20   95-18852
                                                                                          CIP

Contents

Preface

An August 1994 editorial in *The New York Times,* noting that juveniles are the fastest-growing segment of persons arrested in the United States, and that the number of juveniles arrested for violent crimes has nearly quadrupled since 1965, placed the blame on "the lenient juvenile justice system introduced in most states during the 1960s. The message that dysfunctional system sends to violence-prone young people is that actions don't have consequences" (*New York Times,* 18 August 1994). Similarly, a *Wall Street Journal* editorial published in the fall of 1993 reported that "[w]hen asked to name a cause for the increase in youth violence, law enforcement officials largely single out the nation's system of so-called juvenile justice. Set up some 30 years ago to protect immature kids who might get arrested for truancy, shoplifting or joy riding, it is ill equipped to cope with the violent children of the 1990s who are robbing, raping and murdering" (*Wall Street Journal,* 28 September 1993).

In reality, the American system of juvenile justice began nearly a century ago based on the English chancery court, which handled the estates of orphaned children, in an effort to protect children whose parents were unable, unwilling, or simply ineffective as parents to control the behavior of their offspring. Sadly, the situation of youths in juvenile court has not improved from 100 years ago—family issues, poverty and community crime problems overshadow their lives. Only today, the dangers of being young in the United States are much greater. The Centers for Disease Control reported recently that the homicide rate among young men fifteen to nineteen years old more than doubled between 1985 and 1991, and that after accidents, homicide is ranked as the number two cause of death among males in that age group.

Those who are searching for a solution to the juvenile crime problem are not going to find it in most juvenile justice systems of the United States. That is because most juvenile justice systems, in reality, do not function as systems. Their components—police, courts, correctional programs, legislation, constitutional oversight—lack unity of purpose. Competition is more typical than cooperation. Inertia is a common characteristic because the diverse philosophies of stakeholders within and outside of the core agencies paralyze those who run the system. Various agencies working at cross-purposes inevitably render the "system" agonizingly complicated and ineffective.

With vision and cautious optimism, we liken a balanced model in juvenile justice to an effective family model in which punishments and rewards for children satisfy multiple purposes—an ideal taken for granted in most middle-class families. The need for a balanced model that incorporates multiple purposes was captured in a *Time Magazine* article that quoted Los Angeles County District Attorney Gil Garcetti on the subject of juvenile justice: "We need to throw out our entire juvenile justice system. . . . We should replace it with one that both protects society from violent juvenile criminals and efficiently rehabilitates youths who can be saved—and can differentiate between the two" (Lacayo 1994). The same article quoted political scientist James Q. Wilson's sobering observation of the juvenile justice system that, "[n]obody has tracked the process carefully enough to find out who is good at it, in what states and by what means."

Any single interest group espousing a particular philosophy—retribution, deterrence, accountability, rehabilitation, public safety, due process rights for offenders, victims' rights, protection of offenders from conditions of confinement—can easily point to cases that illustrate their cause with drama and conviction. Indeed, single cases make up the "raw materials" of the system. However, single cases, if handled with philosophical bias while diminishing the importance of other interests, invite politicization. Single cases and single issues in an all-too-familiar point-counterpoint format have become grist for election campaigns and the talk show mill, but have shed very little light on what needs to be done.

The reason we wrote this book is to offer an approach for juvenile justice that balances divergent philosophies. We examine states, counties, and local jurisdictions to show how balance is achieved by providing organizational structures that satisfy competing stakeholders.

We also examine reform efforts throughout the United States in which agencies have struggled to match the diversity of youth characteristics with an equal diversity of policies and programs. Typically, in jurisdictions accustomed to stereotypes, the acknowledgment that diversity exists among youthful offenders requires a fundamental shift in philosophy.

We thank the many employees and volunteers who work in "the trenches" of juvenile justice agencies for sharing their experiences with us over the years. We hope that this book can demonstrate some measure of the challenges that they have faced.

Finally, we appreciate the commentary of our colleagues and several anonymous reviewers who read and critiqued early versions of our manuscript. We offer special thanks to Kim Godfrey for her assistance.

1

Trends in Philosophy and Politics

The Context of Juvenile Justice

Juvenile offenders are caught in a multi-causal and largely impenetrable web of economic, community, and family problems. Theories of juvenile crime have focused on many of these problems, alone or in combination. Lawrence Friedman, in his 1993 book *Crime and Punishment in American History,* enumerates the many "wars on crime" which were lost in this country during the last three-and-a-half centuries. Mr. Friedman's analysis underscores the conclusion that many observers have reached: There is very little that the criminal justice system can do about the causes of crime because the system cannot compete with deeply rooted and complex cultural causes of crime in the United States. As a result, the system is reactive, rather than preventive.

Indeed, reacting to crime has become a political opportunity for governors and legislators, and a marketing opportunity for the mass media. Critics have found just cause for reaction in the recent increase in violent juvenile crime—a dramatic increase to be sure when one looks at juvenile crime across the years, but still confined to a small percentage (10 to 15 percent) of all crimes committed each year—which criminologist Howard Snyder has referred to as the tyranny of the small number. Violent crime among juveniles rose 47 percent between 1988 and 1992, and the juvenile murder rate similarly climbed 51 percent during that period. This increase in violence among a relatively small number of juveniles has steered attention away from important developments in juvenile justice during the last twenty years, including privatized community-based programs, a continuum of pro-

1

grams—many of which are highly specialized—available to fit a range of supervision and treatment needs of youths, and balanced decision models to classify offenders into appropriate placements.

The officials and administrators who run even the most well regarded juvenile detention and correctional systems are feeling the impact of a negative reaction to the juvenile justice system, the consequences of which are not usually considered. The political importance of the growing presence of the "violent few," as Donna Hamparian and her colleagues referred to violent juvenile offenders in 1978, has recently been forced onto correctional agencies in the following ways, with unanticipated results:

- Automatic waiver to adult court by lowering the age to thirteen (Georgia) or fourteen (Colorado) for a catalogue of offenses, including mostly violent crimes, but certain property offenses as well. Youths receive a hearing in court to determine if their case should be heard in the juvenile or adult sector. This type of procedural reaction is not new. New York State led the way for adult trials of violent juveniles in 1978 after Willie Bosket killed two poor laborers coming home on the subway late one night and then boasted to the media that the state could do nothing to him because he was only fourteen years old. The state of Florida followed with the most sweeping adult trial mechanism in the nation— the state's attorney decides whether to try youths in juvenile or adult court for certain misdemeanors and all felonies, thereby bypassing the need for a waiver hearing. Many believe that the results of this law have been disastrous: Florida waives thousands of youths a year, only one-third of whom serve any time in the adult system.
- Overcrowding the juvenile system. If there is a single factor which will ultimately destroy an effective juvenile detention or correctional system, it is the overcrowding of programs so that they become dangerous environments for youths, provoking more violent behavior and failing to provide safe opportunities for positive behavioral change. In 1987, 36 percent of confined juveniles were in facilities whose populations exceeded their reported design capacity. By 1991 that increased to 47 percent. Dale Parent, who studied patterns of confinement of 65,000 juveniles in nearly 1,000 juvenile corrections and detention facilities throughout the United States, found that one-third of confined juveniles were in living units with 26 or more juveniles, one-third slept in rooms that were smaller than required by nationally recognized standards, and nearly half of confined juveniles were in facilities whose populations exceeded their reported design capacity. In total, almost three-fourths were in facilities that were crowded in some way (Parent 1994).

Furthermore, resident and staff injury rates were higher in crowded facilities, and higher juvenile-on-juvenile injury rates were associated with large dormitories. Ten percent of confined juveniles were in facilities where at least 8 percent of the residents were injured (and whose injuries were known to staff and were reported) by other residents during a thirty-day time frame. One percent of juveniles were in facilities where 17 percent or more of staff were injured during that period. Injury rates for staff and residents alike were higher in facilities where living units were locked twenty-four hours a day, despite a heavy emphasis on security in such units. The percentage of juveniles convicted for violent crimes was not related to injury rates, which supports the theory that violence in facilities in environmentally induced, rather than caused solely by characteristics of the residents.

- Use of juvenile facilities to support the adult system. Dealing with the severely strained adult court system has forced backlogs and overcrowding problems onto juvenile detention facilities, where juveniles are held pending the outcome of their adult trials, and where such youths are generally co-mingled with less serious youths who are being processed as juveniles. Juvenile justice, which was intended to offer some protection and vigilance over youths, has itself become a detrimental experience that often reproduces youths' defiance against authority. During the summer of 1993 in the aftermath of two particularly heinous crimes by juveniles in North Carolina and Florida—two graduates of North Carolina's juvenile system robbed and killed basketball star Michael Jordan's father, and two teenagers were arrested for the murder of a British tourist in south Florida—a *Wall Street Journal* editorial soundly condemned the juvenile system, using police officials as its authority and source of discontent: *"When asked to name a cause for the increase in youth violence, law enforcement officials largely single out the nation's system of so-called juvenile justice.* Set up 30 years ago to protect immature kids who might get arrested for truancy, shoplifting or joy riding, it is ill equipped to cope with the violent children of the 1990s who are robbing, raping and murdering" (emphasis added).

As reckless as the above statement is in attempting to equate reaction with causation, it is hard to refute the criticism when so many of the juvenile correctional systems around the country are anything but systems, and very few even look systematic or rational in the handling of juvenile offenders. Given the environmental obstacles that youths often face, including increasingly violent subcultures and early childhood traumas caused by abuse, neglect, and exposure to violent communities, correctional officials should balance the competing concerns of protecting youths, on the one hand, with controlling youths, on the other. What is needed is a comprehensive discussion of the primary considerations that policymakers *should* use in striking a balance between holding youths accountable for their past behavior, and providing services and opportunities to change their environments so that future behaviors will be guided by constructive, rather than destructive, forces.

In order to meet the challenges of social problems, youth violence, and elite indifference to conditions in inner cities, programs for juvenile offenders must be creative, flexible, oriented toward community reintegration efforts, accountable for decisions, and, perhaps most importantly, cognizant to public safety risks. As correctional organizations evolve, decision makers become more aware of the differences among youthful offenders and the need for specialized programs and policies to fit characteristics of the offense and the offender. We believe that these concerns will translate into several emerging and expanding trends for juvenile justice into the twenty-first century:

1. expansion of the range of surveillance programs to monitor juvenile offenders
2. expansion of the range of service programs to provide skill-building and other opportunities to youths
3. private sector involvement in designing and managing programs
4. rational decision structures for making accountable placement decisions
5. programmatic emphasis on preparing youths for successful reintegration.

In considering the future of juvenile justice, we need to examine the past. In defining what has constituted "juvenile justice" up to this point, there is a series of answers. This is because, historically, there have been a number of politically ideological groups that have not acknowledged the challenge of balancing support with control, and have devised their own ideologically shaped solutions. The dominant views on the state's role vis-à-vis juvenile offenders have changed from one time period to another, originating with the progressive or liberal view, which survived the longest period from roughly the turn of the century into the 1960s; the libertarian view, which challenged the liberal view and lasted until the late 1970s; the conservative view, which emerged in the late 1970s and persisted through the 1980s; and the fundamentalist view, which co-existed with the conservatives and dominated during the Reagan administration.

The history of juvenile justice reflects the diversity and competition among political interest groups, much as it exists in many other sectors of our society. A thorough analysis of juvenile justice must be able to draw insight from various perspectives on handling juvenile offenders. The lessons of history can be used to help develop an approach that is consistent with recent and foreseeable trends in communities, families, the economy, government, politics, and juvenile offenders themselves.

The Liberal View

Historically, the liberal or "progressive" view of the state as protector of juveniles shaped the early philosophy of separate treatment of juvenile offenders in juvenile courts and correctional placements. Policies to control juvenile offenders in the United States were formulated a century ago as a philosophy that is separate and distinct from "adult justice." Structurally, there are many important and distinct characteristics of an autonomous juvenile justice system. Separate institutional facilities for juveniles were first created in 1848 (in Massachusetts), and a separate juvenile court was first founded in Cook County, Illinois, in 1899. The process began with a separate juvenile court that operated under a different mandate than the adult court, with flexible intake and diversion provisions, and with different laws and vocabularies that defined the legal rights of youths. The *parens patriae* philosophy of the juvenile court was best articulated in the words of Judge Julian Mack in 1909, when thirty states had just established separate courts for juveniles. Mack noted that before the inception of the juvenile court, the aim of punishment for juvenile offenders was no different than punishment for adults—retribution for wrongdoing, or as a deterrence to others (Mack 1909). Punishment was meted out in proportion to the degree of wrongdoing, rather than in a manner intended to improve the offender. Judge Mack (Mack 1909: 107) described punishment that was consistent with progressive thinking:

> Why is it not just and proper to treat these juvenile offenders, as we deal with the neglected children, as a wise and merciful father handles his own child whose errors are not discovered by the authorities? Why is it not the duty of the state, instead of asking merely whether a boy or girl has committed a specific offense, to find out what he is, physically, mentally, morally, and then if it learns that he is treading the path that leads to criminality, to take him in charge, not so much to punish as to reform, not to degrade but to uplift, not to crush but to develop, not to make him a criminal but a worthy citizen.

At the time of the juvenile court's inception around the turn of the century, the court's Progressive creators envisioned a process for handling juvenile offenders that would be informal, highly flexible, child-centered, and scientific. The Progressives' ideas were drawn from a variety of sources that were part of larger societal changes that were taking place at that time. The American culture was changing rapidly as a result of urbanization, industrialization, immigration, and shifting roles within the family. Children were being looked at differently, as was the whole concept of childhood and family. Rather than viewing children as laborers, as many were in rural settings during the 1800s, children during the Progressive era were regarded as "corruptible innocents" who needed protection from the state. Progressive reformers sought scientific solutions to deviant behavior that identified the causes and prescribed the cures. These early rehabilitative efforts demanded discretionary decision-making so that cases could be handled on an individualized basis, with the focus on the child rather than the offense (Feld 1987).

The rehabilitative model allowed for provision of services to juveniles that de-emphasized their offenses and highlighted their treatment needs. The benevolent intention (or guise) of the juvenile court enabled the state to broaden its definition of deviant behavior by means of the "status offense" category, that included smoking, sexuality, truancy, immorality, stubbornness, vagrancy, or living a wayward, idol, and dissolute life (Feld 1987). Many of the children charged with status offenses were in fact homeless, parentless, or economically disadvantaged, and were placed into institutions for indeterminate periods of time on the basis of "expert" judgments about the needs of the child. One legacy of this era is that status offenders who were prosecuted in juvenile court were routinely institutionalized until the federal government intervened in 1974.

In addition to the status offense category, which applies only to minors, the creation of the juvenile court established other differences between juvenile and adult court proceedings. To protect the youth's privacy, most sessions are closed to the public, whereas adult courts allow the public to observe, and records are generally confidential. In juvenile court, there are "hearings" rather than trials, youths are "adjudicated delinquent" rather than found guilty of a particular offense, and the disposition or sentencing options are, in theory, more reforming than are those for adults. The emphasis on reforming juveniles' behavior requires a more detailed assessment of youths and their backgrounds than what is done for adults, and more specialized programs that are tailored to the youth's individual needs. Juvenile offenders are placed into programs that purport to assess and respond to the special characteristics of youths. Such programs are provided or overseen by juvenile correctional agencies at the state or county level. Generally, as with adults, the least serious offenders are maintained at the county level, where they are given a disposition of probation that is supervised by court probation departments, although county correctional programs are becoming more diverse and creative in a few jurisdictions, such as Los Angeles County and Allegheny County, Pennsylvania.

The juvenile court has two broad options with serious offenders. Offenders charged with violent felonies can be transferred to adult court, which in some states is also called certification, bindover, or waiver, for an adult trial and sentence. Alternatively, the juvenile court has the option in most states to dispose of these cases itself, just as it has with any less serious cases, by "committing" the youth to state jurisdiction. In many states, this means that the judge directly sentences a youth to a particular institution. In a growing number of states, however, the judge has more limited control and merely sentences the youth to the state correctional agency, which then determines the placement. If the youth does indeed remain under control of juvenile corrections, as opposed to being convicted and sentenced as an adult offender, there is a presumption that rehabilitative efforts will be made. Traditional efforts include psychological treatment as well as skill building in educational and vocational areas. More recent rehabilitative efforts for juveniles include substance abuse counseling, violence and gang prevention, AIDS education, specialized programs for juvenile sex offenders, and pre-natal health care for pregnant girls.

Although rehabilitation has been widely debated as an appropriate goal for seriously violent juvenile offenders, it is generally believed to be appropriate for the majority of nonviolent juveniles due to their relative receptiveness to outside influences on their behavior, both positive as well as negative. In terms of their psychological and social development, most experts believe that adolescents are clearly different from adults, even though their offense behaviors may make them appear otherwise. The motivations for their offenses are often situational or group-induced. Commonly, juvenile offenders have experienced a series of negative encounters with authority figures as the result, for example, of learning problems in school or parental abuse at home. Correctional practitioners in the field of juvenile corrections hope that their interventions will have a positive and lasting impact on the young, developing individuals with whom they work.

Many psychological perspectives on adolescent behavior have supported the policy of separating and treating youths differently from adults. Psychological research on cognitive and moral development offers an explanation for the observed differences in behavior between juveniles and adults. The focus is on children's and adolescents' ability to make choices and form judgments. The Swiss psychologist Jean Piaget (1948) was one of the first to propose that morality develops in a series of steps or stages, and that the development of morality is based on the intellectual or cognitive ability of the individual along with the quality of his or her social environment.

Other perspectives assume that aggression has a physiological base, and point to biochemical factors (Brown and Goodwin 1984) or neurological factors (Cornwall et al. 1984; Wilson and Herrnstein 1985). Still others point to international comparative evidence of cultural influences on adolescent aggression (Gadpaille 1984). Sociological theories of adolescent offense behavior have focused on peer group interaction (Sutherland and Cressey 1966); weakened bonds to family, school, and other institutions (Hirschi 1969; Reckless 1962); lower-class subcultural values (Miller 1958; Cohen and Short 1958; Sykes and Matza 1957); gaps between goals and means (Merton 1968); unavailability of legitimate opportunities (Cloward and Ohlin 1960); and the self-fulfilling prophecy of labeling youths as offenders (Lemert 1972).

The role of the federal government in juvenile delinquency issues began with the establishment of the United States Children's Bureau in 1912, which collected data on juvenile court cases and distributed reports on juvenile justice topics. However, the federal government did not set a comprehensive policy agenda for juvenile justice until the Kennedy and Johnson administrations. In the 1960s, those administrations funded large-scale delinquency prevention programs in inner cities, such as Mobilization for Youth, that were designed to expand employment opportunities for youths in their communities. Those programs were a reaction to sharp increases in youth crime, and were shaped, in part, by Richard Cloward and Lloyd Ohlin's differential opportunity theory (1960). In 1967, President Johnson's Commission on Law Enforcement and the Administration of Justice organized a comprehensive plan based on policies of diversion and deinstitutionalization. Those policies were given justification by labeling theory, which warned of the counterproductive effects of official intervention.

In their analysis of the different perspectives noted above, in comparing juveniles to adults, Shireman and Reamer observed the following generalities:

> 1. Juveniles characteristically have less capacity than do adults to reckon the results and costs to themselves or to others of their own behavior . . .
> 2. Childhood and youth are periods of experimentation, of ambivalence, of trying out and discarding various . . . self-concepts and values . . .
> 3. Normal adolescent social development includes a considerable component of establishing one's identity as a self separate from adults and, most especially, separate from dependence upon and control by parents and those associated with parents . . .
> 4. The offense behaviors of juveniles are more frequently and more evidently than those of adults immediate outgrowths of family, community, and society breakdown. The most hurtful youngster is generally the one who has been most hurt. Thus, to the concept of individual guilt must be added that of a widely shared, societal guilt. Intervention in the course of the juvenile's misbehavior will often necessitate countering the damage being done to him. (Shireman and Reamer 1986: 55–56).

Consistent with the assumption that there are important characteristics that distinguish youths from adults, there are many legal distinctions between minors and adults that impose legal disabilities on juveniles for their own protection. For example, a 1972 Indiana appeals court reversed a murder conviction of a seventeen-year-old juvenile who had voluntarily waived his right to an attorney (*Lewis v. State,* 1972). The court ruled that because his confession was taken by police before the youth had an opportunity to consult with his parents, the youth's decision to waive his right to avoid self-incrimination did not meet the standard of being voluntary, knowing and intelligent. In its ruling, the court explained that applying the waiver standard differently to juveniles was an accepted legal principle, similar to other legal differences between adults and minors, including executing a binding contract, conveying real property, marrying, purchasing alcoholic beverages, and donating blood.

Despite the rehabilitative paradigm's symbolic goal to protect youths, it remains as true today as it has during the past century that the program of choice for juvenile offenders is the institution. Many of the institutions that were constructed at the turn of the century are still in use today, and some institutions house over 500 juvenile offenders. Many states have not ventured beyond the institutional setting to test other alternatives, although there is no research that ties the rehabilitative model to the institution, and there is considerable evidence that institutions have seriously harmful effects. The negative impact of institutions has been documented regarding incarcerated male and female adult offenders, institutionalized mental patients, and juvenile offenders placed in institutions, many of which are euphemistically referred to as "reform schools" or "training schools."

The Libertarian Perspective

The libertarian perspective was the first challenge to the rehabilitative model in juvenile justice. The libertarian position embodied two main arguments: correctional intervention should be as "least restrictive" and "non-interventionist" as possible, which means that youths should be removed from institutions, and the juvenile court should restore constitutional rights to youths that are available to adults. As Judge Julian Mack foresaw as early as 1909, the appeal of institutions for juvenile offenders in spite of progressive rehabilitative goals contained the seeds of its own destruction. Judge Mack observed that over-incarceration was:

> a real truth, and one which, in the enthusiastic progress of the juvenile-court movement, is in danger of being overlooked. If a child must be taken away from its home, . . . a real school, not a prison in disguise, must be provided . . . . This cannot be done in one great building, with a single dormitory for all of the two or three or four hundred or more children, in which there will be no possibility of classification along the lines of age or degrees of delinquency, in which there will be no individualized attention. (Mack 1909: 114)

Removal of Juveniles from Institutions

In 1974, by overwhelming majorities in both the House and Senate, Congress passed the Juvenile Justice and Delinquency Prevention (JJDP) Act following a string of class-action lawsuits attacking conditions under which juveniles were confined. In 1970, *Pena v. New York State Department of Social Services* sought "relief for children subject to solitary confinement, to the binding or hand-cuffing of their hands and feet, and to the intramuscular use of thorazine or other tranquilizing drugs." In 1972, in Indiana, *Nelson v. Heyne* challenged "supervised beatings, indiscriminate use of tranquilizing drugs without competent medical supervision, solitary confinement without procedural protections, mail censorship, and religious discrimination." In 1973, the federal court decided *Morales v. Turman* against the Texas Youth Council (described in Schwartz 1989: 5):

> The court found that the defendant's practices of physical abuse, use of tear gas, solitary confinement without limitation, imposed silence, and "make work" details violated the Eighth Amendment prohibition against cruel and unusual punishment; that defendants' practices of mail censorship and use of English only violated the First Amendment freedom of expression provisions; that its transfers of juveniles to maximum-security institutions without procedural protections or hearings violated the Fourteenth Amendment due process guarantee; that racial segregation violated the Constitution; and that practices such as homosexual segregation, denial of contact with family and friends, withholding of case work, psychological and other services from children in solitary confinement, lack of grievance procedures, less than twenty-four hour nurse availability, and poor personnel screening and training violated the constitutional right to treatment.

One focus of the JJDP Act concerned the removal of youths from adult jails. In 1973 an estimated 100,000 juveniles were held in adult jails or police lock-ups per year to await court action. Despite recommended standards, and often contrary to state laws, many of those juveniles were not physically separated from adults, but were often forced to share "drunk tanks" with intoxicated and aggressive adult detainees. Reports of suicide, rape, and attacks on youth in adult jails and sheriffs' vans were not uncommon (U.S. Congress, Senate, 1973). During the early 1970s, many of the youths held in confinement were charged only with status offenses, and some were not charged with any offense, but were actually abused or neglected children (Sarri 1974).

Responding to those problems, U.S. Senator Birch Bayh headed the Senate Subcommittee to Investigate Juvenile Delinquency, and drafted the Juvenile Justice and Delinquency Prevention Act of 1973. The draft version called for no juveniles to be held in adult jails under any circumstance. However, the final version of the JJDP Act was a compromise position that allowed juveniles to be confined in jails so long as they were kept separate from adult prisoners. On the one hand, the compromise acknowledged the need to confine certain juvenile offenders prior to court action, and recognized the lack of secure alternatives to adult jails, particularly in rural areas. On the other hand, the compromise permitted increasing numbers of youths to be confined in adult jails. An amendment to the Act in 1980 reinforced the need to remove juveniles from adult jails, but the impact was slow and uneven (Schwartz 1989). Indeed, one-day counts of juveniles in adult jails increased from 1,611 nationwide in 1978 to 1,736 in 1983 (Bureau of Justice Statistics 1982, 1984).

The JJDP Act also required that the newly created Office of Juvenile Justice and Delinquency Prevention coordinate all federal delinquency prevention and control efforts and give leadership and support for research, provide training for juvenile justice professionals, and give technical assistance to state and local policymakers and practitioners. The Act also encouraged the states to develop community-based alternatives to institutions for juvenile offenders. Financial incentives provided the states with seed money to diversify programming, particularly for nonviolent and nondangerous offenders. Labeling theory provided an intellectual basis for recommending the least restrictive alternatives in order to avoid permanently stigmatizing youths. At the same time, treatment experts questioned whether any treatment programs had consistent positive effects (Martinson 1974). As one commentator observed (Hackler 1978):

> Is [delinquency] the price we pay for a creative and individualistic society? Those who are treatment-oriented will resist such a philosophy. Perhaps it is necessary to accept that random delinquency is preferable to organizing these deviants for the purpose of social improvement. . . . The possibility that the cure could be worse than the disease is relevant to a balanced perspective on delinquency.

Although the JJDP Act represented an achievement by libertarian child advocates, many juvenile offenders still remained confined in adult jails and detention centers for long periods of time awaiting trial (Schwartz 1989). Other libertarian efforts on behalf of children's rights were made in the arena of juvenile court procedure. The libertarians argued, and the Supreme Court later agreed, that the legal "protections" of the Progressive era, specifically the informality of court procedure, were insufficient in that they did not afford juveniles the rights that are guaranteed under the Constitution. Indeed, some observers alleged that the so-called Progressive era "protections" were introduced not to serve the interests of children in court, but to mask the role of capitalism in fracturing the American family (Platt 1977) by softening the image of institutionalized youths whose primary characteristic was growing up in poverty.

The Progressive era juvenile court rested on the belief that the needs of juvenile offenders could be addressed through "rehabilitation" by whatever means were employed, even long-term institutionalization for status offenders, dependent or neglected youths. Since institutionalization was in the best interests of the youths, their reasoning went, decisions to institutionalize juveniles did not need to adhere to rigorous criteria or procedures. It was not until the so-called "due process revolution" of the 1960s and 1970s (the key Supreme Court decisions concerning juveniles were *Kent, Gault, Winship, McKeiver,* and *Breed*) that discretionary decision making by the juvenile court was seriously curtailed. The *Kent* decision (*Kent v. United States,* 383 U.S. 541), delivered in 1966, was the first to suggest that constitutional principles might be applicable to juvenile court procedures. *In re Gault* (387 U.S. 1, 1967) granted children the rights to written notice of charges, time to prepare a defense, a right to counsel, a right to appointed counsel if indigent, the right under the Fifth Amendment not to incriminate themselves, and the right to confront and cross-examine any complainants and witnesses. The decision seemed to acknowledge that the *parens patriae* doctrine had not lived up to its expectations, and that the consequences to juveniles of being incarcerated in an institution or training school were punitive in nature.

In re Winship (397 U.S. 358, 1970) expanded juveniles' rights by increasing the standard of proof necessary to sustain a finding of delinquency from a "preponderance of the evidence" to "proof beyond a reasonable doubt." *McKeiver v. Pennsylvania* (403 U.S. 528, 535, 1971) examined the juvenile's right to a jury trial. Unlike the pattern of previous decisions, the Supreme Court rejected the claim that juveniles had the same rights as adults to trial by jury, ruling that jury trials were permissible but not required. In its decision, the Court cited jury costs, time consumption, protection of juveniles' confidentiality and rights to privacy, the problem of determining a jury of peers, and its interest in discouraging plea bargaining from the juvenile court process. Finally, *Breed v. Jones* (421, U.S. 519, 1975) provided to juveniles the same protection against double jeopardy as adults, which meant that juveniles could not be tried as juveniles and then retried as adults. As a result of the due process revolution, juveniles in court now have legal rights that run parallel to adults in most areas of the law, although juvenile courts operate with less formality.

A paradigm shift—from libertarian to conservative—occurred in the mid-1970s, as the news media headlined a frightening increase in violent juvenile crime. Neither least restrictive alternatives nor due process for offenders addressed the criminal justice system's most compelling political problem—controlling crime. Both policies omitted any consideration of offenders' moral wrongdoing, holding offenders accountable for their offenses, or reducing dangers to public safety, what Braithwaite (1989: 156) called the "symbolic emptiness" of libertarian policy. Thus, civil libertarians not only failed to offer a solution to crime on the streets, but, by counseling tolerance and acceptance of offenders they planted the seeds for a paradigm shift toward conservative "get tough" policies that tried to symbolize increased accountability for convicted offenders and enhanced public safety.

The Conservative View

Plagued by peaking rates of juvenile crime in the mid-1970s, courts began confining juveniles to institutional settings in record numbers (Schwartz 1989). The pattern of heavy confinement continued into the 1980s, despite a declining trend in juvenile crime until 1985. Between 1977 and 1985, contrary to expectation based on the crime rates, the rates of youth confined on any given day in juvenile detention centers to await court action increased by more than 50 percent. The rates of juveniles incarcerated in training schools on a given day increased by more than 16 percent. Moral and legal differences between juveniles and adults notwithstanding, policymakers became convinced during the 1980s that serious juvenile crime was not significantly different from serious crimes committed by adults. We heard more accounts of youths who were committing "adult crimes," who were leading adult lives in warring street gangs, who supported their families with drug money, who carried weapons to school.

The desperate, urban life-style of many lower-class neighborhoods was portrayed as the life-style of choice for adolescents. According to the classical model of punishment, free choice should be followed by behavioral consequences in the form of "just deserts" or retributive punishment. The conservative line of reasoning urged that if we were going to punish youths for committing the crimes of adults, then we must do so through the adult system of criminal justice. This is because the philosophy of juvenile courts and juvenile correctional agencies rests on the assumption that the motives, predispositions, and insights of youths are qualitatively different from adults. That assumption translated into policies of diversion and least restrictive placements to protect youths, which seemed to contradict the goal of just deserts and community protection.

From the mid-1970s through the 1980s, a "get tough" mentality pervaded policies that were implemented to strengthen governmental control of serious juvenile offenders. Rather than focusing on juvenile agencies, these policies generally facilitated handling juvenile offenders as adults—that is, trying cases in adult, rather than juvenile court, and sentencing such offenders to adult correctional facilities. There is ample evidence that some sort of change was called for, given the unpredictable and inconsistent response of the juvenile justice agencies to crimes of even the most violent nature during the 1970s. In Columbus, Ohio, Donna Hamparian and her colleagues studied disposition patterns from almost 5,000 offenses committed by 1,138 violent juvenile offenders. Legal variables (nature of offense and prior record) had about as much influence on the disposition as "tossing coins in the courtroom" (Hamparian et al. 1978: 114). Similarly, a study in Massachusetts, which examined Department of Youth Services' placements of all violent juvenile offenders committed in 1975, 1977, and 1979 found that despite the seriousness of their offenses, 85 percent to 100 percent (depending on the year) of committed youths were not placed in long-term secure facilities (Juvenile Justice Advisory Committee 1981), but were instead returned home or placed in community programs. Offenders who were placed in long-term secure facilities were placed on the basis of idiosyncratic criteria that emphasized control factors (e.g., youths who were AWOL risks) as opposed to public safety factors (Rocheleau 1981).

Inconsistencies in decision making, in particular the lack of fit between the seriousness of the crime and the juvenile correctional response, was problematic for at least two reasons. First, stakeholders in the juvenile system (police, legislators, victims' rights advocates) grew increasingly outraged by the lack of administrative credibility shown by decision makers. Much of the criticism was justified; however, some of it was driven by exaggerated perceptions of violent juvenile crime that were fueled by political opportunists. Regardless of its validity, the finger pointing made it clear that organizationally, something needed to be changed. Secondly, the inconsistent and unpredictable correctional responses could only have demonstrated to youths a warped sense of justice. If one of the goals of juvenile justice is to demonstrate the logical consequences of behavior, it failed miserably. As Shireman and Reamer observed (1986: 40–41, emphasis added):

> Indeed, the young person who may have violated the law several times without being caught, who for several violations that have been brought to official attention has received only a dismissal, a warning that some day serious consequences *may* follow if he continues his behavior, or has received nominal probation, can only perceive either that the social order and the state are not actually much concerned about his behavior or that they are simply ineffectual—or both. *There is danger that when, finally, the repeat offender does encounter firm treatment in the form of correctional placement, the sanction will be perceived as almost random, as "bad luck" or as discrimination—perhaps an occasion for deciding to "get even," but hardly an occasion for reform.*

Somewhat desperately, perhaps, the adult system was turned to as an answer to satisfy stakeholders and also to demonstrate rationally escalating consequences to juveniles' offense behavior. These goals would be accomplished by adult courts sending a presumably stronger and more predictable message to offenders, and thereby restoring a sense of justice for other interested parties. While it is true that longer prison sentences are theoretically possible in the adult system compared to juvenile dispositions, practically, however, the assurance of long prison terms for violent juveniles has been impeded by a number of factors, including prison overcrowding, youthful age being treated as a mitigating circumstance, and the lack of uniform guidelines in most jurisdictions governing sentencing decisions in adult courts. Basically, except where there are statutory sentencing guidelines, adult courts operate on an idiosyncratic basis that is disturbingly similar to the very practices that the "get-tough" reformers claimed they would avoid. Therefore, it is not necessarily clear that handling juveniles as adults could achieve satisfactory results.

The juvenile court's waiver of jurisdiction is the most common mechanism for trying youths as adults. The judicial waiver decision is made at a hearing which is analogous to the preliminary hearing in adult court. At a waiver hearing, the prosecutor must only show probable cause that an offense occurred and that the juvenile committed the offense. The prosecutor does not have to prove guilt beyond a reasonable doubt. Proof of guilt is reserved for the trial in adult court if waiver is successful or for the adjudication stage in juvenile court if the waiver motion fails. The juvenile waiver hearing differs from an adult court preliminary hearing in that the prosecutor must go further and establish that the juvenile is not amenable to juvenile court intervention or that the juvenile is a threat to public safety. An example of nonamenability would be the case of a youth who is already on parole from a state training school for an earlier delinquent act who then commits another serious offense (e.g., armed robbery). If probable cause were established that the youth committed the robbery, then the judge would have to find that the juvenile court had a history of contacts with the boy dating back several years, and that one more juvenile court effort to deal with the boy's problems would be futile.

Nationally, the number of judicially waived cases increased 68 percent from 1988 to 1992 to a total of 11,700 cases (Sickmund 1994), but the judicial waiver hearing is only one mechanism for transferring jurisdiction from juvenile to adult court. The second mechanism is known as "concurrent jurisdiction," whereby prosecutors have discretion to file cases in either juvenile or adult court. (Procedural issues are discussed more fully in chapter 4.) Although there are no national data on the exact number of youths tried as adults by way of concurrent jurisdiction provisions, 17,000 cases were estimated in 1990 (Office of Juvenile Justice and Delinquency Prevention 1993). The third mechanism is amendment of state statutes so that certain offense types are automatically excluded from juvenile court jurisdiction. Those provisions are believed to account for a few thousand cases each year (Wilson 1994). It should be noted that specific offense exclusions are in addition to the upper age boundaries of juvenile court jurisdiction that automatically exclude all juveniles beyond age fifteen, sixteen, or seventeen, depending on the state. Such age boundaries are believed to account for 176,000 youths per year under the age of eighteen, regardless of their offense (Sickmund 1994).

Since expanded waiver or transfer policies only became established in recent years, it is probably too early to determine if they are effective strategies, but there is anecdotal evidence that the publicity of tough laws does not materialize into a deterrent effect. Three Massachusetts teenage boys recently left home on a week-long crime spree in a stolen Chevrolet Caprice. Their odyssey led them north to Maine, and then they proceeded all the way down the east coast to Tampa,

Florida, where they burglarized and murdered a retired bus driver (*Boston Globe,* 12 June 1994). In Massachusetts, the juveniles, aged fifteen and sixteen, would have been automatically subject to a transfer hearing, but not necessarily transferred to adult court, and there is no death penalty in Massachusetts. In Florida, they will be automatically tried as adults and, if convicted, they will be subject to the death penalty.

Recent scholarly studies have offered mainly negative assessments of the effectiveness of transfer. The severity of juvenile and adult criminal court sanctions were compared in a study of sixteen- and seventeen-year-olds charged with burglary and robbery in New York and New Jersey (Fagan, Schiff, Brisben, and Orden 1991). The study found that juvenile court dispositions were not less severe than those in adult court. Furthermore, over time, youths adjudicated in the juvenile court were rearrested less often, at a lower rate, and after more time had elapsed.

Dean Champion studied the use of waivers and transfers in four states (Virginia, Tennessee, Mississippi, and Georgia) between 1980 and 1988. He found an increase in waivers and transfers during that time period of 104.3 percent, which included a disproportionate rate of increase for property offenders as compared with violent offenders. During the study period, juvenile arrests neither rose nor fell significantly. Furthermore, as time went on, more and more juvenile offenders convicted as adults received probation as opposed to a prison, jail, or an alternative sentence. In none of the years did the combined proportion of offenders sentenced to jail or prison exceed 14 percent. Champion explains his findings as follows (Champion 1989: 583):

> If waivers are not resulting in more severe penalties for juveniles, then what are they accomplishing? These findings suggest that their use in the present jurisdictions is primarily cosmetic. In defense of juvenile court prosecutors, however, it should be noted that several of them are consistently disappointed about how juveniles are treated after being waived to criminal courts. It is clear that their intentions are to make it possible for transferred juveniles to receive more severe penalties than they otherwise could. However, criminal courts seem inclined to treat less seriously those cases waived to their jurisdiction by juvenile courts. One important explanation for this extensive leniency toward youthful offenders transferred to criminal courts is that their age becomes a mitigating circumstance. Furthermore, offenses considered serious by juvenile courts may be considered less serious by criminal court judges. When transferred to criminal courts, youthful burglars and thieves become part of a large adult aggregate that is often extended probation as a means of alleviating jail overcrowding and allocating scarce prison space for more dangerous offenders.

Rudman, Hartstone, Fagan, and Moore (1986), on the other hand, looked at 138 violent youths considered for transfer between 1981 and 1984 in Boston, Newark, and Phoenix and found that 94 percent of the transferred youths were convicted of crimes of violence in adult court and 90 percent of the convicted youths were incarcerated. Furthermore, youths convicted and sentenced to incarceration in adult criminal court received substantially longer sentences (about five times longer) than youths who were not transferred but received a sentence of incarceration in juvenile court. Rudman and his colleagues concluded that transfer of violent juveniles was indeed a punitive response and that it resulted in "longer terms of more secure confinement" (Rudman et al. 1986: 3). However, an update to that study, which included an additional site (Detroit), found that violent youths accounted for less than one-third of all youths who were transferred. Moreover, the researchers were unable to identify any strong or consistent determinants of the judicial transfer decision (Fagan and Deschenes 1990).

In other important research conducted by Barry Feld, problems were identified in Minnesota's waiver policy, which is similar to waiver policies in other states. After reviewing the cases of 17,195 juveniles who were formally petitioned in juvenile courts in 1986, Feld concluded that decisions to waive and sentence were highly idiosyncratic because too much discretion was permitted under the existing statutes (Feld 1989). In general, Feld's review of the research concluded that the exercise of discretion is rampant in the waiver decision (Feld 1987: 492). Statistics compiled by the National Center for Juvenile Justice support Feld's conclusion: only 34 percent of delinquency cases waived by juvenile court judges in 1992 involved an offense against a person. Nearly half were property offenses (45 percent), followed by drug (12 percent) and public order crimes (9 percent) (Wilson 1994).

Because of the problems of discretion inherent in the judicial waiver process, a few states have experimented with concurrent jurisdiction provisions, which permit prosecutors to waive juveniles to adult court without a hearing. Florida's concurrent jurisdiction laws were evaluated based on data from 1981 and 1984 (Bishop, Frazier, and Henretta 1989; Bishop and Frazier 1991). The statistical analysis of juveniles transferred to adult court by prosecutors revealed that over time, increasing proportions of nonviolent felons and misdemeanants were transferred, so that by 1984, only 20 percent of youths waived by prosecutors were charged with felony person offenses. Many of the inappropriate transfers were the direct result of insufficient programs available within the juvenile system. The authors recommended against the use of concurrent jurisdiction because of the high likelihood of inappropriate prosecutorial decisions that are not reviewable due to the lack of a hearing process.

An additional study examined a related area of juvenile waiver—namely, how well juvenile offenders adjust to adult prisons (McShane and Williams 1989). The study compared fifty-five male juvenile offenders committed to Texas prisons between 1984 and 1987 with a similar group of ninety-one young adults between the ages of seventeen and twenty-one. They found significantly more adjustment problems among the younger group, even though all of the juveniles were previously exposed to institutional confinement because they began their sentences in the juvenile system. Juvenile offenders in prison were nearly twice as likely as the older group to be classified as "problem inmates" who neither worked nor earned good time credits, resulting in longer prison stays. They were almost three times as likely to be placed in the most restrictive security levels. The authors warned that young offenders would continue to be highly disruptive, to require the most costly security levels, and to serve more time in prison (due to the loss of good time) unless creative strategies are developed—a possibility we view as remote. The broad-based criticisms of present waiver and adult sentencing policies lead us to the conclusion that we need to reconsider the path that led us away from the juvenile justice system. An important twist in that path—led by religious fundamentalists—grossly distorted the purpose of juvenile justice.

The Fundamentalist View

As discussed above, one intended result of the federal Juvenile Justice Delinquency and Prevention Act of 1974 was that local juvenile justice systems lost federal funding if they detained runaways, or other status offenders, in state institutions, local jails, or secure juvenile facilities. When placed in housing by the police or the juvenile court, the Act required that status offenders be kept in nonsecure settings—shelters, group homes, or foster care. Those states that have revised their laws to prohibit the institutionalization of status offenders could, as provided by the Act, continue to receive federal funding for their juvenile justice systems, and could receive additional funds to develop innovative, alternative programs for status offenders. Those states that did not pass "DSO" (deinstitutionalization of status offenders) laws lost federal funding. By 1991, all but five states (Hawaii, Nevada, North Dakota, South Dakota, and Wyoming) had complied (Forst and Blomquist 1991).

From the fundamentalist point of view, the Act was a policy disaster because it was "anti-family" (Schwartz 1989: 108). Admittedly, without secured entrances and exits, the alternatives to institutions are placements from which youths can easily run again. Even more significant is the fact that roughly half of all status offender complaints are filed by parents. Confinement of status offenders can thereby be perceived in two possible ways. The fundamentalist position viewed confinement of status offenders as a tool for parents, to help them regain control of defiant youths. The libertarian position viewed confinement of status offenders as a traumatic experience for troubled youth, by mixing them with more serious offenders and depriving them of their liberty, when the reasons why they have run may not be their fault. This issue clearly bisected religious fundamentalists—who were courted by the Reagan administration—and libertarians, who retained the support of most Democratic and Republican legislators during the 1980s.

The Reagan years (1981–1988) were characterized by three major patterns: first, administrators of the Office of Juvenile Justice and Delinquency Prevention (OJJDP), which oversees all federal juvenile justice policies and initiatives including the JJDP Act, worked hard to eliminate their own agency, under directives from the White House; second, research grants were awarded by OJJDP through scandalous procedures, for ideological subjects that were irrelevant to policy; third, the Reagan administration tried to reverse the JJDP Act so that status offenders could once again be incarcerated. A key administrative strategy for signaling the need to incarcerate status offenders was to link the problem of child runaways with stranger abduction cases of missing children, which were already being grossly exaggerated by advocates for missing children.

In October 1981, Reagan's first year in office, the administration proposed that OJJDP funds be deferred, so that money appropriated for the agency could not be spent. In response, in December 1981 the Senate passed Senate Resolution 260, expressing its disapproval of the deferral request. In 1983, Alfred S. Regnery was appointed by Reagan to direct the OJJDP. For each year thereafter, Regnery's administration requested zero funding for OJJDP, but each year Congress resisted the administration and provided level funding of $70 million. Administrative pressure on Congress to eliminate funding for OJJDP continued throughout both terms of office. For example, Regnery refused to spend all appropriated funds from the $60 million FY 1985 budget. In December of that fiscal year, he used an obscure law known as the Impoundment Control Act of 1974 to impose an "informal freeze" on all OJJDP funds, which was a clear violation of a directive of Congress. By April, the funding was finally released as a result of a Senate resolution submitted by Senator Arlen Specter, amended by Senator Joseph Biden, and co-sponsored by a majority of the senators, which sent a strong message to the White House that the Senate would reject any further attempts to eliminate funding from the agency (*Juvenile Justice Digest*, 21 April 1986).

In 1986, Regnery made a statement to the Senate Judiciary Committee Subcommittee on Juvenile Justice that articulated the administration's position to eliminate federal funding for juvenile justice programs. His rationale was twofold: in his view, the federal obligation was only to assist states in removing juveniles from adult jails and deinstitutionalizing status offenders; however, the states were using most of the federal money for other programs, demonstrating— as far as he was concerned—that they did not need federal support because their programs were based on local philosophy that would continue without federal support.

> In FY '85, states spent only 23 percent—roughly $9.3 million—for preadjudicatory alternatives in support of jail removal and the deinstitutionalization of status offenders. The largest percentage of funds—27 percent or $10.8 million—is spent on treatment and rehabilitation programs. Another 23 percent ($9.1 million) is spent on prevention programs; 20 percent ($7.8 million) is spent on system improvement programs, training, for example; and 2.5 percent ($960,000) is spent on advocacy programs. Thus, states are using Federal funds to finance programs they would support, and do, in fact, support, regardless of Federal assistance. (*Juvenile Justice Digest*, 10 March 1986: 7)

Regnery thereby redirected both the spirit and the letter of the JJDP Act, narrowing its focus to only those programs that states did not want, which characterized the Act as obsolete.

On 6 June 1986 Alfred S. Regnery left office as administrator of OJJDP after a three-year term, denying rumors that he was pressured out of office due to scandals that he awarded noncompetitive grants to professed fundamentalists who failed to produce usable research (Waas 1986). Verne Speirs was named acting administrator of OJJDP, and he continued fighting Congress to abolish OJJDP. In 1990, Robert Sweet took over as head of OJJDP, and to the surprise of juvenile justice practitioners, took an active leadership position in such areas as correctional education, child abuse and neglect, sex offender treatment, crime and gang prevention. Ironically, in April 1992 Sweet was dismissed shortly after being praised by the National Council of Juvenile and Family Court Judges.

Another area of mismanagement at the federal level due to fundamentalist pressures to promote "family values" were the policies developed for missing children. It is now believed that the Reagan administration manipulated the problem of missing children for political gain. The administration released exaggerated statistics on children kidnapped by strangers, encouraged private sector involvement to increase awareness of the kidnapping "crisis" (pictures on milk cartons, etc.), and created an $8 million agency run by OJJDP, the National Center on Missing and Exploited Children. The administration then connected the missing children "crisis" to their proposed "solution," namely, to restore the policy of incarcerating status offenders. A report released in March 1986 by the U.S. Attorney General's (Edwin Meese III) Advisory Board on Missing Children recommended that Congress reverse the Juvenile Justice and Delinquency Prevention Act (JJDP) so that parents and courts in each state would regain the legal authority to confine runaway and homeless children. The report was highly critical of the JJDP Act because it

> influenced states to create a child's right of freedom from both parental and appropriate government control. A law that was intended to benefit America's children, in fact, handcuffs those most able to help them and contributes to the very hazards it seeks to eliminate. As children are set free to a life on the street—one that often includes drugs, street crime, sexual exploitation, prostitution and grave physical danger—frustrated parents, police, and juvenile judges are denied authority to exercise effective control over them. (U.S. Attorney General's Advisory Board on Missing Children 1986: 19)

The Meese report also criticized government influence in families and used the theme of "family values" to deny rights of liberty to adolescents. The report recommended laws that would support the maintenance or reunification of families "without undue government interference. We believe the first step is to bolster family values and to stop the continued disintegration of the family. Caring parents or legal guardians who give children love, discipline, and support can be powerful influences" (U.S. Attorney General's Advisory Board on Missing Children 1986: i).

In taking that position, the administration failed to acknowledge studies, including several that were overseen by the Department of Justice, that contradicted the claim that runaways were confused children who simply needed the guidance of their wise and caring families. Study after study identified the majority of runaways as victims of parental violence or neglect (Farber 1984; Goldmeier and Dean 1973; Forst and Blomquist 1991). Data indicated that the family of the typical runaway was far closer to Huck Finn's story—whose father was alcoholic and physically abusive—than the concerned Ozzie and Harriet that the administration attempted to portray. But the official position of the Justice Department on the reason why youths run away from home was that they are drawn by outside influences, not pushed by family problems:

There has been a proliferation of material in records, videos, motion pictures, and magazines that would have been considered obscene or dangerous even for adults a generation ago. The apparent glorification of drugs, suicide, murder, rape, incest, torture, bondage, and blood rituals and rites raises serious questions about the images and values held out to children as counterculture attractions. Would children be less vulnerable to running away, to sexual exploitation, to sex rings, and destructive cults if they were more sheltered from lurid, everyday depictions of perversion? Granted that most children choose not to identify with perverse and antisocial imagery, are those who are least secure in their homes more likely to be lured into destructive escapes? (U.S. Attorney General's Advisory Board on Missing Children 1986: 30)

As a result of the politicization of missing children as victims of the streets, rather than youths in fear of family abuse or neglect, policy changes focused on police investigation of all missing children as if they were abduction cases, and penalties increased for individuals who kidnapped or molested children. Meanwhile, programs that were truly needed by runaways—shelters, social services, assistance for emancipation—were either ignored or grossly underfunded (Forst and Blomquist 1991). William Treanor, the executive director, American

Youth Work Center, Washington, D.C., commented on the connection between missing children and runaway youths (*Juvenile Justice Digest*, 25 August 1986: 7–10). Treanor had started one of the nation's earliest programs for runaway youth in 1968 called the D.C. Runaway House. He had also proposed the Missing Children's Assistance Act in 1983. He noted, first, that runaway juveniles are different than missing children, but, secondly, that distinction was not made or understood by the OJJDP and its "wholly-owned and controlled subsidiary," the National Center on Missing and Exploited Children.

> I envisioned a modest federally-financed effort to operate a national toll-free hotline to aid in the recovery of truly missing children, principally those 13 and under. . . . In addition, I expected a substantive Federal leadership effort to promote a wide range of services to parents of missing children. . . .

> Apparently, the Attorney General's Advisory Board has discovered the true scope of the truly missing children's problem and, being unable to find those kids, has decided to lock up some others [namely, runaways]. . . .

> The merchants of fear originally claimed that more than 5,000 unidentified dead children are buried each year! . . . According to the College of American Pathologists' national study of 1983 unidentified dead, less than 200 children—dead from all causes such as accidents, disease, or crime—were buried that year.

> Up to 50,000 stranger abductions have been claimed by numerous people in the missing children's business such as Denny Abbott, executive director of the Adam Walsh Child Resource Center and the Justice Department's NCMEC (1984 brochure). In truth, . . . there are under 300 cases each year.

In summary, stagnation of federal leadership in the area of juvenile justice encouraged a morass of approaches based on process (how to try juveniles) rather than substance (what their sanctions should consist of). Innovative programs to reduce crime were not promoted under Reagan, whose administration used hollow policies to promote political and ideological interests, at the price of endangering the public.

Lessons Learned

In retrospect, we have learned several important lessons from the clash of ideological perspectives that has constituted the history of juvenile justice:

1. The liberal assumption that rehabilitation can be imposed on adoles-

cents by the state lacks the activism needed to prevent problems of violent families and communities. Rehabilitative services without a plan for prevention merely ensures the reproduction of a victimized, and victimizing cohort of juvenile offenders. The liberal perspective also fails to focus on key issues of public safety, offender accountability and victims' concerns.

2. The libertarian view that juvenile offenders should not be incarcerated is valid for low- to medium-risk offenders, status offenders and for many pre-trial detainees. However, the experience of "liberty" at home and on the streets, for many youths, is every bit as frightening and hardening as confinement to an institution. The streets and homes from which court-involved juveniles emerge are often unsupportive and traumatizing. Moreover, a growing number of serious offenders need to be held accountable for their offenses, and confinement may be the most appropriately penalizing recourse. Offenders who have committed serious crimes and who pose a danger to society need to be confined for reasons of public safety. But confinement does not necessarily mean large-scale institutions where abuse is more likely and skill development is often lacking. The same public protection goals can be accomplished in small settings with intensive programming designed to reorient youths away from life-styles that are destructive to themselves and others.

3. The conservative view that juveniles must be held accountable for their crimes and recognize their impact on victims needs to be an important component of juvenile justice policy. However, the idea of imposing suffering or *retribution* at the expense of programs designed to control crime is dangerously archaic. The promise that *deterrence* would be achieved through greater *severity* of punishment, with little or no adjustment to the *uncertainty* of punishment, was an empty promise, since most offenders correctly observe that the probability of being caught is exceedingly low.

The assumption that *incapacitating* offenders is guaranteed to reduce crime overlooks four caveats. For incapacitation to be effective as a crime reduction policy, incapacitated offenders:

• must be allowed gradual access to the community through reintegration programs, which result in lower recidivism than strict incapacitation (LeClair and Guarino-Ghezzi 1991);
• need to be selected carefully, so that only those who would have continued offending are incapacitated, while those who are at low risk of offending are not using resources unnecessarily;
• must not be replaced in the community by other, new offenders in order to supply illegal activities or products to meet public demand;
• must not become appreciably "worse" as a result of the experience of being incapacitated.

Recent legal and procedural reforms to facilitate the trial of juveniles in adult court have overlooked several critical considerations:

- Juveniles in adult court are subject to substantial variation in case outcome;
- They are often given probation or fines (for a number of reasons, theoretically, unrelated to the actual offense record, including: the length of time awaiting adult trial is longer than in juvenile court, so youths are released upon conviction; it is inconvenient for the adult court prosecutors to locate the juvenile offense record; plea bargaining is more likely in adult court; an adversarial defense is more likely in adult court; age is viewed as a mitigating circumstance);
- They often commit crimes in groups in which different youths play different roles—some leaders, others followers. Many youths are brought into situations without planning or knowledge. Statutorily excluded offenses mean that no process exists for determining whether youths are, in fact, initiators and full participants, or at the periphery of a crime.
- Most serious juvenile offenders have serious family and personal problems. Many of them need more help than the adult system can provide.
- Most adult prisons are already overcrowded and are ill-equipped to handle the additional management burden posed by young offenders.

4. The fundamentalist view that government should serve merely as a conduit for religious morality, rather than address social problems through government policy, denies the necessity of political leadership in education, community and job development, and is an impossibly narrow solution, particularly for inner-city or repeat offenders.

Taken as a coherent package, the lessons that we have learned provide invaluable understanding in shaping a future agenda for juvenile justice. However, the road ahead is further confounded by the lack of a balanced system. As history reveals, societal concern with youthful offenders as actors—who have individual weaknesses and strengths, and who are the products of non-nurturing, often dangerous environments—was replaced by conservatives' eagerness to punish their acts. At the same time, many taxpayers have shown a growing indifference to treatment and prevention issues, allowing their attention to be diverted away from the social conditions that produce juvenile offenders.

Concomitant with societal indifference toward juvenile justice, our nation has witnessed indifference to the needs of children, adolescents, and families who are without adequate resources. As a nation, we have experienced a growth in children living in poverty; abused and neglected children; children who are witnesses to acts of violence in their communities; children whose desperate needs as actors, in addition to their acts as offenders, fall into the machinery of juvenile justice agencies. When correctional agencies fail to acknowledge years of societal indifference, the neediest youths are often categorized as the most deserving of punishment in our increasingly punitive society.

Many observers are beginning to make the discovery that our overcrowded prisons, jails, and institutions—for adults and juveniles—are the result not of too few facilities, but of avoidable patterns of institutional over-incarceration. These discoveries come on the heels of the law-and-order decade of the 1980s in which unprecedented numbers of offenders were placed in prisons, jails, and juvenile detention centers and institutions. Particularly in the adult sector, the heavy reliance on incarceration is persisting into the 1990s with no discernible impact on crime. There are now active signs of discontent; a recent *New York Times Magazine* article proclaimed that "lock 'em up" is a failed crime control strategy (12 June 1994: 56). The purpose of incarceration is being questioned by critics who observe that many of those individuals who are incarcerated are not a threat to public safety, nor have they committed a violent crime. This theme is being reiterated particularly by advocates for juvenile offenders (Krisberg, Litsky, and Schwartz 1982; Schwartz 1989), female offenders (Immarigeon and Chesney-Lind 1992; Schwartz, Steketee, and Schneider 1990), and also by activists favoring the deincarceration of nonviolent adult offenders (Morris and Tonry 1990) or the reduction of their sentences (Treaster 1993). Their reasoning relates to the negative impact of overcrowded institutions on offenders, as well as the need to protect public safety by preserving prison space for chronically violent offenders.

Furthermore, victims' advocates are discovering many more opportunities for restitution and community service when offenders are placed in the community than when they are confined to a secure facility (Klein 1988). One reason that courts and correctional systems use long-term security for other than the most serious offenders is that many offenders are "control" problems who defy authority by running away from home or failing to meet with probation officers. Examples of youths commonly labeled as control problems include status offenders, female prostitutes and drug addicts, probation violators, unadjudicated persons awaiting trial, and many juvenile offenders who commit relatively minor offenses but who lack stable family controls. Most of these individuals present no public safety threat, so their incarceration is contestable on utilitarian grounds—it is simply an inefficient and potentially counterproductive use of scarce resources.

Other major criticisms of institutions boil down to the brutality inflicted on those individuals who are subjected to their unnatural and isolated environments. Specifically, observers contend that institutions foster staff brutality (Bartollas, Miller, and Dinitz 1976; Bowker 1991; Chase 1976; John Howard Association 1974), overcrowded conditions (Giari 1991; Parent 1993a), violence among residents (Braswell, Dillingham, and Montgomery 1985), corruption of staff (Sykes 1958), sexual aggression (Lockwood 1980), consensual homosexual behavior (Sagarin 1976), rioting (Braswell, Dillingham, and Montgomery 1985), limited access to treatment programs (Irwin 1980; Parent et al. 1994), and hardened institutional personality types (Abbott 1981). These conditions are present in most, if not all, of our adult prisons today and historically have been discovered and rediscovered in juvenile institutions as well.

There is a myth that institutions are capable of controlling behavior. However, even a cursory examination of our nation's prisons and jails will uncover the organized gang activity, the easy availability of drugs, and the vulnerability of unaggressive inmates to violence and sexual assault that encourages the weak to become violent (Lockwood 1985). Indeed, during 1988 a total of thirty-three juveniles died while in U.S. public custody facilities, including six homicides and seventeen suicides (Allen-Hagan 1991). More than 11,000 confined juveniles engage in more than 17,000 acts of suicidal behavior per year (attempted suicide, suicidal gestures, or self-mutilation) (Parent et al. 1994). The high number of juvenile institutions now under court order, as well as pervasive gaps in security and programming throughout the juvenile system (Parent et al. 1994), is further testimony to the misplaced confidence that many have had in the institutional model of control.

Our position for shaping justice into the twenty-first century is what we term a balanced model of juvenile corrections. It is striking to us that in active war zones throughout the world, as James Garbarino and his colleagues (1992) discovered, the vast majority of children learn to overcome chronic experiences with violence and trauma by relying on a few resilient traits or resources. Using a developmental theory of children, Garbarino and his associates examined patterns of adaptation and achievement in war-torn countries, where children learned to manage their environments by finding meaning and purpose even in the worst tragedies. For some children, the best revenge was becoming a good person. How, the authors ask, can we communicate that message to children in our own war zones, the inner cities of the United States, where families live in ever-deepening poverty, children live in constant danger, and public schools have grown violent?

It is clear that our nation's social problems have correlated with higher rates of violent juveniles entering the system. According to the FBI, the rate of violent crimes by juveniles in the United States increased by more than 25 percent during the 1980s decade. The rate of arrests of juveniles for violent offenses in 1990 was 430 per 100,000— a 27 percent increase over 1980. The FBI also reported a 79 percent increase in the number of juveniles committing murder with guns. The majority of the violent crime increase occurred after 1985, ironically, after most states had implemented their "get tough" juvenile justice legislation. For instance, the number of waived offenders increased 45 percent between 1984 and 1988, from 4274 to 6211 (Snyder et al. 1990), and the number of cases tried automatically as adults, without a waiver hearing, increased substantially as well. Even if present conditions do not worsen, demographic trends predict an increase in juvenile crime through the 1990s simply because the number of juveniles is increasing.

Programs for adolescent offenders must emphasize that in fact it is the program residents and their peers who make up an ever-growing segment of "the environment"; it is they whose threatening behavior on the street contributes to the fear of other members of their community; it is they who are negative role models for younger children. At the same time, programs must be able to identify and develop sources of resiliency in youths, develop skills and establish positive behaviors.

In addition to the various political perspectives outlined in this chapter, juvenile justice intervention cuts across state and local lines. The dominant expression of juvenile justice at the national level is not necessarily the same as what is operating at the state level, and the two may be at odds with local programming and policies. In chapter 2 we examine the geographical phenomenon of "justice by geography," comparing patterns and trends across sixteen states.

Adding to the states' geographical boundaries of justice are local (county and city) systems, which, in some areas, are developing model approaches for handling juvenile offenders. Chapter 3 describes how developments in several counties and cities have become models of program innovation.

Further complicating the geographic mosaic of correctional programming is the powerful entity of the juvenile court, which has different interests organizationally from juvenile corrections, and may be supportive or detrimental to the development of a system which balances the goals of offender accountability, or punishment, along with rehabilitation and crime prevention (deterrence and incapacitation). The complex history of the juvenile court is described in chapter 4.

Striking a balanced approach in juvenile justice requires that the multiple "stakeholders"—courts, corrections, police, victims, legislators and other politicians, schools, churches, community groups, youth advocacy groups, and so on—have an investment in the system which serves their cause. One of the most fundamental components of a balanced system is a classification system for making decisions on precisely how to intervene with juvenile offenders—what messages to send, what lessons to teach, what service needs to address, what public safety risks to neutralize. A multifaceted classification system is essential for considering each of the varying concerns on a case-by-case basis. The development of balanced classification models is described in chapter 5.

A balanced system requires not only the coherence of multiple decision factors, but that the intervention itself—the program to which the youth is assigned—represents an equilibrium of diverse goals. Chapter 6 examines innovations in balanced programs and policies throughout the United States, including boot camps with treatment components, reintegrative treatment facilities for sex offenders, and community-based programs which provide both surveillance and services to low- to medium-risk juvenile offenders.

Even a cursory scanning of juvenile justice systems throughout the United States reveals many signs that systems are out of balance. Finally, chapter 7 discusses how to identify those signs, what they mean, and what to do to establish or restore a balanced approach which satisfies a diversity of interests and goals within a given jurisdiction.

2

State Reforms in Juvenile Corrections

The Non-System of Juvenile Justice

Progress is difficult to achieve when the different juvenile justice organizations vary so much by state and locality. In addition, some observers scoff at the use of the word "justice" in the phrase "juvenile justice system," claiming that there are hidden systems used to incarcerate youths, many of which are in violation of laws and standards and need to be addressed immediately (Schwartz 1989). Others bristle at the term "system," noting the confusing morass of legislation that has followed different patterns in different states. Still others are stopped short by the word "juvenile" due to the ambivalence that it evokes. Many of us feel the ambivalence of both outrage and sympathy for juvenile offenders in part because of the marginality of adolescence, and this confusion clouds our thinking about juvenile crime, juveniles' needs, and criminal culpability (McDermott and Laub 1986; Shireman and Reamer 1986).

In short, most caretakers are not sure what behaviors to demand from juveniles, they are not convinced that crimes are handled with justice, and they cannot perceive any existing infrastructure that resembles a system. Clearly, the path toward understanding the "juvenile justice system" is impeded by its very title. It is perhaps rare that the better a phenomenon is understood, the more complicated it becomes. Yet, this is the case with juvenile justice.

To compound the conceptual confusion, matters related to juvenile offenses are handled by several interconnected entities. The first is the juvenile court, which, in addition to hearing cases, has the discretionary authority to detain youths pending their hearings, to transfer youths to adult court for trial, and to set the disposition (or sentence) of juveniles who are adjudicated delinquent within the juvenile court. Another functionary is the juvenile probation department, which in some states is composed of individually managed county or court-level probation services for juvenile offenders, while in other states probation is overseen by a statewide executive agency. Another component in most states is the agency responsible for family services, which handles youths who are referred from the courts for status offenses (truants, runaways, and other disciplinary problems). The final entity in virtually all states is the juvenile correctional agency, which handles the most serious youthful offenders who are committed by the juvenile courts. Although these basic pieces exist in most states, no two states are completely alike as far as mandates, legislation, policies, or programs. The result is that differential approaches to handling offenders vary dramatically by state, as pointed out by Barry Krisberg, Paul Litsky, and Ira Schwartz in their 1984 article "Youths in Confinement: Justice by Geography," which compares juvenile incarceration practices by state.

The various agencies that are mandated to provide services and supervision for juvenile offenders have collectively experienced more than a decade of powerlessness. Substantive mandates focusing on problems of youths, families, and communities have ceded to political manipulation. The credibility that any type of "system" exists for juvenile offenders is near zero. In actuality, the progress that was necessary for developing an integrated system was thwarted on the national level throughout the Reagan administration, at times flagrantly. Progress in developing theoretically based programs for juvenile offenders also was impeded by the rise in serious juvenile crime, which peaked in the mid-1970s, only to increase again during the 1980s.

Attempts by policymakers and researchers to analyze trends in juvenile justice—to identify what "the system" is—have been hampered by the idiosyncrasies of individual states. For example, Donna Hamparian and colleagues from the Academy for Contemporary Problems (1982) identified a wide array of states' policies for prosecuting juveniles as adults that displayed as many contrasts as commonalities. Similarly, research on trends in secure programming identified four different patterns of organizational change within a research sample of only ten states (Guarino-Ghezzi and Kimball 1986). Some observers have noted that part of the problem appears to be a mixture of differ-

TABLE 2.1
Purposes for State Youth Corrections Programs

Purposes Stated in the Statute	Number of States with Stated Purpose*
Protect society	25
Substitute offender rehabilitation for retribution	22
Meet the needs of delinquent youths	11
Establish fair and constitutional procedures	18
Punish or hold accountable delinquent youths	4

* The numbers add up to more than 50 because more than one purpose can be in the state's statute.
Source: Streit and Barton 1990.

ent statutory purposes for state youth corrections programs (Streit and Barton 1990). For example, the individual states' enabling legislation that created youth correctional agencies in forty-nine states and the District of Columbia was examined and the purposes for those agencies compared (see table 2.1). Five distinct purposes were found, and not even one purpose transcended all jurisdictions.

Perhaps our nation's policies for juvenile offenders defy coherent national goals and standards. For example, after the passage of the 1974 Juvenile Justice and Delinquency Prevention Act, programs calling themselves "community-based alternatives" emerged throughout the nation. However, it is clear that these programs were not necessarily used as "alternatives to institutions," that is, to prevent the institutionalization of offenders who would otherwise be confined. As Shireman and Reimer (1986) point out, the states were given nearly complete autonomy in developing their own guidelines for these programs in terms of client contact, supervision, community involvement, security, size, staffing patterns, treatment model, services, admission and discharge criteria, and length of stay. Rather than being viewed as true alternatives to institutions, to many people "community-based" meant "nearly any program operated outside a traditional correctional facility, that is, a synonym for non-institutional" (Shireman and Reamer 1986: 148). The vagueness of the federal legislation and its limited guidelines encouraged the practice of net-widening, or expanding the net of control to include low-risk offenders who previously might have only received probation, rather than using the programs for youths who previously would have been institutionalized.

A related problem is the need for initiatives that provide a continuous range of community-based programs on a punitive scale in between probation and incarceration (Klein 1988; Morris and Tonry 1990). Many observers and practitioners are calling for new "alternative sentences" or "intermediate sanctions" to handle the bulk of middle-range offenders in both the adult and juvenile sectors. A balanced approach to sentencing would indeed provide a continuum of community-based programs with increasing penalties in addition to existing secure facilities. In the juvenile correctional system, the range of programs should be sufficiently comprehensive to satisfy each of the goals of punishment—incapacitation, retribution, rehabilitation, and deterrence—while taking into account the special characteristics of the juvenile offender population.

That realization grew among juvenile corrections planners in several states during the 1980s. A number of states began to reformulate their juvenile correctional models so that programs could become more diverse and flexible. An array of programs matching offenders' risks, offenses, and service needs began to replace the traditional, one-dimensional model of the institution.

It should be noted that both the Bush and Clinton administrations began to catch up with program reforms that took place in states at the grass-roots level during the Reagan years. Under the Bush administration, the Office of Juvenile Justice and Delinquency Prevention gave grants to Johns Hopkins University to provide technical assistance to states for managing offenders in the community, and to the National Council on Crime and Delinquency to provide assistance with community-based intensive supervision programs. Training and technical assistance was also provided by the National Institute of Corrections, which convened juvenile justice administrators from around the nation to develop a long-term vision and mission statement.

Under the Clinton administration, United States Attorney General Janet Reno and Acting Administrator of the Office of Juvenile Justice and Delinquency Prevention John J. Wilson have captured the philosophy of a balanced model in their agenda for juvenile justice, "A Comprehensive Strategy for Serious, Violent, and Chronic Juvenile Offenders" (OJJDP, December 1993). The strategy outlines six principles for preventing and reducing delinquency that include "a broad spectrum of graduated sanctions" to hold youths accountable for their offenses, as well as a continuum of service programs corresponding to offenders' needs. Under Reno and Wilson, OJJDP provided $4 million in grants in 1993 and 1994 for the development of comprehensive programs based on multiple goals: offender accountability, increased community-based intervention, treatment, and rehabilitation services in four sites including Allegheny County, Pennsylvania, and Washington, D.C.

State Trends in a Non-System

As we discussed in the first chapter, the "get tough" philosophy of the mid- to late-1970s and 1980s replaced the short-lived agenda for deinstitutionalization during the late 1960s and early 1970s. The conservative agenda resulted in more juveniles detained prior to trial in locked facilities, more juveniles in adult prisons, and more juveniles in juvenile correctional institutions. While the first two results clearly continued into the 1990s, the third did not—at least, not in some states. Ironically, following the "get-tough" adult court policies for the most serious juvenile offenders, what emerged from some states' juvenile correctional agencies was a renewed interest in deinstitutionalization. Notably, states' interests in deinstitutionalization seemed not to be impeded by serious crime rates. In fact, in 1993, states that were planning or implementing deinstitutionalization were most likely to be ranked in the top twenty for index crime arrests.

Massachusetts' juvenile correctional system is invariably cited as the "founding father" of deinstitutionalization, having accomplished wide-scale reforms that began twenty years ago. The Massachusetts Department of Youth Services' closure of its large-scale training schools for youths in 1970–71 predated the events that are now unfolding in some states. The history of the Massachusetts juvenile justice system reveals a cyclical process that repeated itself for the 126–year existence of the reform schools. At first, the agency enjoyed a period of calm where staff and youths interacted, and youths made progress. That was usually followed by overcrowding of the institutions. In fact, within a decade of opening the first institution, its population soared to 600 youths. The next period was marked by older, predatory youths attacking younger, more vulnerable ones, escapes, youth assaulting staff, and intimidated staff turning on youth. Next followed exposure of incidents and problems by the media, which usually triggered an investigation by state and federal authorities. Ultimately, a period of reform began in the early 1970s.

The previous chapter documented a lack of national leadership in supporting juvenile justice programs and reforms throughout most of the 1980s. The impact, both in retrospect and in assessing the future of juvenile justice, has been dramatic. For one thing, during the last decade states had to struggle to provide programs for juvenile offenders with an absence of federal leadership in technical assistance, training, or substantive design. Despite this, drawing on remarkable initiative not commonly associated with government agencies, many states' juvenile correctional systems developed and reformed during that time, relying on shared technical assistance and nongovernmental forms of support.

By our accounting, at least a dozen states were involved in some stage of an effort to reform their juvenile correctional systems in the early 1990s. This chapter describes the nature of the reform efforts—some established, some fledgling, others actually retrenching. Reforms were at least under discussion in Alabama, Delaware, Florida, Georgia, Maryland, Missouri, Montana, Nebraska, New Hampshire, North Dakota, Ohio, Oklahoma, Oregon, and Virginia as of mid-1993, although Georgia and Virginia reversed their efforts by late 1994. The states varied considerably with regard to the exact policies that they were implementing, or attempted to implement. Some reorganized their juvenile correctional agencies in an effort to establish a "youth authority" model, whereby the juvenile correctional agency, not the court or the legislature, determines placement and sentence length for offenders under their jurisdiction. That reorganization allowed the most important individual case decisions to be made by executive branch agencies. It also meant that the agencies that are ultimately responsible for juvenile offenders are able to decide where the youths should be placed and for how long, rather than being so ordered by the courts.

Some states made significant changes, or were in the process of so doing, to the types of programming in which youths are placed. In particular, several states sought to end their reliance on the traditional institutional model for youthful offenders and substitute smaller-scale, community-based programs that often involved the participation of the private sector. Private sector management of programs for youths grew particularly in the area of community-based programs as opposed to secure, institutionalized settings, which continued to be operated by state employees. Some institutional systems attempted to downsize facilities to a level that is more easily managed, generally under 100 beds, and at the same time develop alternative sanctions in the community.

In post-reform states, correctional administrators faced a new set of substantive problems concerning such critical issues as offender classification, case management, and development of a private sector system of community programs to handle youths who would previously have been placed in institutions. Fortunately, administrators did not work in a vacuum, due to the fact that so many states were tackling very similar problems. One planning strategy was to tap into a grapevine of shared technology that developed informally from one state to the next. Privately funded sources of technical assistance were also accessed, most notably from the Annie E. Casey Foundation, the Edna McConnell Clark Foundation, and the National Council on Crime and Delinquency.

One characteristic of juvenile justice reforms that cannot be overemphasized is the fragility of reform initiatives. For example, a reform agenda was extremely short-lived in the state of Georgia, lasting just three years. Beginning in September 1991, Governor Zell Miller proclaimed a new era for juvenile justice in Georgia when he commissioned a Joint Study on Children and Youth in the General Assembly. In his charge to the committee he said, "Pick any young offender from any youth detention center and look in his file. You will find a whole history of problems: poverty, substance abuse, difficulties at school, a troubled family at home." He then went on to criticize government's traditional approach to young offenders. "We address problems by establishing institutions and putting people in them, rather than pursuing alternative treatment programs that can be individually tailored." Governor Miller promised to awaken Georgia from the institutional neglect in its handling of young offenders and move it forward (State of Georgia 1991).

He subsequently reorganized the state's juvenile correctional agency by creating a new and more focused department, and in 1992 appointed a proven administrator and leader, former Atlanta Police Chief and Public Safety Commissioner, George Napper. Those events signaled a new day for juvenile justice in Georgia. Many juvenile justice professionals around the country took note and eagerly awaited Governor Miller's reforms: a movement away from large institutions to a balanced system of juvenile corrections with the proper mix of secure confinement for the dangerous few and an array of community-based alternatives for nonviolent offenders.

Then, in early 1994, on the eve of his re-election campaign, Governor Miller politicized juvenile crime by drafting legislation that transfers youth as young as thirteen to adult court, although widened transfer policies have been negatively evaluated in many jurisdictions (Champion 1989; McShane and Williams 1989). In September 1994, just two months away from election day in a close gubernatorial race, Commissioner Napper was fired by the governor after an eleven-year-old sex offender was mistakenly returned home by his mother for a haircut, which provoked well-publicized outrage by the victim's family. Investigation into the case confirmed, however, that the agency itself was not at fault, and had acted swiftly to detain the youth after learning about the incident (Schwartzkopff 1994).

The firing of George Napper is just one more indication of Governor Miller's retreat from his reform strategy. The circumstances of Commissioner Napper's termination—a single incident made volatile by a heated political campaign—will likely result in a long and inefficient learning process for a new administration unfamiliar with the structure of the juvenile system and unaware of how to correct the existing gaps in programs and policies, since the new appointee to the commissioner's position was a former Drug Enforcement Agency supervisor, lacking experience in the juvenile justice system (McDonald 1994). Our information was last collected in 1993–1994, with updates provided in late 1994 by respondents from New Hampshire, Virginia, Delaware, Missouri, North Dakota, Ohio, and Florida. All of the information presented is subject to the volatility of the juvenile justice system.

Programmatic Trends in State Juvenile Corrections

The juvenile correctional agencies of fifteen states were surveyed by us in 1990, 1993, and 1994 to obtain answers to the following questions:

- What states were contemplating or implementing reforms?
- What was the scope and nature of the reforms?
- What obstacles did states encounter in attempting to make changes, and what strategies were successful in instituting reforms?
- What ongoing management issues have states tried to overcome?

Specifically, agency administrators were questioned about the ratio of institutional, or training-school, placements to community-based placements; their methods for classifying offenders into different levels of programming; where the decision-making authority for determining client placements was located among different parties in their state; the impact of transfer policies; the impact of status offenders; the use of private program providers; trends in expansion or reduction of different types of programming; and strategies used by agency administrators to market the expansion of community-based programs. The following states were surveyed: Texas, California, Ohio, Montana, Alabama, Oregon, Delaware, Florida, Missouri, New Hampshire, Maryland, Virginia, Georgia, North Dakota, and Mississippi. In addition, comparative background information was obtained from several other states.

Most states have, by now, created separate and autonomous juvenile correctional agencies. In the past, many juvenile correctional agencies fell under the jurisdiction of adult corrections, which generally indicated a lack of specialized programming for juvenile offenders. Now, most states' juvenile correctional agencies share equal footing with the adult correctional agency in their state, meaning that they are not governed by the philosophies or management styles of adult correctional administrators. Of course, to achieve desired policy changes, these "autonomous" juvenile correctional agencies still need the support of their parent agency, which is usually the agency in charge of either human services or public safety departments, the governor, the legislature, the judiciary, the child advocates, and the remaining host of stakeholders who share an interest in juvenile justice.

In 1994, some states continued to rely primarily on the century-old institutional model for punishing juvenile offenders, while others attempted to diversify programming by providing different levels of security and individualized treatment. Three of the states with established juvenile correctional agencies (Texas, California, and Ohio) based their correctional programming primarily on an institutional model, and neither Texas nor California reported any movement toward a more diversified system. Ohio has diversified programming by funding counties to provide community-based programming at the county level. Montana's legislature recently created a separate juvenile correctional agency that relies primarily on existing institutions, but program plans indicate that some community-based expansion is foreseeable. Georgia's legislature recently created a separated juvenile correctional agency also, but restrictive placement legislation will guarantee the expansion of institutional placements. Five other states with established juvenile correctional agencies (Alabama, Oregon, Delaware, Maryland, and Florida) have responded to litigation, or threatened litigation, to reduce institutional overcrowding by implementing tighter management policies and creating greater program diversity.

Other states not in legal jeopardy nonetheless down-scaled their traditional reliance on institutions, in part voluntarily following the lead of Massachusetts' first institutional closures in the early 1970s. These states include Missouri, New Hampshire, North Dakota, and Virginia. Virginia, however, stepped back from reforms in 1994 and is now projecting substantial increases in institutional capacity. In 1993, New York, which since the 1970s has provided a full range of program levels from institutions to group care, shifted slightly toward increasing the numbers of at-home intensive supervision placements due to the high cost of residential facilities, but represented such a mixed model that we do not discuss it in detail in this chapter (see chapter 5 for a description of the New York placement decision model; see also McGarrell 1988). Mississippi's former institutional model was undergoing changes out of fiscal necessity.

The critical issue of which branch of government has authority to make "sentencing" decisions—including type of placement, length of stay, discharge decision—has created a turf struggle in various states. In 1994, at least three of the states that were experimenting with expanded community-based programming (Maryland, Virginia, and Delaware) were waging battle against the juvenile courts for the authority to place youths in programs that they believed were most appropriate. Those correctional agencies that were emerging from litigation were abiding by legislatively mandated caps, or limits, on institutional populations to control their offender population, but—as we describe in Oregon and Florida—the caps were creating new problems unto themselves. We also note that legislatures in several states have recently mandated that a portion of the correctional budget be spent on early delinquency prevention programs. Finally, we particularly commend efforts through 1994 in North Dakota to develop and manage a balanced program model.

Five States Managing Institutions—Texas, California, Ohio, Montana, and Georgia

Among the states that we surveyed, five (Texas, California, Ohio, Montana, and Georgia) can be considered "institutional" because of their reliance on training schools over such alternatives as group care, intensive supervision, and specialized treatment. With the exception of Georgia, those states were not trying to reform their correctional systems, although certain incremental changes were planned. In 1993, all but Texas were contemplating incremental program changes. The Texas juvenile correctional system, holding fast to its institutional model, placed 70 percent of its youth population in training schools, and the remainder into community settings. In total, 20 percent of the programs were privately contracted, including two-thirds of the community-based programs. The Texas Youth Commission (TYC) had statutory authority to make decisions concerning placement, length of stay and parole in juvenile corrections for all but a few select offenders who are committed by juvenile judges for a specific sentence. The TYC uses a standardized risk assessment instrument to classify youths.

The California Youth Authority (CYA), also an institutional agency, confined 95 percent of its youths in training schools; only 5 percent were placed in community settings, and only 1 percent of all programs are privately contracted. Chronic overcrowding has plagued the CYA and is projected to continue in the years ahead. By 1996, if no other plans are implemented, the institutional population will reach 9,287, nearly 2,600 over capacity. Overcrowding was, in part, caused by the Youth Offender Parole Board (YOPB), an agency separate from the CYA. The parole board in California had expansive authority to not only increase a juvenile's sentence with either discretionary add-on time or disciplinary add-on time, thus lengthening the stay of institutionalized offenders, but also to make decisions concerning type of placement. Due to overcrowding and the related threat of litigation, the CYA has implemented a five-year plan to manage overcrowding by building new institutions. Community-based program plans include drug treatment programs for parolees and supervised electronic monitoring, but these programs are limited in scope.

Turning to Ohio, a number of different placement options were used for the youths committed to the Department of Youth Services (DYS), including state-run and private contracted programs. In 1994, the state operated eight training schools and two residential treatment facilities, and also contracted with two private facilities and numerous privately run community-based programs. On any given day in 1994, there were approximately 2,000 committed youths, of whom 1,800 were in an institutional setting and the remaining 200 in a community-based program. The DYS also oversaw approximately 2,400 youths who were on parole. In late 1992, the total population of DYS training schools was nearly double their capacity. To alleviate overcrowding, DYS funded the construction of eleven regional rehabilitation centers as well as other diversion programs.

In 1994, DYS was focusing on two main policy areas: institutional programming and community alternatives. DYS had implemented measures for improving security and treatment in institutions including unit management, expanded drug testing and security procedures, and specialized treatment for sex offenders and substance abusers. The department had also developed an innovative program for drug traffickers, which included community service with crack babies and business training in legitimate areas.

DYS had also replaced three aging facilities with two new state-of-the-art institutions designed to maximize programming and improve security. A third facility was in the construction stage. In an effort to downsize, these facilities have lower bed capacity (200 beds) than the ones they replaced. One of the facilities will specifically work with youths with mental health or medical issues to address a longstanding service need in the department. Another will be used as a centralized assessment center.

In addition, DYS is implementing a plan titled "Reclaim Ohio" (Reasoned and Equitable Community and Local Alternatives to Incarceration of Minors). This is a model by which state funds put resources into the front end of the system, so that courts can provide services to more youths at the local level, diverting them from DYS. The plan targets nonviolent felons and provides financial incentives for local counties to develop or purchase community-based programs, including day treatment, electronic monitoring, specialized residential treatment, and intensive supervision, in lieu of commitment to DYS. Funding is allocated to counties based on their historical felony adjudication rate. The intent is to give judges the resources to provide an intermediate range of programs for youths whose behavior does not warrant a DYS commitment. Judges will continue to have the option

of making a commitment to DYS, at 75 percent of the per diem allot-
ment.

Unlike California, Texas, and Ohio, whose youth correctional agencies are well established, the Montana state legislature created the
Department of Family Services (DFS) in 1987. Despite a rocky start
(within three years DFS was almost abolished by the governor but was
saved with the appointment of a new director), DFS is still in existence and faces no major opposition. Prior to the creation of DFS,
judges sentenced youths directly to the only two institutions in the
state, the Mountain View School for Girls and the Pine Hills School
for Boys. Laws were changed so that, following adjudication, the judges
remanded youths to the custody of DFS, giving DFS control over
placement and length of stay. That policy change was important in
increasing DFS's authority vis-à-vis the courts. There are exceptions
to that authority, however. If the judge labels a youth as a "serious
offender," that label mandates DFS to send the youth into an institutional placement, but the release date is set at the discretion of DFS.
On the other hand, the transfer laws loosened over this same time
period, enabling youths to be transferred to adult jurisdiction at the
age of twelve for such crimes as murder and rape. In 1993, DFS was
placing 80 percent of its youths in training school facilities, 5 percent
in psychiatric placements, and the remainder in the community. Other
than private hospitals, no private providers were operating programs
for DFS.

The placement decisions made by DFS are guided in part by the use
of a risk assessment instrument that was developed with technical
assistance from Ira Schwartz, former director of the U.S. Office of
Juvenile Justice and Delinquency Prevention (OJJDP) and the University of Michigan's Center for Youth Policy. Each institution contained
an evaluation unit which makes the placement determination within
forty-five days. If a youth was not retained in the institution, he or she
was placed in the community. When DFS was first created, it contained a full complement of community programs, and the average
daily population in the Pine Hills School, which is capped at 100, was
down to 70. However, by 1990, the facility was 140 percent over
capacity, up to 140 residents. The number of beds in community residential programs decreased by 30–40 percent by 1990, causing an
increase in institutional population. Reasons for the loss were twofold:
(1) the state was hit by a severe loss of federal funds, and the state's

own economy slowed, which translated into major budget cuts; (2) DFS had just been created, and the pieces were not yet in place to manage the new system and guarantee that community-based programs, in particular, would not be lost due to budget cuts. However, those funds were restored and a new sixteen-bed transitional community-based program was opened in 1991. In addition, a risk/needs classification program was being piloted and future expansion of community-based programs was under consideration. Specialized programming for sex offenders and mentally ill offenders was also under discussion.

Turning to Georgia, throughout the 1980s, the Alliance for Children, which was the state's sole advocacy group for juvenile offenders, unsuccessfully pressed the state legislature to close Georgia's antiquated and overcrowded institutions. One of the overcrowded facilities was built in 1905, an era that produced dungeon-like structures. In 1990, the University of Michigan's Center for the Study of Youth Policy conducted an assessment that recommended institutional downsizing. Their data showed that high numbers of low-risk youths were being institutionalized unnecessarily. In addition, the *Atlanta Constitution* editorialized about the state's desperate needs for reform. Between 1989 and 1991, changes began to occur. Georgia opened a twenty-five-bed community-based residential program, increased foster home contracts, and expanded nonresidential programs.

Most significantly, the 1992 legislative session created the Department of Children and Youth Services (DCYS) as a separate state agency, moving it from division status under the Department of Human Resources. The legislation also mandated downsizing of the large institutions, directed that funds be moved to the "front end" of the system for expanding community-based alternatives, and gave the department a mandate for prevention activities. Those reforms were supported by judges, legislators, the governor, and the youth services' division, with no specific opposition by other interest groups. In 1993, a study by the National Council on Crime and Delinquency provided additional support for system-wide changes. The study, "The Georgia Department of Children and Youth Services: A New Vision, Mandate and an Agenda for Reform," described the institutions as severely neglected and out of touch with contemporary advances in programming and policies. At the time, Georgia's prosecutors had concurrent jurisdiction over certain serious offenders, meaning that the prosecutors decided where those cases would be tried—in adult or juvenile court. In addition, most violent offenses retained in the juvenile court were known as "designated felonies" and required automatic placement in DCYS institutions for up to eighteen months.

However, in 1994, a bill introduced by Governor Zell Miller, candidate for re-election, was passed by the state legislature which placed the reform efforts in serious jeopardy. The new law provided that youths aged thirteen to seventeen be automatically tried as adults, rather than considered "designated felons" in the juvenile system, for seven violent offenses: murder, rape, voluntary manslaughter, armed robbery with a firearm, aggravated sodomy, aggravated child molestation, and aggravated sexual battery. Subject to a voters' referendum, which passed in November 1994, the law recommended that minimum sentences of ten years be set for those offenders. Other designated felony offenses remained in the juvenile system, such as second-time possession of a firearm, but the law mandated a five-year sentence, rather than the previous eighteen-month sentence to an institution.

The law also allowed judges to directly sentence adjudicated youths to institutions for up to ninety days without committing them to the Department. This forced the Department to reopen cottages they had closed during the downsizing period in 1993. In late 1994, the Department was unable to handle the volume of youths who were sentenced under the ninety-day provision, as youths were coming in at an average of forty per week, while there were only 120 institutional beds set aside for such offenders. Consequently, those youths were backing up in detention for approximately eight weeks awaiting institutional placement. Some judges were further specifying that good-time credits could not be applied for time spent in detention.

As a result of the law, the state's juvenile detention facilities, already overcrowded in 1994, will need to be expanded significantly to hold youths who are awaiting trial in Superior Court for an average of nine to twelve months, and to absorb the new category of short-term detainees. In late 1994, there were over 1200 youths in 669 detention beds. The critical need to expand detention capacity is expected to take resources away from community-based programs.

Five States Responding to Litigation—Alabama, Oregon, Florida, Delaware, and Maryland

The process of litigation can be a long and painful one that is generally prompted by institutional overcrowding and problems linked to overcrowding, such as program deficiencies and constitutional rights violations. In some states, litigation was avoided, but the threat of lawsuit led to changes. Class action lawsuits and system-wide court orders are generally signs of extreme, longstanding mismanagement that often requires years to address. The experience of the following five states demonstrates the varying impact of litigation on juvenile correctional agencies.

Alabama—Taking a Long-Term Approach

In the state of Alabama, the director of the Department of Youth Services (DYS) reports to an eighteen-member Youth Service Board that is appointed by the governor. In 1987, DYS was placed under court order as the result of overcrowding in juvenile facilities. The court order encouraged the chief justice of the Supreme Court, an elected position, to run on a juvenile justice platform that included a progressive expansion of community-based programs, but no downsizing of their training school capacity, then at 385. The legislative leadership and the Youth Service Board were supportive of the plan and sold it as a public safety measure. The emphasis of the plan was on serious offenders, because it was commonly believed that serious offenders were being released from institutions too quickly due to overcrowding in detention and the lack of alternative placements. Rather than recommend expanding the institutional capacity, the framers of the reforms were able to sell the public on expanding only community-based capacity.

Ironically, community program advocates were helped in their efforts to curtail institutional expansion by a notorious case in late 1989 in which a youth escaped from an institution and committed murder in the community. The incident was used to send the message that institutions were not necessarily in the best interests of public safety; policymakers were deterred also by the costs of building new institutions. DYS located outside funding for institutional alternatives from the Edna McConnell Clark Foundation, which provided $650,000 for outreach and tracking, diversion from detention, and the development and monitoring of detention criteria. Two hundred and fifty nonresidential slots were added in 1989. However, state budget cuts hampered further any expansion plans other than a boot camp program, which increased from 20 to 100 beds between 1990 and 1993, comprising 20 percent of residential placements in 1993, while community-based slots made up only 10 percent of residential placements. Overcrowding problems were further aggravated in 1990 when a new law was passed that removed disposition authority from DYS in cases involving second-time Class A felony offenders, permitting courts to impose twelve-month minimum institutional sentences. The legislation was a response to the overcrowding problem and consequential early release of serious offenders.

In mid-1993 a consent decree addressing the institutional overcrowding issue was signed by all parties. Two reforms were decreed: first, DYS would adopt all American Correctional Association standards for monitoring correctional programs. Second, DYS would work more closely with the community to develop community-based programs, favored by the Alabama legislature because they are less costly than institutionalizing offenders. In order to accommodate the second goal, DYS retained the services of a local consulting group to survey the various local communities and to establish a priority list of needed programs, focusing on early intervention and educational programs.

Oregon—Managing State/County Partnerships

The state of Oregon experienced changes that were also inspired, in part, by legal action. The Juvenile Rights Project, an association of legal aid lawyers based in St. Louis, Missouri, brought a lawsuit against the Oregon Children's Services Division (CSD) during the 1980s that focused on overcrowding and the conspicuous absence of mental health professionals in the Hillcrest and MacLaren Schools, the only training schools in the state. At the time of the suit, there were over 500 youths housed in just one of those schools. As part of the court settlement, a cap of 513 was placed on all secure placements, which included the two training schools and five 20–bed work/study camps for boys (since changed to four 25–bed camps). In addition, the court ordered that mental health professionals be added to the institutional staff. In order to meet the specifications of the court-ordered cap, a "downsizing" policy for the training school population was implemented in 1986.

The mechanism for downsizing was worked out so that state control over the training schools was shared with the county courts. The Children's Services Division apportioned state money to county juvenile courts to offer community programming through their probation departments. Secure beds were appropriated to each county according to the population size of children at risk within that county, with 140 beds held in reserve by CSD for Class A violent felons. The allocation policy was designed to give the county courts incentive to release youths in order to make space for incoming youths. This was similar to courts having direct sentencing authority, except that courts were also made responsible for utilizing scarce secure resources. The release decision from secure placements, until recently, was based on a recommendation from a CSD parole officer to the centralized Close Custody Review Board, which included representatives from county parole as well as state corrections. By 1993, the Close Custody Review Board was replaced by a decentralized process in which each county created a separate "CAP" committee where release decisions were mutually determined by state and county workers.

Despite the 513 cap, institutional placements exceeded 550 in 1993 due to an increasing number of serious juvenile offenders. Although community-based beds comprised 40 percent of all residential slots, there was no community-based program expansion since 1984. In 1993, state budget cuts were threatening even the existing community beds. As a result of those pressures, and of the recognition that 513 was an arbitrary limit, efforts were launched to roll back the original court order. Proposed legislation was being considered that would relax the 513 cap, allowing it to "flex" up or down with fluctuations in the state's youth population. Another strategy to expand the cap was a legislative proposal that would prevent serious offenders who are sentenced as adults and transferred back to CSD from being counted against the cap.

In mid-1993, a unified case management system was piloted so that each youth would have one CSD worker who would follow his or her case from begining to end. Although funds for these pilot caseworkers existed in the state budget, there were tentative plans to shift them to county control. County participation in corrections was clearly emphasized in Oregon, and although the combined decision process was cumbersome, one advantage of bringing courts into the correctional process was the breakdown of traditional turf barriers between courts and corrections, because the court became a partner in deciding how to control resources.

However, the fact that the county courts shared administrative authority over placement and release decisions caused divisions between state and county administrators, depending on the county. Counties varied considerably not only as to the types of youths who were sent to the institutions, but also to the decision criteria that they used. Several of Oregon's three dozen counties used an objective risk assessment instrument to distinguish high-risk, institution-bound offenders; the remainder used more subjective and idiosyncratic criteria. As decision procedures continue to decentralize, it seems that geographic variability will continue to dominate the management of resources in Oregon.

Florida—Battling for Credibility

A class action lawsuit, *Bobby M. v. Martinez,* was filed in federal court in 1983. The suit alleged that conditions in the four juvenile institutions that confined 1,000 juveniles violated the constitutional rights of those confined youths. Such conditions included overcrowded and below standard living conditions, lack of security and discipline, inadequate medical and psychological care, cruel use of isolation, inadequacies in education and other programming, and inappropriate placements. A consent decree was signed by the plaintiffs and the Department of Health and Rehabilitative Services (DHRS), the agency responsible for all committed juvenile offenders. A court master was appointed by the federal court to oversee the implementation of the consent decree. Elements of the negotiated settlement included the following mandates for the DHRS (Streit 1988):

1. Confront the need for effective programming, meaning small intensive treatment and supervision programs; specialized treatment programs for special needs youth, including sex offenders and mentally ill offenders; and generally improve the quality of care for all committed youths.
2. Establish an assessment, classification, and placement process to guide decision makers, and establish a case management system.
3. Stop the overreliance on deep-end training school programs by providing community-based alternatives for youths who are not violent or chronic offenders.

4. Confront the reality of high recidivism by providing family services and substitute care arrangements for youths returning to their communities.

The suit resulted in a training school population cap of 250 youths. Between 1988 and 1992, the training school capacity was forced down from 405 in 1988 to 260 in 1992, thereby achieving virtually uncrowded conditions. In addition, 50 secure treatment beds were created along with hundreds of nonresidential programs. However, the state's liberal transfer policies encouraged prosecutors to transfer juveniles to adult court, rather than risk the 250 bed cap. For example, a twelve-year-old boy was reportedly waived to adult court and convicted of armed robbery and assault because the prosecutor feared an inappropriate placement in DHRS. Indeed, the pattern of court statistics confirm that such examples were widespread. The number of delinquency cases that was transferred to adult court was 3,162 in 1982/83, when the Bobby M. suit was filed. Transfer cases then increased somewhat, by 22 percent, between 1982/83 and 1987/88, before the cap was in place. Then, between 1987/88 and 1991/92, the number of transfer cases swelled by 65 percent, to 6,352 (Governor's Juvenile Justice and Delinquency Prevention Advisory Committee 1992).

Ironically, the adult system was not necessarily a better alternative for punishing juvenile offenders. Florida's experience with transferring thousands of youths annually to adult court resulted in a seriously overcrowded detention system, as youths spent more time waiting for adult trials than they waited for juvenile hearings. Ironically, fewer than one-fourth of the youths were charged with a violent offense (Bishop, Frazier, and Henretta 1989). In addition, due to severe overcrowding in the adult prison system, a far lower than expected proportion of youths served time in state prison, and a lower than expected amount of time was actually served. Approximately 50 percent of youths in adult court had their charges dismissed or received no jail time due to credit for time served in detention while awaiting trial.

In order to further comply with the consent decree, DHRS attempted to expand educational, medical, and legal services while decreasing the training school overcrowding problem. One positive consequence of the cap on training school beds has been the creation of a variety of community-based programs, wilderness camps, and day treatment programs. In October 1994, the Department of Juvenile Justice (DJJ) was established as a separate entity. The DJJ assumed responsibility for managing the continuum of programs for delinquent juvenile offenders that was previously the responsibility of the Department of Health and Rehabilitative Services.

The new agency is expected to have more focus on punishment than its predecessor. Although the identification of youths' treatment needs will continue to be a priority, two policy changes deserve mention. First, whereas juvenile commitment programs were previously categorized into four levels of restrictiveness, a fifth level was added to serve as the maximum-risk residential level. Second, judges became empowered in 1994 to order youths into pretrial detention facilities as punishment for contempt of court. To alleviate some of the impact on detention facilities, "alternative sanction coordinators" will be responsible for providing contempt sanction options as alternatives to placement in a secure detention facility (Florida Advisory Council on Intergovernmental Relations 1994).

Delaware—Expanding Community-Based Programs

In 1993, the state's Division of Youth Rehabilitive Services (DYRS) was continuing to implement the so-called Delaware Plan, which passed in 1987, calling for a more community-based approach in juvenile corrections. The Delaware Plan was an outgrowth of a 1986 decision by the state attorney general that prohibited the state's practice of mixing delinquent youths in the same programs with abused, dependent, and neglected youths. A subsequent task force appointed by Governor Michael Castle determined that mixing delinquent and nondelinquent youths together in residential placements was the result of the general unavailability of adequate services and resources for youths in the state, particularly alternatives to institutions. Between 1987 and 1991, the allocation of state funding for alternative programs (such as in-home counseling and residential group care) increased from $800,000 to over $4 million (Brandau 1992).

By 1988, the new funding enabled DYRS to contract with more than thirty-five day and residential treatment programs as well as family therapy specialists. In FY 1989, DYRS added contracts with four private Pennsylvania community-based programs and an additional private group home in Delaware. In addition, DYRS established contracts with residential and nonresidential substance abuse programs, as well as nontraditional minority psychologists who work directly in the community.

The Division of Youth Rehabilitative Services was successful in procuring funding for community-based alternatives, in part because of an assessment conducted by the National Council on Crime and Delinquency. Although the assessment did not examine the chronicity of the youths' prior offense records, it recommended that only 6 to 10 of the youths then in institutions needed maximum security, while 30 others were appropriate for either an institutional or alternative setting, and the remainder could be placed in the community. These figures seemed to symbolize minimum, rather than realistic, numbers of secure beds needed in Delaware, but nonetheless were useful in negotiating the release of nonserious offenders from institutions.

The transition to a more community-based system in Delaware was not without controversy. Although the Ferris School (the state's institution for boys) reduced its numbers, conditions remained unsatisfactory, and the American Civil Liberties Union was pressed into filing a lawsuit. The state planned to close the Ferris School and replace it with a new facility in 1996, along with implementing disposition guidelines to limit the types of offenders placed into the training school, in order to settle the concerns named in the suit. Inattention to the conditions in a separate detention facility, another longstanding problem in Delaware, led to the resignation of the director of the Division in 1989. There was no court order citing a need to ameliorate the existing conditions and, finding no other sources of support, the director resigned in protest. His replacement, Patrick McCarthy, worked diligently on case management of detainees in order to move them out as quickly as possible. In addition, the 1990 legislative session passed a bill limiting the categories of youths who could be detained on pretrial status. Although youths charged with a felony or with one of six serious misdemeanors could be detained by the court until adjudication, all others needed to be released. The legislation took effect in December 1990, and was credited with reducing detention admissions by removing all nonviolent misdemeanor cases.

Maryland—Battling for Credibility

Maryland's Department of Juvenile Service (DJS) is unique among the fifty state juvenile correctional agencies. Under Maryland law,

DJS is assigned full responsibility for a continuum of juvenile justice services including intake, pretrial detention, probation, confinement, and aftercare/parole supervision. That is, DJS intake workers collect information on youths' backgrounds, and then make placement recommendations to the court. Other DJS workers supervise probation and parole. At the same time, the state's DJS oversees pretrial detention. In most other states, intake and probation operate from the court level. In all but a handful of states, pretrial detention is managed by individual counties, rather than by state government. In two states (California and Illinois), decisions on institutional release and aftercare are made by distinct parole boards. As a result of their broad mandate, DJS is responsible for making decisions and delivering varying degrees of service to nearly 52,000 youths annually.

In 1993, the state of Maryland had many juvenile justice issues on the table. Linda Rossi was appointed by the governor to head the Department of Juvenile Services (DJS) in 1987. One of her first challenges as secretary was to close the Montrose School, a dilapidated facility designed for 212 youths that held approximately 250. The process took nearly a year, as reluctant private providers were gradually persuaded to accept Montrose youths into their group homes and residential treatment facilities. Montrose had been the target of a class action suit in 1986 following two suicides and several more attempted suicides by youths in less than a three-year period. The suit was initiated by law professors from the University of Maryland who had represented Montrose residents and had periodically taken tours of the facility. Along with Mark Soler of the Youth Law Center in San Francisco, they charged Montrose with denying the civil and constitutional rights of its residents, including failure to provide minimally adequate medical or psychological care, denial of opportunities for youths to visit or even communicate with their families, and arbitrary use of isolation. One plaintiff was sent to Montrose at age eleven for stealing a bicycle. During his six-month stay, he was raped repeatedly by older boys in his cottage, restrained with handcuffs, stripped of his clothing in isolation, and denied adequate medical treatment (Butts 1988).

A second suit was brought in 1987 by the Sierra Club concerning the Montrose facility's sewage system, which was in violation of federal water-quality standards. The suit was settled when the state agreed to fix the system. However, the repair cost of $2 million, along with another $10 million in needed renovations, provided additional justification for simply closing the school (Butts 1988).

In addition to closing Montrose, Secretary Rossi also reduced the average daily population of the Hickey School from 500 residents in 1987 to 340 by 1993. The state of Maryland developed a range of community programs including family shelter care, specialized foster care, group homes, wilderness programs, and addiction and mental health treatment programs. The Ten Year Master Facility Plan (Maryland Department of Juvenile Services 1990) further specified the construction of more community programs, and had as one objective to increase the average daily population in community residential programs from 1,029 to 1,235 during the 1990s.

Despite those efforts, since the closure of Montrose and the downsizing of Hickey, some courts managed to resist efforts on the part of the Department of Juvenile Services to divert youths out of institutions. For example, a DJS study showed that 14 percent of the youths committed to Maryland's Hickey School did not meet the Hickey admissions criteria and were committed against the Department's recommendation. In addition, judges repeatedly overstepped their commitment authority by placing youths out-of-state in the nearby Glen Mills institution in Pennsylvania. Glen Mills is a privately operated, 600–700 bed facility on an open campus. Many old-line judges viewed Glen Mills as a preferred alternative to placing youths into community-based residential programs in their own state, arguing that it was more convenient geographically for youths from northern Maryland than Maryland's own programs.

It appeared that by mid-1993, the time of our survey, the overstepping of judicial authority was reduced through better communication between the juvenile court judges, federal court overseers, the DJS advisory board, and DJS. In addition, DJS won the passage of legislation banning out-of-state commitments. The legislation reportedly increased the willingness of judges to consider in-state community-based alternatives. Moreover, efforts by the DJS helped to defeat a legislative effort known as the "Bishop Bill" calling for a 300–bed juvenile prison with a minimum determinate sentence of two years. The Department sought to reduce the number of youths waived to the adult system and fight the Bishop Bill by calling for 150 new beds in small secure programs to accommodate the types of serious youths who would otherwise be waived. However, the small secure programs did not materialize, and, at the time of our survey, community protection advocates were proposing a new eighteen-month secure facility at the Hickey School for serious offenders.

Another development in the operation of the Hickey School resulted from two 1991 legislative reports that recommended the closing of the school because of its unsafe conditions. After a subsequent threat of a lawsuit, Governor Schaefer called for private companies to bid on the operation of Hickey. Rebound Corporation from Colorado won a $50 million contract to operate Hickey for three years. However, Rebound lasted only fourteen months before DJS Secretary Saar terminated their contract. No reasons were published for the termination of the contract, but DJS communicated its disappointment that Rebound had not implemented as many youth programs as promised (*Juvenile Justice Digest* 1992b, 1992c).

Five States That Have Downsized Institutions: Missouri, New Hampshire, Virginia, North Dakota, Mississippi

In mid-1993, institutional downsizing or closure had occurred in a variety of ways among several states' juvenile correctional systems. "Institutional downsizing" should not be equated with expansion of community-based alternatives, as Mississippi's skeletal system illustrates, nor need it even mean that fewer youths are placed into secure confinement. For example, Oklahoma's youth correctional agency closed 800 institutional beds in 1979 as a result of a lawsuit that found the state in violation of civil rights. Nonetheless, about the same number of youths were placed in secure beds in 1990 as in 1979. This was due to the fact that on any given day there were approximately 500 youths in in-patient psychiatric care. That is, psychiatric hospital placements had merely substituted for the lost institutional space. Despite such experiences in some states, a number of other states have actively created a wide array of community-based alternatives, modeling themselves after such states as Massachusetts, Utah, and Colorado.

Missouri—Measured Progress

Community-based residential programming began developing in the state of Missouri in 1972. This movement developed to the point that in 1980 and 1983, the Division of Youth Services (DYS) closed the Training School for Girls and the Training School for Boys (they were not under any court order to do so), leaving no large state-run institutions in 1983. Following that closure, small residential community programs were expanded and in 1988, the division developed a plan to serve a significant portion of its commitments in nonresidential programs. The nonresidential service system consisted of day treatment, proctor care, and intensive supervision to closely track youths and receiving services in the community.

A case management system was implemented in 1991, whereby each committed youth was assessed using an eight-item risk assessment form and placed accordingly into six categories of placements. Additional reforms were aimed toward increasing the number of nonresidential program community slots. In 1994, Missouri passed a bond issue which allocated $20 million to establish 160 new secure bed spaces; replace one existing 20–bed facility; and fund an additional 20–bed program. These facilities were needed for the most serious juvenile offenders, so that their average length of stay could be increased from six months to a year, and waiting time for openings in secure facilities could be reduced. On any given day, there were approximately 580 youths committed to the agency. When the bond issue passed, there were 160 secure beds in 20– to 30–bed programs around the state. To balance the increase in secure capacity, Missouri is also adding more community-based and nonresidential programs with strong support for these programs from diverse community groups.

New Hampshire—Determining Resource Needs

Efforts in the state of New Hampshire to shift from a residentially based system to a community-based system reach back to the mid-1970s. These efforts were accelerated in the late 1980s and have reached their peak in the past several years. Up until the mid-1970s, commitment to the state's only juvenile training school, the Youth Development Center (YDC), was the primary way in which juvenile delinquency was addressed. In 1976, through efforts of the legislature, judges, police, and child advocates, the bed capacity of the YDC was reduced from 180 beds to 107. In 1983, the Division for Children and Youth Services was formed (whose name has been changed to the Division for Children, Youth and Families, or DCYF). At that time there were a total of 26 residential programs (470 beds) available statewide and few if any community-based nonresidential services available. By 1990 there was a marked increase in both the number of community-based residential care facilities and a significant increase in nonresidential community-based services such as tracking, family-based services, and juvenile diversion programs.

Since 1992, DCYF has been purposefully recognizing, through its practices, that in order to address the massive increase in the number of juveniles entering the system, meaningful intervention as well as prevention can best be achieved by increasing the collaboration with local communities. Long-term intrinsic changes in a family system which may serve to reduce the likelihood of continued juvenile delinquency is a goal DCYF believes can best be attained by adhering to the principle of "local solutions to local problems."

This effort has resulted in a further increase in nonresidential community-based services such as crisis intervention services, intensive day programming, adolescent and family support services, family mediation services, multidisciplinary teams, respite care, and parent aid services. Based on a trend analysis completed in July 1994, the Division was then experiencing a decreasing utilization rate of residential care and a significant increase in the utilization of nonresidential community-based services. This resulted in a shift in where dollars were expended. In the late 1980s over 80 percent of the Division's budget was used to purchase residential care and institutional placements. By 1994 that figure had decreased to 45 percent. In 1994 over 3,000 youths in the juvenile justice system were served through nonresidential community-based services.

In late 1994, the Division was facing an unprecedented increase in juvenile service caseloads. Earlier that year, a statewide effort was undertaken to ensure the availability of juvenile diversion programs in every community. Those programs include components such as restitution, community service, family counseling, substance abuse groups, challenge courses, and conflict resolution training. It was the expectation of the Division that increased availability of community diversion programs would slow the numbers of juveniles entering the system.

In the late 1980s, the Division was forced to thoroughly scrutinize its usage of the Youth Development Center. Studies conducted by the University of Michigan's Center for Youth Policy (Butts and DeMuro 1989) revealed longstanding patterns of over-institutionalization in New

Hampshire, based on offenders' expected risk of recidivism. In 1993, disposition guidelines were adopted by the judiciary to encourage courts and juvenile services officers employed by the Division to follow uniform criteria when recommending YDC placement. Assessments of instant offense severity, prior offense severity, and offense chronicity were to be completed by juvenile service officers as they developed their disposition recommendations whenever YDC placement was a possibility. Just as the new policies were implemented, a new director, Lorrie Lutz, was appointed to head the DCYF.

Compliance with the guidelines was evaluated by William Barton after they had been in use for about one year (Barton 1994a). The evaluation study found that the guidelines had little or no impact on the number and type of youths committed to the YDC. In fact, 69 percent of the YDC commitments in 1993 fell outside of the guidelines and were committed to the YDC only as a result of overrides to the scoring instrument. In the majority of cases, overrides were made due to perceptions that youths were not complying with, or had failed in, their community-based placements (Barton 1994a). Consequently, an acceleration of staff training and education, and the establishment of clear commitment criteria for the YDC, were major priorities of the Division for 1995.

Virginia—Rapid Reversals

The Department of Youth and Family Services (DYFS) was created as a separate agency on 1 July 1990, apart from the adult Department of Corrections, its former parent. In its first three years, DYFS pursued a community-oriented approach. As in Montana, the DYFS became a separate agency because diverse groups wanted to give juvenile corrections its own identity and resources. The reform advocates were broad-based and included legislators, the former governor, judges, private provider associates, the Virginia juvenile officers union, and other local groups. The Division of Youth Services estimated that their operating costs would go down by becoming an independent Department of Youth and Family Services. Reportedly, the only group that resisted their efforts was their former parent agency, the Virginia Department of Correction.

In 1985 an 80–bed training school was closed, and over the past ten years community-based residential capacity expanded by 400 beds. A continuing problem was that DYFS lacked full authority to decide where youths would be placed. Until 1993, the courts had complete authority to place youths directly into all programs, bypassing DYFS, which reportedly resulted in inappropriate use of community-based alternatives. DYFS's lack of placement authority continued after 1993, when the Comprehensive Services Act (CSA) was implemented. The act pooled funding from several child-serving agencies (education, social services, mental health, health, and DYFS) and allocated those funds directly to the communities based on a funding formula. The act also created local community assessment teams, made up of representatives from the various child-serving agencies, parents, and court officials. Those teams received the funding and determined how it should be spent. When a youth needed services, she/he would be referred to the community team closest to the youth's home, and that team would assign a case manager to prepare a service plan. The funding would be allocated depending on the youth's service needs.

If the local community assessment team rejected a youth, then the youth was forced to be committed to the care of DYFS. A potential future problem is that only a judge can place a youth in a DYFS training school, or "learning center," not DYFS. In 1993, DYFS no longer had the funding to purchase private residential and nonresidential programs as a result of the CSA model. Therefore, the placement of those juveniles who were not court ordered into a learning center, but who were rejected by the local community assessment teams, was unclear.

The Comprehensive Services Act's changes to the structure of Virginia's juvenile justice system marked an attempt to allow for more local community control, encourage more interagency cooperation, and eliminate the duplication of services. Those changes spurred the opening of new group homes in the last few years. However, as of 1993, Virginia continued to rely primarily on learning center/training school beds (for 68 percent of their placements). In 1994, a new governor assumed office and a more conservative philosophy took hold. Learning centers were renamed "Youth Correctional Centers," and the number of those institutional programs was projected to increase.

North Dakota—Expanding Community-Based Programs

The Division of Juvenile Services (DJS) was first established in 1989 as a division within the Department of Corrections. That followed two years of development of community-based programs and regional offices. Prior to 1989, all juveniles were sentenced directly by the courts to the state's single institution. The 1989 legislation provided courts with the choice of committing youths to the division for a term of eighteen to twenty-four months, giving the division authority to decide where youths should be placed, or directly committing youths to the division's 90–bed institution, the North Dakota Industrial School.

Although courts retained the option of making direct commitments within their own authority, in 1994 the courts authorized the division to make placement decisions in approximately 90 percent of the cases, demonstrating their confidence in DJS's abilities to make appropriate placement decisions. On any given day, there were 450–500 youths under DJS care and custody. Approximately 40 percent remained in their homes with nonresidential services or casework supervision. Another 28 percent were placed in group homes, 8 percent in therapeutic foster care, 10 percent in various residential placements including mental health or an evaluation unit, and 14 percent at the North Dakota Industrial School. Initially, the courts had concerns about authorizing the DJS to make placement decisions, but those concerns had diminished within just a few years of aggressive management by DJS.

The new DJS policies were fashioned around a case management system and the development of community-based alternatives. DJS worked with schools, human service agencies, and criminal justice agencies to develop programs such as school day treatment programs, intensive supervision, and therapeutic foster care. DJS also developed especially innovative programs for the short-term detention of nonserious offenders (mainly curfew violators) who had previously been jailed by police. In 1985, police in North Dakota placed over 1,800 juveniles in county jails because the juvenile detention facilities were spread out inconveniently over the state's rural landscape. Working with the counties, DJS designed and funded twenty-six nonsecure shelters, sited in convenient locations, and furnished with couches, television, VCR, and reading material, so that police could drop off youths for ninety-six hours or until retrieved by their parents. In 1993, all but fifty youths were diverted out of the county jails.

Mississippi—Reluctantly Downsized

Mississippi is a state that clearly has not voluntarily deinstitutionalized, although the only two residential programs for juveniles (both institutions) were downsized significantly prior to 1993. The sole reason for the institutional downsizing was a statewide budget crisis, not a philosophical shift. There was no development of new, alternative programs, aside from pilot Boy Scout programs, to replace the lost capacity. Furthermore, the Office of Youth Services' (OYS) central office staff was cut drastically, from a staff of twenty-two down to seven. In 1993, OYS pursued a plan of simply placing most youths with their families or passing them onto other agencies. A new director of OYS, Donald R. Taylor, who favored the disciplined approach of boot camps, recommended the adoption of a statewide boot-camp program, both for its low cost and its discipline. With such limited programming, the questions of who had placement authority and what placement criteria were used were not controversial. In Mississippi, the judge made an institutional commitment, but did not specify the institution or the sentence length. The OYS decided where to place the youth and for how long based on two criteria: age and sex. There were only two choices available: the Columbia Campus, an antiquated facility built in 1917 for younger males and all females, and the Oakley Campus, opened in 1943, for sixteen- to seventeen-year-old males.

Summary

The issues that state juvenile correctional systems tackle seem to reflect the underlying characteristics of each state. In some states, the battle was with more powerful courts over placement authority. In others, it was with parole over release authority. In yet others, it was more clearly a battle with powerful legislation such as mandatory sentences or court transfer policies. Many state correctional agencies were fighting to reduce overcrowding as a result of not being in control of placement and length of stay. Some were experiencing frustration with budget constraints, while others had located funding for institutional and/or community-based program expansion.

In general, developing balanced systems of programs that match the supervision and programming needs of offenders is confounded by the irrationality of fluctuating resources, organizational interests, politics, and philosophies. Plans to develop balanced systems can be easily undermined as in the case of Georgia. Even without the added impact of political election campaigns, entrenched organizations can often work at cross-purposes and defeat chances for a rational continuum of programs. Risk and needs assessment models seemed to be of benefit to states in their struggle to reform, because they demonstrated how offender characteristics needed to be matched with appropriate programs in order to maximize public safety and most efficiently control resources.

Actually mobilizing systems to develop a balanced approach may require that mechanisms to motivate reluctant stakeholders be firmly implanted into reform strategies. Among several recent juvenile detention initiatives reviewed by Barton (1994b), the presence of external rewards and sanctions had a bearing on their short-term success. In particular, challenges to detention practices that included lawsuits (sanctions for noncompliance) or were accompanied by external funding (rewards for compliance) were more likely to result in successfully implemented reform efforts, although they may not be long-lasting. Consensus building with stakeholders was a more effective long-term strategy for achieving permanent change. Among the reform states that we reviewed, the North Dakota youth correctional agency's approach of building consensus with stakeholders by encouraging interagency collaboration and providing resources for police departments appears to fit Barton's recommendations for accomplishing permanent reforms.

3

Local Reforms in Juvenile Corrections

Local Corrections Defined

Generally, we are defining "local corrections" as juvenile correctional systems or programs in jurisdictions smaller than states—that is, in counties or cities. Local corrections would include city or county-run court programs, police initiatives, and programs or systems developed by county executive offices. As we have shown, the geography of juvenile justice by states alone is overwhelmingly complex. The state level has typically been the level of government capable of providing innovative programming for juvenile offenders. However, because local correctional agencies are smaller and more geographically focused than those at the state level, their programs can sometimes respond more intensively to community problems, particularly those in major urban areas. There is a great deal of variation across counties in terms of their legal authority and resources to provide correctional programs. Strong county governments combined with local initiative have produced notable programs for juvenile offenders in Cuyahoga County, Ohio (Cleveland); Los Angeles County; Multnomah County, Oregon (Portland); Broward County, Florida; and Allegheny County, Pennsylvania (Pittsburgh), among others.

In particular, detention overcrowding solutions have emanated from county-based policies and programming. There is a growing trend among counties to go beyond the tradition of merely providing pretrial detention services and probation by expanding programs for post-adjudicated youths up to and including intermediate sanctions and secure residential programs. This replicates the continuum of care model that is found in some state systems. In a few areas, local police have been

65

pressed into service to conduct joint programs with state or local correctional systems in what may become a growing trend in community- or problem-oriented policing of juvenile offenders.

Reasons for Local Correctional Reform

Overlapping layers of correctional systems may seem redundant or unnecessary. However, there are several reasons why local correctional systems have developed important and innovative programming. First, the virtual absence of federal resources and leadership during the 1980s created a desperate situation in many local jurisdictions, and out of that situation a handful of local jurisdictions were compelled to innovate on their own.

Second, several states have passed legislation designed to encourage local counties to share the burden of absorbing offenders into their systems. Usually called "Community Corrections Acts," the legislation provides for states to pay a share of the cost of local corrections if counties agree to retain offenders in their own local systems. Community Corrections Acts (CCAs) were passed in at least eighteen states between 1973 and 1991, including: Minnesota, Iowa, and Colorado (1973–1974); Oregon, New Mexico, Indiana, Ohio, Connecticut, Virginia, and Texas (1977–1981); Tennessee (1984); and Arizona, Michigan, Pennsylvania, Alabama, and Florida (1988–1991). All CCAs require that participating local governments prepare a community corrections plan for review by the state. Typically, the plan includes an analysis of offenders incarcerated in state facilities and proposes local alternatives to incarceration (U.S. Advisory Commission on Intergovernmental Relations 1993). States whose CCAs specifically refer to juvenile offenders include Florida, Indiana, Kansas, and Minnesota, although other states may make funding available for local programs as well (Florida Advisory Council on Intergovernmental Relations 1994).

States vary in their provisions for reimbursing counties that divert state-bound offenders into local programs. The way CCAs are structured financially reflects each state's tradition of determining state and local responsibility. For example, in Michigan, prior to their CCA, the state made direct payments to community-based programs; after the CCA, local governments were paid by the state to contract with community-based programs on their own. In some areas, CCAs have encouraged local governments to counterbalance state policies that over-incarcerate offenders by developing effective community prevention and reintegration programs (U.S. Advisory Commission on Intergovernmental Relations 1993). The experience of community program development in Wayne County (Detroit) Michigan, for example, suggests that the roots of delinquency in inner cities are less easily ignored by local officials in Detroit than by state correctional officials in Lansing, the state capital.

Third, over the last two decades, local court probation has been criticized for being ineffective and insufficiently "tough" on offenders due to heavy caseloads averaging 150 offenders and, consequentially, limited abilities to monitor and sanction behavior (Morris and Tonry 1990). During the 1980s, many local jurisdictions developed intermediate sanctions that included house arrest, intensive probation supervision, day reporting centers, electronic monitoring, and restitution and community service programs (for a review of these programs for juveniles see Armstrong 1991). Prior to that, and still the case in many jurisdictions, a juvenile offender might receive numerous consecutive sentences of regular probation and then, upon the next adjudication, be abruptly committed to a secure facility in the state system. Now, some local courts can access an array of intermediate sanctions which allow the court to gradually increase sanctions in a more rational and effective manner (Morris and Tonry 1990).

Finally, efforts at the state level to rehabilitate juvenile offenders have been frustrated by the fact that youths are frequently hard-core by the time they reach state programs. Recidivism rates have shown disappointing results, particularly in states lacking a strong community-based component (National Council on Crime and Delinquency 1991). Geno Natalucci-Persichetti, director of the state of Ohio's Department of Youth Services, recently called for more resources and programs in not only state agencies but at the local level of government (1991: 26):

> The most important correction we must make is a systems correction. Corrections and juvenile justice professionals must not settle for anything less than a social system that inhibits the factors that lead to crime and strengthens the community supports that encourage respect for others. We need local sanctions and treatment that redirect first-time and non-violent youthful offenders.

The Problem of Detention Overcrowding

Detention overcrowding has been an important reason for counties to develop new ways of handling youthful offenders as they await their juvenile hearing. In a few states, the state juvenile correctional agency is responsible for pretrial detention. However, most states divide the pretrial detention responsibilities among all of the individual counties, so that each county controls its own pretrial detention programs. Regardless of how it is organized, pretrial detention is associated with a multitude of problems, including inappropriate placements, the use of adult facilities (jails) for juveniles, and lengthy confinement periods.

The latitude of discretion in the decision to detain juveniles prior to their court hearing was decried as a national problem by the American Bar Association (1980), leading to standards that prohibit the control or detention of accused juveniles for the following reasons (Institute of Judicial Administration-American Bar Association 1980: 51-52):

- to punish, treat, or rehabilitate the juvenile;
- to allow parents to avoid their legal responsibilities;
- to satisfy demands by a victim, the police, or the community;
- to permit more convenient administrative access to the juvenile;
- to facilitate further interrogation or investigation; or
- due to a lack of a more appropriate facility or status alternative.

However, a number of law-enforcement pressures that compromise these standards have been cited in the literature, including:

- the presence or absence of alternative diversions (Coffey 1975:159);
- avoidance of criticism should the minor commit another offense (Coffey 1975:160);
- to deter the criticism that the juvenile court is soft on crime (Norman 1960:11);
- to protect the community from future dangerousness, a standard that was upheld by the U.S. Supreme Court in 1984 (Schall v. *Martin,* 467 U.S. 253). (For a discussion of preventive detention in juvenile court, see Feld 1984: 191-209.)

Many pretrial detention facilities do not provide programs for youths because the assumption is that the youths are innocent of the offense with which they are charged, and programs should not be forced upon them. Also, the American Bar Association is concerned that the provision of programs and services to pretrial detainees would increase the inclination of well-intending judges to detain youths who are simply needy, rather than youths who are likely to flee or who have been charged with serious offenses.

Local or state correctional agencies, at first glance, have no recourse but to accept pretrial detainees into their facilities, even though their placement may not be appropriate or deserved. The juvenile court can guarantee control over pretrial detainees by ordering a temporary commitment into a detention facility or setting a high bail. Once adjudicated, however, juvenile courts in many states lose their authority to order a secure placement, particularly for nonserious offenders, after commitment to a youth services agency. This creates a temptation for the court to confine youths before the adjudication hearing, while it still has the authority to do so.

A key issue in pretrial detention concerns its overuse by courts, specifically the secure detention of youths who do not require a locked setting in order to guarantee their appearance in court. Pointed criticisms have been launched against detention practices in recent years throughout the nation, including the increased use of pretrial detention for increasingly less serious offenses (Schwartz 1989; Schwartz, Steketee, and Butts 1991); the confinement of juveniles in adult jails (Schwartz 1989; Schwartz, Steketee, and Butts 1991); the disproportionate growth in the detention of African-American and Hispanic youths (Snyder 1990); and the disproportionate use of detention by urban courts for both felonies and misdemeanors (Feld 1991).

In Massachusetts, pretrial detention practices have been examined in several studies. The first, conducted by the Massachusetts Advocacy Center (1980), raised several important concerns. Pretrial detainees were frequently returned again and again to Department of Youth Services' detention facilities, as often as five or more times without being committed. Pretrial detainees waited in detention for months at a time. Cases were continued well beyond the statutory guidelines of fifteen days or forty-five days under extenuating circumstances.

A follow-up study (Massachusetts Department of Youth Services 1987) identified similar patterns that indicated that the courts were continuing to inappropriately exercise their authority to detain. For example, fully one-third of the youths who were detained had their charges continued without a finding, continued indefinitely, or dismissed. Also, one-third of the cases were held on less than $100 bail (several on only $1.00 bail), indicating not dangerousness or crime seriousness, but lack of parental support or financial means. In some courts, as many as 60 percent of the youths who were detained were charged with minor misdemeanor offenses. Indeed, although it is a violation of the federal Juvenile Justice and Delinquency Prevention Act, some states continue to hold not only misdemeanants, but status offenders in detention facilities. For example, 13 percent of youths arrested as runaways were held in a detention facility prior to disposition (Snyder et al. 1990).

In Massachusetts, although no status offenders are officially ordered into pretrial detention, half of the youths in pretrial detention were previously involved with the Department of Social Services, the agency that provides services for status offenders. Along with anecdotal information from caseworkers and court personnel, this suggests that Massachusetts judges use pretrial detention as a way to control children who need help that other social agencies (e.g., the Department of Social Services) cannot or will not provide. Not coincidentally, this very group of indigent, nonserious offenders is the group that critics of the juvenile court claim pushed the court into its original existence (Bernard 1992). Indeed, the Massachusetts Advocacy Center's (1980) report on detention in Massachusetts made it clear that a disproportionate number of girls, runaways, and generally needy children were being detained because the courts had no better alternatives. The action of detaining a youth may be well-intended, particularly if the child appears to the court to be in need of care, supervision, or protection—most likely a girl on the run from an abusive home. Many judges cannot, in good conscience, release even a status offender to the kind of environment that caused the youth to be referred to the court in the first place. Yet, the focus on the youth as the problem, rather than adult caretakers in the family or school, is often misguided. More than 60 percent of the status offenders in shelters and transitional living facilities nationwide were physically or sexually abused by parents, and one out of four experienced violence by other family members (National Association of Social Workers 1991). Public schools in some areas are notorious for focusing too late on misbehavior and truancy—long after behavioral patterns have become established; reintegrative school discipline needs to begin in the primary grades (National Council of Juvenile and Family Court Judges 1990).

Several studies have demonstrated that pretrial detention has an independent effect on subsequent disposition, meaning that if offense records are equal, youths who have been detained awaiting trial are perceived more harshly and are given more severe sanctions (Feld 1991: 194, fn. 97). Although detention tends to be used "for punishment, for administrative convenience, or because a jurisdiction lacks alternatives" (Schwartz, Barton, and Orlando 1991: 21), experts are adamant that it not be used for such purposes. Finally, utilizing scarce secure resources for any offenders other than serious offenders raises a vital issue of public safety. *Non-dangerous juvenile offenders are occupying secure residential slots that could otherwise be used for serious offenders who threaten the public's safety.*

Overcoming Detention Overcrowding in Cuyahoga County, Ohio, Broward County, Florida, and Wayne County, Michigan

Because of growing social problems and shrinking budgets for social programs, overcrowding in detention facilities is worsening in virtually all jurisdictions. Frustrated by the number of inappropriate detainees in the state of Delaware, which because of its small size consists of one sole county, their DYS Commissioner recently championed legislation to limit the court's authority to detain youths by establishing a threshold of seriousness of both the current charge and the prior offense record. This is the first legislation of its kind in the United States. More typically, correctional agencies rely on attempts to persuade the court to follow guidelines, although guidelines obviously lack the command of law.

Cuyahoga County, Ohio, was the first local jurisdiction in the nation to receive widespread recognition for successfully diverting preadjudicatory youths from secure detention facilities into an alternative program. The county government worked with the courts to develop a home detention program in 1984, which provided casework services to families of youths awaiting adjudication. An evaluation, published two years later (Huff 1986), showed that nearly 3,000 youths were released to home detention by judges in 1984. Nearly all (94 percent) of those youths who were released to home detention complied with agreements set by the court and appeared in court for their adjudicatory hearing. At roughly one-third the cost of secure detention, the program was clearly cost-effective, and with the high compliance rate, it received strong support from the judiciary (Huff 1986).

A similar solution to the over use of secure detention was developed in Broward County, Florida (Schwartz, Barton, and Orlando 1991). In 1988, the Broward County Juvenile Detention Center was unacceptably overcrowded and was the target of a class action lawsuit alleging overcrowded and unsafe conditions. The 109-bed facility, the only secure detention facility in the county, held an average of 161 youths daily. One of the keys to reducing overcrowding was the knowledge that more than two-thirds of the detained youths were charged with nonviolent offenses, which suggested that many placements were needlessly incapacitating. An analysis of the situation was conducted by the University of Michigan's Center for the Study of Youth Policy. Their study revealed that

> 10 to 15 youths were placed in secure detention each month because they lacked a suitable home. Sometimes as many as 10 youths who spent the daytime in the lobby of child welfare offices were sent to the detention center at night because no foster homes were available. In addition, a small number of dependency and neglect cases were held in secure detention because of a lack of suitable resources and programs. . . . As in many jurisdictions, juvenile detention in Broward County was serving—inappropriately—as a child welfare resource. (Schwartz, Barton, and Orlando 1991: 23)

A plan was formulated to develop alternatives to secure detention and manage placement decisions in order to reduce the detention center's population to the capacity for which it was designed. The police, prosecutors, and judges who had the authority to order youths into secure detention were found to be unaware of, or unimpressed by, nonsecure alternatives. One such alternative was a home detention program that already existed but was being severely underutilized despite success rates of more than 90 percent—that is, fewer than 10 percent of youths who were living at home committed new violations or failed to appear for court hearings (Schwartz, Barton, and Orlando 1991).

Staff from the home detention program in Cuyahoga County, Ohio, were brought to Broward County to publicize their own successes and provide training to staff of the Broward home detention program. A day center consisting of educational and recreational services was established with the Boys Clubs of Broward to supervise youths in the home detention program. The Lutheran Ministries was recruited to manage a six-bed residential program for low-risk youths. As a result of these efforts, yearly admissions to secure detention declined by roughly 800 youths, or 22 percent, while admissions to home detention increased by roughly the same number of youths. The success of Broward County in managing its detention population was not lost on Florida's state legislature, which incorporated the home detention model as part of the 1990 Juvenile Justice Reform Act so that the model could be enacted on a statewide basis (Schwartz, Barton, and Orlando 1991).

In Wayne County, Michigan, a three-prong strategy was launched in 1993 to combat overcrowding in its Juvenile Detention Facility, the county's sole pretrial detention facility, which had a rated capacity of 146 but routinely held over 200 youths per day. Studies conducted by the Wayne County Executive Office showed that up to 80 percent of the youths in the secure facility did not pose sufficient risk to require a secure placement and would be more appropriately served in the community. However, the county detention facility was vulnerable to inappropriate placements on at least two levels. First, the juvenile court, not the operators of the detention facility, made all determinations regarding individual placement decisions. In other words, the detention facility's intake officer was physically assigned to the detention facility, but in reality was an employee of the court, which then lacked a stake in reducing overcrowding. Second, the Michigan Department of Social Services, which is the state's juvenile correctional agency, was inappropriately placing post-adjudicated youths—youths awaiting placement or on parole status—into the detention facility, accounting for approximately one-third of the youths in residence on an average day.

The strategy developed by the County Executive Office was as follows: First, the county executive put legal pressure on the state Department of Social Services to withdraw state-committed youths from the Juvenile Detention Facility. The state-committed youths were not appropriate for the county's detention facility, argued the county, because they were not on pretrial status; instead, they had already been adjudicated delinquent and were waiting for the state to place them into a state-run facility, which often ran into delays.

Second, the county executive worked with the county courts to divert low-risk youths into home detention programs. A risk assessment instrument was developed with an outside consultant and training was conducted with the court intake staff. An agreement was signed between the county executive and the court to exclude youths who were low risk or low seriousness from the detention facility. Alternatives to detention placement, including three models of home detention that provided a gradation of supervision, were agreed to by the court as substitutes for placing youths who did not meet the new threshold of the detention facility. Finally, the county executive worked to develop a downtown prevention program, known as the Work & Learn Institute, with a focus on providing practical educational and job-related skills to post-adjudicated youths, such as computer literacy. Each of these initiatives was developed with the help of a committee made up of representatives from the county executive, the court, and the Department of Social Services.

Despite these efforts, however, the federal Justice Department initiated an investigation of the facility in 1994 after learning of reports of mismanagement and continued overcrowding. The Justice Department has several options, including appointing a federal overseer to bring the facility into compliance with federal standards. Therefore, both the immediate and long-term future of the facility, as of late 1994, was unresolved.

Over-representation of Minority Youths and a Solution: Allegheny County (Pittsburgh), PA

Over-representation of minority youths is apparent in each stage of corrections, from probation to secure confinement, but the problem of over-representation is especially pronounced in the more restrictive placements (Schwartz 1989). At the same time, the more restrictive placements tend to provide the least comprehensive treatment programs (Parent et al. 1994), although the service needs of incarcerated youths are often, if anything, more critical than the services needs of youths who are placed in the community.

The Community Intensive Supervision Project (CISP), located in Allegheny County, Pennsylvania, was developed in 1987 by the juvenile court for post-adjudicated male youths. The factors that precipitated the project were a significant increase in African-American referrals to the Allegheny County Juvenile Court, the disproportionate residential placement of minority youths, the under-representation of minority youths in drug and alcohol treatment, and the rising costs of institutional placements. Unlike previous local examples, it was the court, rather than the county executive branch, that initiated this project.

The court had to convince the local government officials that the program would be cost effective and decrease institutionalization, and the court also needed to confront community opposition and zoning issues. The CISP project has received local, state, and federal awards for excellence in programming.

The program contains three inner-city community centers with a capacity of thirty-five youths each, which operate between 4:00 P.M. and midnight, seven days a week, as well as an intensive supervision project. The youths targeted for the program are predominantly African-Americans adjudicated for violations of probation, drug charges, and motor vehicle-related theft. The community centers are staffed by residents of the community to provide effective role modeling and supervision.

The CISP youths are strictly regimented when first assigned to the program. Although they are permitted to live at home, they must attend school and after school, their attendance at their community center is required at 4:00 P.M. Between 9:30–10:30 P.M., all youths are driven home by staff. Between 10:30 P.M. and midnight, staff return to the youths' homes to make random checks and contact with parents. Overnight, youths are monitored at home by parents and an active electronic monitoring system.

In the community center, where youths spend a total of forty-two hours per week, they receive the following services: homework supervision, literacy tutoring, group and individual counseling, dinner, in-center recreation, drug/alcohol counseling, parent support groups, and guest speakers. A drug/alcohol specialist is assigned to each center, and random drug testing is conducted inside the center. Outside of the center, youths are under twenty-four-hour supervision which includes electronic monitoring, participation in community recreation and cultural events (e.g., YMCA, professional sporting events, community theater), and community service (e.g., neighborhood clean-up efforts, food bank volunteer service, painting elderly persons' homes.

The length of stay is a minimum of 180 "good days," with "good time" evaluated each day. If youths misbehave they are immediately sanctioned by withdrawing privileges, overnight lock-up, or an eight-day residential program. Behavioral violations include not attending school, school suspensions, not attending CISP, electronic monitoring violations, major behavior problems in the center, and positive drug/alcohol tests. The program model incorporates efforts to reduce supervision gradually. Electronic monitoring is removed at day 165. After 180 days, youths remain on aftercare status under court supervision for a minimum of 30 days.

The CISP program was evaluated in 1993 (Kinder and Speight 1994). In general, the results were highly promising, although they were not based on a controlled study. However, more formal evaluations are pending, which should provide more valid indicators of effectiveness, including the extent to which the program truly diverts youths from residential programs, or merely "widens the net" of youths receiving intensive supervision. Among the preliminary findings, very small percentages of youths tested positive for drug/alcohol while in the program (2.5 percent). Program costs were lower, at $55.00 per day, than residential alternatives, without factoring in the additional costs of program non-completers. Fifty-one percent successfully completed the program. Of the unsuccessful youths, 20 percent committed a new offense, while the remainder simply failed to comply with the program rules, resulting in a residential placement.

A Role for Local Police in Juvenile Corrections[*]

The "juvenile justice process" conception of formal control locates police at the front end of a three-stage process. In other words, the formal process moves from police to courts and ends with corrections. In their metaphoric formal role, police do little more than "feed the system" by making arrests and are discouraged from work that is preventive or reintegrative vis-à-vis juvenile offenders. The image of police as formal processors of juveniles stands in stark contrast to August Vollmer's 1930s traditional vision of police work, which included the goal of providing moral education. Vollmer envisioned that police would develop programs well beyond the Police Athletic League recreational programs for youths which were then just evolving (Kelling 1987). Vollmer's vision was never realized. Instead, a variety of narrowly specialized units within police departments proliferated, some of which related to juveniles but with far less penetrating goals than Vollmer conceived.

For instance, Needle and Stapleton (1983) observed that a prominent feature of gang control programming in the United States was its

---

[*] Adapted from Guarino-Ghezzi 1994.

similarity to general police programming. Gang units consisted of recreation programs, preventive patrol and other traditional suppression activities, school-based crime prevention programs, and "streetwork" oriented to suppression and prevention of gang activity. Standard patrol, investigation, and disposition procedures were used to apprehend and process gang members in most cities. In some cities special "gang-breaking" strategies were implemented, which targeted gang leaders for arrest, prosecution, and incarceration, based on the assumption that removing leaders weakens gangs for at least some period of time. It appeared that cities that employed gang-breaking strategies used a youth services model with younger adolescents, and a more aggressive "gang-breaking" approach with older teenagers. This suggests that services were used as the "carrot" for compliance with one population and gang-breaking as the "stick" of control with the other. However, dividing strategies in that way has received neither empirical support (Spergel 1990) nor the endorsement of the National Youth Gang Suppression and Intervention Program, which recommends a combination of surveillance and services (Spergel et al. 1993).

As juvenile correctional practitioners are well aware, juvenile offenders with service needs should not be expected to embrace services without a measure of control, nor should services be omitted from control strategies. For example, in well-run correctional programs, services, controls, and surveillance augment one another (Gendreau and Ross 1991; Guarino-Ghezzi and Byrne 1989; U.S. Department of Justice 1993). Moreover, the impersonality of police encounters, caused in part by centralized, reactive management, has placed practical limits on the perceived legitimacy of police authority (see Hummel 1977; Lipsky 1980).

In part as a result of the failures of over-centralized, reactive police management, many jurisdictions have been rapidly implementing community policing or problem-oriented policing models that do a great deal more than simply dispatch cars to street corners in response to a civilian 911 call. Among the theoretical advantages of community policing is incorporation of the values and needs of community residents into police goals. The experience of police-citizen contacts demonstrates how those contacts are susceptible to demographic influences. Although the general citizenry has positive feelings toward police, members of racial minority groups tend to have more negative opinions (Jamieson and Flanagan 1987; McGarrell and Flanagan 1985).

That is not surprising, given the evidence of differential treatment depending on the race of the officer, complainant, and victim that disfavors black suspects, particularly when the complainant and officer are both white (Black 1980), and the routine questioning and detention to which teenagers, African-Americans, and lower-income persons are subjected (Boston Police Department Management Review Committee 1992; Wilson 1975). A number of studies have documented inner-city blacks' hostility toward the police and the police's negative attitude toward black inner-city dwellers (e.g., Reuss-Ianni 1984).

Age seems to aggravate already strained relationships between police and inner-city residents. Bynum, Cordner, and Greene (1982) studied the hierarchy of victim status according to age of the victim, and they found that the probability of police follow-up investigation of a reported crime is lower for victims under age 21. An additional problem for improving policies for inner-city youths is that police seem to hold a one-dimensional, negative perception of youth gangs (Hagedorn 1988), which impedes their communication with youths despite numerous studies identifying the varied social, psychological, and economic functions of gangs (Cohen 1955; Jankowski 1991; Miller 1976; Moore 1978; Thrasher 1963). One critic of the police has charged that the criminal image of Chicano gangs was exaggerated mainly to justify applications for federal grants to support specialized gang units in police departments (Zatz 1987). Stereotypical images of lower-class youths may have helped justify police in targeting them as a threat (Cashmore and McLaughlin 1991).

Some jurisdictions are attempting to reduce the antagonism between police and juvenile offenders and reformulate the role of police vis-à-vis juvenile offenders. In those jurisdictions, community outreach groups, social workers, and correctional agencies are working with police to develop mutually compatible roles for supervising the prevention of delinquency and the reintegration of youthful offenders back into the community. Various types of programs following a problem-oriented model are in early stages, including gang control, preventive policing, and reintegrative policing.

Gang Control

More and more eight- to twelve-year-olds are being swept up in the excitement and status that accompany gang membership and urban violence. To counter the influence of gang leaders and reduce incidents of violence among these youngsters, some cities have hired full time "streetworkers"—residents of target areas who are street-savvy and who want change in their neighborhood. Streetworkers counsel youths in their natural environment, occupy them with activities and events, advocate for community programs tailored to their interests and needs, and act as liaisons between youths and police by sharing information and representing authority in a nonthreatening way.

In cities with emerging or existing gang problems, a dual strategy of combining services with surveillance is recommended by the National Youth Gang Information Center. A comprehensive model for gang control, the Community-Based Youth Authority (CBYA), would provide specialized training to CBYA staff, community residents, and representatives of schools and justice system agencies. The model would increase the frequency and quality of contacts between gang members, "wannabes," and trained workers. The CBYA mission would consist of six objectives: socialization, education, family support, training and employment, social control, and community mobilization and agency coordination. CBYA staff, based in communities, would perform both a case management and a surveillance function, and they would be responsible for consistent rule enforcement, as well as for the protection of youths, in order to demonstrate their authority as legitimate. CBYA workers would also serve as intermediaries between criminal justice agencies, schools, and neighborhood groups (Spergel et al. 1993). At the same time, a role for specially trained police officers would include reporting technical violations to probation and parole officers, and developing close liaisons with schools and service agencies (Ehrensaft and Spergel 1993).

In Aurora, Colorado, a community-based gang prevention effort includes a victim/witness program established to support victims and witnesses of gang-related crimes and train police officers in assisting them. Gang Intervention Unit police officers wear modified uniforms so that they are not perceived as traditional police officers. They generally contact between ten and thirty gang members on a daily patrol (from 4 P.M. to 2 A.M., seven days a week). The unit attempts to give the gangs the impression that the police are constantly watching them. Indeed, the gang members and intervention unit members have gotten to know each other on a first-name basis and reportedly gang members have developed into information sources about rival gangs (U.S. Department of Justice 1992b).

Preventive Policing

It is now recognized that police departments that provide services to communities produce benefits for residents and enhance the authority of police (Sparrow, Moore, and Kennedy 1990). This point has been demonstrated with juvenile offenders in innovative police departments throughout the United States. A police program in Carlsbad, California, administers punishment to juveniles who have committed misdemeanors based on the theory that youths often learned it was "acceptable" to commit a minor crime because they received a "slap on the wrist" penalty. Youths often lost respect for society's institutions and the personnel who served the community such as court and police officials. Also, victims of crime felt frustrated that the courts and police department did not adequately punish or prevent youth from committing such crimes. First-time offenders were slipping through the courts, with no certainty of punishment. The new program oversees a tribunal composed of community members to determine guilt or innocence and assign from eight to forty hours of community service and/or counseling (U.S. Department of Justice 1992b).

The innovative School Resource Officer (SRO) Program in St. Petersburg, Florida, is also being implemented in over forty of Florida's sixty-seven school districts and in many cities in the United States. Police officers in uniform (with a firearm) are stationed in secondary schools, where they serve as law enforcers, counselors, and instructors. In addition to helping maintain a safe school environment, the SRO program is designed to promote a positive relationship between students and police officers and to provide 200 hours per year of classroom instruction in law-related topics. Officers also counsel students who seek assistance, who are referred by teachers, and who are involved in the juvenile justice system. Officers may call on parents or make referrals to other school or community resources. Strategically, SROs figure prominently in city-sponsored youth activities. For example, they help organize "pool parties," which are particularly popular among youths and therefore provide the kind of reward for involvement with police that is often missing in communities. The (free) admission tickets are in demand, but only SROs and other uniformed police officers can distribute them, so young people who want to attend need to interact with the officers to obtain the tickets (U.S. Department of Justice 1992b).

The Police Citizens Youth Clubs in New South Wales, Australia, evolved in the late 1980s as a crime prevention program. The clubs arrange dozens of sports activities, music classes, and other lessons for youths, and they also work with police in several ways. Police officers conduct lectures on law and police roles during "law week," they offer crime prevention workshops, they provide transportation to youths under court order to attend substance abuse counseling, and they supervise court-referred youths who perform community service work at the youth clubs. Court-involved youths become familiar with youth club activities and learn from the positive involvement of other youths (Carter 1989). This model seems to be a significant improvement over other community-service sentencing programs supervised by police, such as the Newark program, which was lacking in positive alternative activities for youths or provision of role models (for a description of the program, see Skolnick and Bayley 1986).

Reintegrative Policing

Reintegrative policing involves a partnership between correctional agencies and police for the purpose of supervising juvenile offenders who are on aftercare or parole status following a commitment to a correctional agency. Although reintegration of offenders back into their communities is the most critical period for offenders because it allows them to "test reality" while still under supervision, the resources for reintegrative programs have been in short supply (Altschuler and Armstrong 1991). Reintegrative programming has been particularly insufficient for the most difficult populations of youths to monitor. For example, neither intensive community supervision by correctional agencies, nor community policing, are designed to handle sex offenders or chronically delinquent inner-city youths. However, two reintegration programs have been developed for those populations using an interagency model that combines resources from agencies with overlapping jurisdictions.

San Francisco sex offender program. The San Francisco Sex Offender Program was implemented in April 1985 by the California Youth Authority (CYA), the state juvenile correctional agency, first in the city of San Francisco and then statewide. The program was designed for youths who were returning to the community on parole status from CYA facilities. The program supervised sex offenders and provided treatment in the community using a model of interagency cooperation and information sharing that included representatives from the local police, parole board, probation office, district attorney's office, public defender's office, child protective services, rape crisis center, and local victim/witness assistance agencies (Greer 1991).

The program developed contacts with local police departments to access police internal data concerning any field interviews conducted with the targeted youths or any arrests. Aftercare workers kept current with other police information, gang intelligence, or sightings of offenders in high-risk situations or areas, such as loitering around children's playgrounds, "cruising" with negative or gang-oriented peers, drinking, or substance abuse. The cooperative relationship between aftercare workers and police allowed a higher level of surveillance ability and resulted in more immediate confrontations with clients when they exhibited dangerous behaviors (Greer 1991).

In addition to reinforcing supervision, the interagency model also helped to neutralize negative reaction to the release of sex offenders back to their communities. Much of the negative reaction to previous cases was based on a lack of knowledge or distrust of the processes that were in place. The aftercare field supervisor in the San Francisco project was in a position to inform public officials about the treatment progress that high-profile offenders made while incarcerated, because they were required to make monthly visits to institutions and attend case reviews prior to release and aftercare planning. Aftercare workers shared that treatment information with the judge, district attorney, public defender, and the police investigators who were involved in the arrest and conviction of the offender (Greer 1991).

Boston's "make peace with police" program. Around the nation, the "reactive" model of police protection, which relies on citizen-initiated calls to police, is generally considered to be a failed model by experts in policing. The model is particularly unresponsive to the needs of inner-city residents. In Bynum, Cordner, and Greene's (1982) study of a medium-sized midwestern city, 82 percent of reported serious crimes that were brought to detectives' attention actually received little or no investigative effort. Indeed, the rate of homicide cases resulting in arrest in large cities has fallen considerably over the past two decades. The clearance rate for murders and non-negligent man-slaughters in cities with populations of 250,000 and over declined by nearly one-fourth between 1971 and 1991, from 82 percent to 63 percent (U.S. Department of Justice 1972, 1992a). The clearance rates for such crimes in smaller cities and rural areas declined by only a few percentage points, indicating that large city murders have become in-creasingly difficult to solve due to factors present in major urban areas. The mayor of Washington, D.C., claimed that violent crime levels had surpassed the authority of police, and proposed that the control of violent crime be escalated to the National Guard (Berke 1993).

The reactive model of policing is also particularly unresponsive to young people in inner cities. A dangerous adaptive style of retaliation against acquaintance aggressors, rather than cooperation with police, has emerged among inner-city youths (Garbarino et al. 1992). Prison researchers have studied a similar relationship between victimization and offending within institutional walls where inmates are in fear of one another due to reactive intervention (or no intervention) by correc-tional officers. Daniel Lockwood (1991) coined the term "target ag-gression" to explain how inmates who sense they are probable future victims of sexual assault learn to initiate physical aggression against others as a form of defense. Like prison inmates, inner-city children and adolescents learn to adapt to patterns of unprotected victimization by defining themselves not as victims, but as aggressors (Bell 1991; Bandura 1973). This may be, in part, a result of youths' perceptions that police are indifferent to the chronic danger of their environments.

The City of Boston's Police Department experienced several highly visible confrontations involving African Americans in inner-city neigh-borhoods in the early 1990s. Philosophically, the Boston Police De-partment had been operating along a reactive model for which it was lambasted by a mayoral committee known as the "St. Clair Commis-sion" (Boston Police Department Management Review Committee 1992). Among the problems cited by the commission was the fear of residents living in the most crime-ridden communities to report crimes to the police. Also cited was a pattern in which a small number of officers with a long record of alleged misconduct, including physical abuse of citizens, remained on the force largely unidentified and unsu-pervised. The commission called for an overhaul of the Internal Affairs complaint review process, including the creation of a Community Appeals Board.

At the same time, adolescents' fear of police retaliation and of police inability to protect them emerged as central problems. A local rap song, "One in the Chamba," described the true incident of James Hall, a Boston police officer on patrol but traveling within his own neighborhood, who fatally shot a male youth who was hiding underneath a car. Hall tried unsuccessfully to leave the scene but was stopped by neighbors. Two years later Hall was convicted of manslaughter, but by then he had been dismissed from the force for an unrelated incident. The Boston Police Patrolman's Association then sued the group for writing a song about cop killing, since the refrain advised listeners to keep one bullet in the chamber for corrupt cops like James Hall (Grant 1992).

During the same time period, Charles Stuart, a white suburbanite who murdered his pregnant wife in the Mission Hill district of Boston, alleged that the killer was a black man who had jumped into their car while they were driving to the hospital for a childbirth class. His claim produced a massive police investigation of African-American men in Mission Hill, involving strong-arm techniques to pressure residents into cooperating in the search, and ultimately producing a suspect fitting the description (Murphy and Ellement 1992). In addition, the Boston Police Department had initiated a policy to "stop and frisk" suspected gang members (i.e., African-American males in black hooded sweatshirts) to confiscate weapons in high-crime neighborhoods. Interviews with Boston youths suggested that stop and frisk policies increased defiance and frustration, weakening police–youth relations (Guarino-Ghezzi 1993).

As a result of national trends as well as local pressures, the City of Boston's Police Department recently began to design a community-policing approach and in 1993 appointed a new chief of police. In 1994, most of their community-policing initiatives were still in the developmental stage. One of their initiatives involved working with the Massachusetts Department of Youth Services to create interagency programs for inner-city youths committed to DYS to help them reintegrate back to their communities.

A theoretical model of "reintegrative policing" was developed with input from DYS, police, and evaluations of pilot communication sessions between police and youths at a DYS secure treatment program

(Guarino-Ghezzi 1994). Subsequently, further sessions were held and a planning process created to specify the objectives of the program, known as "Make Peace With Police." The objectives were to: increase interaction between youths and police in non-incident encounters; enhance mutual understanding by probing into the sources of negative perceptions and stereotypes on both sides; resolve role conflicts by teaching youths about police work and helping police to define their role with respect to youths who are reintegrating out of DYS programs; and reduce fear in the communities. Neighbors who saw young people misbehaving in the community needed to feel unafraid to call police or contact parents. Parents who saw older youths recruit younger children into criminal behavior needed to take action without fear of retribution. Thus, the program was directed at high-risk youths not as isolated individuals, but as members of communities where the level of community reintegration reduced their risk of recidivism.

Summary

Most innovations in local correctional programs are not part of an integrated system reform effort. This chapter has discussed some of the exceptions to that rule, including initiatives encouraged by Community Corrections Acts, aggressive courts, and interagency partnerships. As societal indifference to the problems of inner cities continues to manifest in policies of over-incarceration of inner-city youths, local communities may seek answers that are creative and effective, and that directly address issues within their communities. With the victimization of inner-city youths by other youths at an all-time high, criminal justice and social service agencies may be compelled to work cooperatively and to share resources in efforts to reduce crime, disorder, and fear. The next chapter examines the history and current status of one of the partners needed to reach a balance in juvenile justice, the juvenile court.

4

The Changing Role of the Juvenile Court

History of the Juvenile Court

Age and class are two of the major cleavages in society that stratify its members, and social stratification was central to the development of a separate juvenile court. Underlying the juvenile court is the assumption that children have different interests compared with adults and that they behave differently. Adults have always controlled perceptions of how children "ought" to behave, although their ideas frequently ran counter to children's natural proclivities. When child misbehavior became a social issue in the late 1800s, adults turned beyond the family—to the legal system—to control children, presumably for the betterment of society as a whole. A question that is frequently raised by social historians and legal scholars is, "Just who were those adults who pressured the juvenile court into existence back in the late 1880s?" Were they parents of uncontrollable children seeking help from the state? The answer to that question is, "No." The chief lobbyists who pressured the first juvenile court into existence were, in fact, well-to-do groups composed primarily of women who had concerns about the family and parenting practices of the poor.

Anthony Platt (1977) describes these "progressives" as elitists who, in his view, misrepresented themselves as social reformers. Unlike their (accurately termed) progressive sisters, who were being arrested during the same time period for supporting radical ideas like birth control and women's right to vote, the women who founded the first juvenile court in Chicago were relatively conservative. They were socially and economically privileged—wealthy, white, Anglo-Saxon, and Protestant—and therefore held the dominant views about the proper roles for women, children, and families. Initially, they entered the slums of Chicago to work with the children themselves. In their view, poverty and bad parenting went hand in hand. Rather than rectify poverty, however, they advocated a separate court system to remove children from parents who were undeserving of them, as evidenced by their children's poverty or misbehavior.

Tom Bernard (1992) explains that by the end of the nineteenth century, the singular criminal justice system that characterized the United States as a whole was stalled in its tracks in Illinois as a consequence of a court ruling known as the Daniel O'Connell decision *(People v. Turner,* 55 Ill. 280, 1870). Prior to that decision, throughout most of the 1800s, poor children who appeared before the court were generally ordered into reform schools. However, the case of Daniel O'Connell in 1870 changed history. That case, which was heard before the Illinois Supreme Court, involved a boy who was committed to a House of Refuge simply because he appeared to be in danger of growing up to become a pauper. Such institutionalization of children in poverty was a typical court practice at that time.

What was unusual about this case was that Daniel O'Connell's parents, although poor and relatively powerless, had the courage to challenge this practice. The boy's parents objected and filed a writ of *habeus corpus* so that the appeals court could examine the process that resulted in his commitment. The Illinois Supreme Court concluded that Daniel was being punished, rather than helped, by the House of Refuge, and would be better off at home. The significance of the O'Connell ruling was that it outlawed the practice of placing youths, other than those who committed felony offenses, in institutions without due process of law. The ruling thereby made it impossible to control the vast majority of youths by institutionalizing them via the court system. As a result, the Illinois court system was ripe for a new mechanism—the "juvenile" court—to process and control juveniles who were deemed troublesome, although most had not gone so far as to commit a felony offense.

This is an important piece of history because it explains the conflicting priorities in the juvenile court today. Is the juvenile court designed to help children? To help their parents? To punish their parents by taking away their children? To punish children by locking them up? The original answer that was given to these questions is today met with some skepticism: that the court was designed to help children by locking them up. Just as homeless people sleeping in the streets make us uncomfortable today, the sight of pauper children in the 1800s provoked a sense of shame and embarrassment and reflected negatively on the state. Children were confined for crimes that were so minor, they would be overlooked today. Many had committed no crime at all, other than the crime of being poor. Clearly, there were other interests at stake than the interests of these children.

The control of poor children by confining them to houses of refuge solved two dilemmas: the need for social reform, and the need to move victims of poverty out of sight. Had houses of refuge not been utilized to feed and shelter poor children, someone might have persuasively questioned why such a great nation could permit abject poverty to exist alongside excessive wealth. The house of refuge model allowed so-called social reformers to believe—and to persuade others— that they were working in the best interests of children. It was also a way for the state to inexpensively manage the social problem of poverty as an individual problem, by dividing families and providing shelter and food for children. In some cases, parents were punished for their poverty by having *wanted* children removed from their homes, much as if poverty had been their chosen life-style. In other cases, children were punished for having parents who did not want them. The state benefited because parents in poverty were made to feel responsible for perpetuating poverty onto the next generation, rather than questioning the distribution of property and wealth as a matter of social policy.

Thus, the first juvenile court in the United States was established in Illinois in 1899. Because of the O'Connell ruling, some structural change was needed, or else the new juvenile court would not be allowed to institutionalize juvenile offenders unless they had committed a felony offense. The O'Connell ruling meant that the court would have to create a new method of incarcerating children who had committed lesser (or no) offenses. The solution to the problem was to define the juvenile court as a "chancery court," an English system for administering the property of orphaned children. Legally, chancery courts were designed to protect the interests of children until they became old enough to manage their own estates. Even if the new juvenile court did nothing more than continue to institutionalize children against their will in houses of refuge (which it did), its definition as a chancery court legally entitled the juvenile court to do so under the guise of acting in the "best interests" of the child without following due process accorded to adults (Bernard 1992).

The *parens patriae* doctrine of the chancery court was specifically invoked to justify the juvenile court by empowering the state to act as the ultimate parent in acting on behalf of the child. *Parens patriae* was the rationale for state intervention because it depicted the court as a kindly parent, and it drew no distinction between criminal and non-criminal youth conduct. The jurisdiction of the first juvenile court was expansive and, in fact, would have permitted the court to assume the supervision of "every single poor child in the city of Chicago" (Bernard 1992: 90). Any of the following types of children could be arrested, brought before the court, and placed in a house of refuge until age twenty-one: those who were destitute, homeless, abandoned, dependent on public support, lacking in proper parental care, beggars, victims of neglect or abuse, street peddlers or street musicians. Clearly, these products of society were all too painful to grace our city streets. Today, the juvenile court continues the practice of incarcerating poor children—many of whom have not committed serious offenses—whose common bond is poverty. It is rare that a middle-class "problem child" has to confront the legal system; private mental health solutions such as counseling or in-patient treatment in psychiatric hospitals are preferred by parents who have the income, or the health insurance, to afford such services.

Children in juvenile court were subject to tremendous discretion in judges' decision making, based on the theory that individualized treatment was beneficial for the child. A psychological casework approach allowed the courts to collect more information about the child's "needs," including his character and life-style, than his offense behavior. There was no goal of matching the offense to a proportionate punishment. The juvenile court procedures and vocabulary emphasized informality and the avoidance of stigma. Because the important issues involved the child's background and welfare rather than his offense, juries, lawyers, rules of evidence, and formal procedures were considered unnecessary. "Hearings," rather than trials, were confidential and private. Access to court records was limited. Youths were found to be generally "delinquent" rather than guilty of a specific offense. "Dispositions," rather than sentences, were indeterminate and could continue until the age of majority.

Perhaps because of their informality and perhaps because they are associated with relatively unpowerful offenders, juvenile courts have borne the stigma of being inferior to adult criminal courts, mirroring the subordinant role of children to adults. A juvenile court judge whose career spanned nearly half of this century (from the mid-1930s to 1973) complained that from its inception, juvenile court judges were discriminated against by state legal systems (Polier 1989). They received less compensation than judges appointed or elected to other courts. They were not given law clerks, nor were they asked to write legal opinions. Neither law reports nor legal periodicals were provided for their use. Because it was assumed that any judge could do justice to a child, the rotation of judges allowed cases to shuffle among as many as a dozen judges. A 1965 study found that about one-fourth of juvenile court judges had no law school training; one-third had no probation or social work staff available to them, and 89–90 percent had no available psychologist or psychiatrist (McCune 1965); a 1967 study found that one-fifth of all juvenile judges did not even have a college degree (President's Commission on Law Enforcement and Administration of Justice 1967).

Bernard (1992) explains that by the 1950s, optimism about the juvenile court had broken down and a more realistic view began to emerge. This view was based on an assessment of the actual performance of the juvenile court rather than the good intentions of its founders. In practice, the juvenile court often neither "treated" juveniles for their problems, nor did it "punish" them for their crimes, but rather seemed to "punish" them for their problems. In other words, not only were quality services lacking, but little attention was paid to adjusting the punishment to fit the offense.

Furthermore, the 1950s highlighted the negative side of the juvenile court's "social work" image. During the cold war period of the 1950s, social services were threatening to our government. For example, the Mid-Century White House Conference on Children made its primary recommendations for improving policies in three areas: opposing communist imperialism, building character in youth, and strengthening belief in God. The social roots of delinquency causation and prevention "were brushed aside as having no importance except to 'bleeding hearts' or radicals" (Polier 1989: 8). At the same time, juvenile court judges were criticized for taking independent stands on school desegregation by dismissing charges of neglect against black parents who refused to send their children to segregated (and inferior) schools (Polier 1989). From the perspective of activist juvenile judges who were concerned about social conditions and civil rights, the need for due process—particularly juveniles' right to counsel—was acute.

The first formal recognition of juveniles' right to counsel occurred in the state of New York, when the New York State Legislature enacted a model Family Court Act (1962) requiring that children be represented in the juvenile court by counsel. The New York Family Court Act was largely a response to influential memorandum reports published by the Bar Association of the City of New York (Polier 1989). One such report (Schinitsky 1961) presented the case of a young teenaged girl who was committed to the mental ward of a city hospital, apparently due to the fact that she had run away from home on two occasions. Her father charged her with being delinquent and his position prevailed in court, despite the girl's angry protests that he often beat her, that he no longer wanted her because of his new wife, and that he threatened to kill her if she ran away again.

> Confining ourselves to the question of when should a child be remanded for observation, we ask: What behavior by the child indicated she was psychotic? What justification was there for [the probation officer] to suggest clinical observation at a hospital? In what appeared to [the child] a hostile atmosphere, how could her reaction be considered outside the range of normalcy? (Schinitsky 1961: 2)

By 1967, one-third of the states had followed New York State's lead in mandating a juvenile's right to counsel. In that year, the U.S. Supreme Court reached a decision in the case of a juvenile named Gerald Gault, which is considered the single most influential Supreme Court decision in the area of juvenile justice, spurring a "due process revolution" that transformed the policies of juvenile courts. The context of this decision included the following key components:

- disappointment that the juvenile court had failed to live up to its optimistic intentions (see, for example, Wheeler and Cottrell 1965);
- enormous discretionary control over decisions affecting the institutionalization of youths, including numerous youths whose crimes were minor; and
- the recognition that family and social problems were hurting youths, and that the juvenile courts could not (or would not) always act in the best interests of children.

The Due Process "Revolution": The Case of Gerald Gault

As in the above case of the teenaged girl, Gerald Gault's case illustrates the enormous discretion and lack of criteria in juvenile court decisions. Gerald was different from the young runaway girl in terms of his behavior, but more importantly (as in the Daniel O'Connell case) because his parents were supportive of him. Gerald Gault was adjudicated delinquent in the state of Arizona for making obscene phone calls. The Gault case was significant because it highlighted the blatant absence of formal procedure in the juvenile court's manner of finding Gerald delinquent and committing him to the State Industrial School up until the age of majority (21), which could have resulted in Gerald's institutional confinement for as many as six years. The maximum sentence that an adult could have received for the same offense in Arizona was two months imprisonment. The facts of the case were as follows:

> On Monday, June 8, 1964, at about 10 a.m., Gerald Francis Gault and a friend, Ronald Lewis, were taken into custody by the Sheriff of Gila County. Gerald was then still subject to a six months' probation order which has been entered on February 25, 1964, as a result of his having been in the company of another boy who had stolen a wallet from a lady's purse. The police action on June 8 was taken as the result of a verbal complaint by a neighbor of the boys, Mrs. Cook, about a telephone call made to her in which the caller or callers made lewd or indecent remarks. It will suffice for purposes of this opinion to say that the remarks or questions put to her were of the irritatingly offensive, adolescent variety. (*In re Gault*, 387 U.S. 1, 1967: 1431–32)

A local child advocate by the name of Amelia Lewis represented the Gault family and argued for Gerald's release in the Arizona Supreme Court. However, the Arizona Supreme Court decided that the juvenile court had done nothing to violate the "due process concept" for juveniles, and Gerald's confinement was upheld. Amelia Lewis turned to a friend of her son's, Norman Dorsen, a New York University law professor who had founded the Arthur Garfield Hayes Civil Liberties Program in New York, to take the case to the U.S. Supreme Court. Mr. Dorsen did so, and succeeded in winning a favorable ruling for Gerald Gault, with one justice dissenting (Justice Stewart), and another justice dissenting in part (Justice Harlan). Justice Fortas wrote the majority opinion, which held that juveniles have a right to formal notice of charges, to legal counsel, to confrontation and cross-examination of witnesses, and to privilege against self-incrimination. Their decision was a reaction to what had happened to Gerald Gault in each of these procedural areas:

Notice of Charges

No notice was given to Gerald's parents when he was taken into custody on Monday, June 8. On that night, when Mrs. Gault went to the Detention Home, she was orally informed that there would be a hearing the next afternoon and was told the reason why Gerald was in custody. The only written notice Gerald's parents received at any time was a note on plain paper from Officer Flagg (the probation officer involved in this case) delivered on Thursday or Friday, June 11 or 12, to the effect that the judge had set Monday, June 15, "for further Hearings on Gerald's delinquency." The Supreme Court ruled that this was insufficient notice, and that juveniles and their parents must be formally notified of charges against them.

Right to Counsel

The Arizona courts were proceeding on the assumption that due process for juveniles did not include a right to legal counsel, that the parents or probation officer could be relied on to protect the child's interests. The Supreme Court reasoned that probation officers are not objective parties, but may represent the court or the detention facility rather than the interests of the child. As a result, the Court ruled that juveniles are no different from adults in that they have a constitutional right to obtain legal counsel, or have counsel appointed for them if they are indigent.

Confrontation, Self-Incrimination, and Cross-Examination

The juvenile court judge admitted that he found Gerald delinquent based solely on Gerald's own admissions at two hearings. Mrs. Cook, the complainant, was never called to testify. Neither of Gerald's statements of admission were written down, and all of the parties present had conflicting recollections of just what Gerald had said. Gerald was not advised to protect himself against self-incrimination, an omission that was supported by the Arizona Supreme Court on the theory that confession is good for the child because he should be encouraged to assume an attitude of trust and confidence toward the officials of the juvenile process. The Supreme Court disagreed with this theory, pointing out that it is more probable that when children are induced to confess by "paternal" urgings on the part of officials and the confession is followed by disciplinary action, the child would feel that he has been led or tricked into confession, because he is punished despite having confessed. Although the Gault Court did not directly consider police investigative procedures, in making the privilege against self-incrimination applicable to juvenile court proceedings, the Court also made the procedural safeguards developed in *Miranda v. Arizona* available to juveniles. Following the Gault decision, virtually all of the courts that have considered the applicability of the Miranda requirements for police encounters with juveniles have concluded that the requirements do indeed apply, although courts have disagreed on whether a parent or attorney must be present and waive the rights also (Davis 1994).

The application of Miranda safeguards means that at the initial police questioning or at any point in the investigative procedures, if a minor decides to waive fifth amendment rights, confess to a crime, or waive any other constitutional right, the validity of that decision must be determined by the court. In assessing the validity of the minor's decision, the court needs to determine if there was a "knowing, intelligent, and voluntary waiver" under the "totality of circumstances" (for example, given the youth's state of mind or comprehension ability). Prior to Miranda, only the "voluntariness" of a confession needed to be determined by judicial review. Although Miranda, in principle, protects juveniles from self-incrimination, there is empirical evidence that indicates that juveniles may not understand the Miranda warning well enough to waive their constitutional rights in a "knowing and intelligent" manner, and yet it is only in extreme cases (such as where the youth is mentally retarded) that confessions are disallowed by the court (for further discussion of this issue, see Davis 1994).

The Gault decision, although sweeping in its implications, was not unanimous among the members of the Supreme Court. Justice Harlan dissented from the majority opinion in part. Although he agreed with the notification of charges and right to counsel, he raised concerns that the majority ruling would merely transplant adult court procedure into juvenile courts, thereby raising the question of whether separate juvenile courts are even necessary. He argued that the requirements of confrontation and cross-examination, and the privilege against self-incrimination, may not be necessary if adequate notice were given and counsel were made available. "I very much fear that this Court, by imposing these rigid procedural requirements, may inadvertently have served to discourage . . . efforts to find more satisfactory solutions for the problems of juvenile crime" (*In re Gault,* 387 U.S. 1, 1967: 1470). Justice Stewart dissented in full from the ruling because, in his opinion, "[j]uvenile proceedings are not criminal trials. They are not civil trials. They are simply not adversary proceedings" (*In re Gault,* 387 U.S. 1, 1967: 1470). He argued that this ruling represented:

> a long step backwards into the nineteenth century. In that era there were no juvenile proceedings, and a child was tried in a conventional criminal court with all the trappings of a conventional criminal trial. So it was that a 12–year-old boy named James Guild was tried in New Jersey for killing Catharine Beakes. A jury found him guilty of murder, and he was sentenced to death by hanging. The sentence was executed. It was all very constitutional. (*In re Gault,* 387 U.S. 1, 1967: 1471)

Limitations of the Gault Decision

The Gault decision has been cited throughout the literature on juvenile justice as the greatest milestone since the creation of the juvenile court itself. However, although certain procedural changes resulted from the decision (see, for example, Willey, 1985: 496–97), any idealistic hopes that the Gault case would somehow transform the juvenile justice system were sorely misplaced. When one considers that, following Gault, the majority of children still failed to receive legal representation, and regardless, that children were increasingly institutionalized "for their own good," the limitations of Gault become evident. One of the reasons why the Gault case failed to revolutionize juvenile justice policy is that it focused exclusively on adjudication procedure, but was not concerned with the lack of procedure in rendering the correctional disposition. In other words, even if due process were exercised to the letter of the law in every juvenile court, the disposition choices for adjudicated youths—where they are placed, the conditions of confinement, and whether placements satisfy the goals of the juvenile justice system—remained antiquated. Shireman and Reamer state this problem as follows (1986: 37–38):

> Important though the victories in moving toward procedural due process have

been, they do not reach to the possibly more substantive question of what should be done once state jurisdiction is assumed. The danger is in becoming so engrossed with procedural issues in ruling, for example, whether the youngster actually stole the car that the usually much more complex issue of what is to be done with him once he has been found to have done so is barely considered . . . .

[A]fter a hearing grossly wanting in protection of due process . . . , Gerald [Gault] was committed at age 15 to a state institution until his twenty-first birthday unless earlier released at the initiative of the institution. The entire procedure was shocking, illustrative though it was of entirely too frequent juvenile court abuse of due process. *But it is rarely observed that it is quite possible that exactly the same disposition of Gerald's case might have been made following an adjudicatory hearing including all the traditional due process protections.* Such disposition would probably have resulted in very little outcry. After all, a large proportion of the population of the nation's juvenile correctional institutions at the time was made up of "status offenders," convicted of behaviors that are legal offenses only when committed by children: truancy, running away, being ungovernable, and similar acts even less "criminal" than was Gerald's. (emphasis in the original)

Indeed, the issue of placement is all the more critical when we consider the issue of private versus state programs. In most states, private programs for delinquent youths tend to be smaller and more treatment oriented than state institutions (or state "training schools," as the institutions are euphemistically referred to). A problem arises because each private program tends to have its own criteria for accepting or rejecting youths, and youths can be rejected for any number of behavioral or character traits. As Schinitsky (1961: 5) observed over thirty years ago, "[c]hildren are often rejected for the very reasons which brought them to the Court's attention and for which they need help." As in 1961, youths who are rejected today by more treatment-oriented programs end up being committed to the state training schools, regardless of how appropriate the training school may be for them.

A second limitation of the Gault decision concerns the absence of compliance with the ruling itself. It is apparent from anecdotal as well as systematic evidence that due process protections are highly uneven across juvenile courts. For example, a study conducted in Arkansas of forty-six county courts in 1983 found that:

1. In at least 15 percent of the cases, juveniles who appeared for their adjudicatory hearing without an attorney were not advised of their right to counsel.
2. The right to remain silent . . . was not announced at approximately 30 percent of the plea and adjudication hearings observed. . . . [Also,] juveniles were required to testify at more than one-third of the adjudication hearings.
3. Prosecutors . . . presented the state's case only about 20 percent of the time while probation officers—persons in whom the juveniles were expected to place their confidence—presented the state's case against juveniles twice as often. Ref-

erees and county judges—the impartial officers of the court—also presented the case against the juveniles at some hearings.

4. Defense attorneys . . . were not present at about two out of three hearings. Even some juveniles sentenced to the training school were not represented by an attorney.

5. The ramifications of entering a plea of guilty were not explained to the juvenile at about three out of ten plea hearings.

6. Neither the complainant nor the complainant's witnesses were present at close to 40 percent of the judicial hearings at which the defense normally should be able to confront its accuser. Most witnesses for the prosecution were placed under oath and the defense given an opportunity to question them, but such was not the case at more than one-fourth of the hearings. (Arkansas Advocates for Children and Families 1983, quoted in Schwartz 1989)

Similarly, a recent examination of juvenile representation in six states (California, Minnesota, Nebraska, New York, North Dakota, and Pennsylvania) yielded the finding that three out of the six (Minnesota, Nebraska, and North Dakota) did not provide representation for approximately half of the juveniles in court for delinquency and status offenses (Feld 1988), including many juveniles who were given out-of-home placement and even secure confinement. Former juvenile court judge Ted Rubin notes that there are ways that judges can encourage youths to waive their right to counsel: "'Johnny, you can have a lawyer, but I believe you're the kind of kid who would like to speak for yourself'; 'Mrs. Jones, Johnny can have a lawyer, but then you would have to take off work and come back here again'" (Rubin 1976: 137). Why do certain jurisdictions resist the constitutional entitlement of counsel for youths who are adjudicated for delinquency? Barry Feld suggests several reasons (1988: 395):

[P]arental reluctance to retain an attorney; inadequate public-defender legal services in nonurban areas; a judicial encouragement of and readiness to find waivers of the right to counsel in order to ease administrative burdens on the courts; a continuing judicial hostility to an advocacy role in a traditional, treatment-oriented court; or a judicial predetermination of dispositions with nonappointment of counsel where probation is the anticipated outcome.

Even when youths are provided with lawyers, that does not guarantee a quality defense. For example, a two-year study of the Law Guardian Program in New York State found that many of the attorneys outside of New York City were not adequately trained in juvenile matters, nor were they familiar with important changes in juvenile justice legislation and case law (Knitzer and Sobie 1984; Schwartz 1989). Problems such as these are undoubtedly true in other states as well, but few systematic studies have been performed. Barry Feld (1988) suggests that public defender offices appoint their least capable or newest lawyers to juvenile courts to obtain trial experience, which results in weak representation for their clients. When private attorneys are appointed by the court, Feld suggests they may be more concerned with catering to the judge, rather than protecting the interests of their clients, in order to maintain an ongoing relationship with the court.

A third limitation of the Gault case concerns the myriad social problems that the juvenile court was purportedly established to ameliorate. The fact that the jurisdiction of the juvenile court includes all types of children—most of them poor, but otherwise widely varying in their behaviors and problems—creates inherent contradictions that cannot be solved merely by expanding due process protections through the adjudication stage. The catch-all nature of the juvenile court was described succinctly in 1961:

> It would appear to me that the neglected, and some delinquent children (when a parent is the petitioner), are no more a [Juvenile] Court problem, than the disturbed adult (not insane) is a Supreme Court problem. No one would think of asking the Supreme Court to assume jurisdiction of all disturbed adults, yet the [Juvenile] Court is asked to do just that with all disturbed children. The welfare of the disturbed adult is a community social problem and recognized as such. The neglected and less serious delinquent children are also a community social problem. If the Court could divest itself of jurisdiction of the . . . neglect and minor delinquency cases . . . , it might be able to work effectively with a larger number of the more serious delinquents: the children who have committed robberies, larcenies, assaults and rapes. These need the immediate attention of the Court to shatter, at their inception, any developing pattern of criminality. (Schinitsky 1961: 7)

Since 1961, all of the due process enhancements required by the Supreme Court, in theory and practice, have not had any impact (nor should they have been expected to) on the diverse caseload of juveniles appearing before the court, nor on the difficult questions of how youths should be handled following an adjudication of delinquency. On the other hand, due process has turned attention away from services needed by children and families. The frustration of a juvenile court judge *after* the Gault ruling had increased due process—and thereby reduced the court's ability to intervene in some cases—was expressed as follows (Polier 1989: 11):

> Counsel bent on preventing intervention overlooked suffering that called for help. Like the accused man with a rope around his neck, for whom the judge demanded a trial before hanging, few youths in the ghetto won a new lease on life through

due process. In court one could sense the bitterness of parents and of youth hurt by discrimination that dominated every aspect of their lives in school, in seeking work and on the streets—left unnoticed by the court and counsel.

Major Post-Gault Supreme Court Decisions in Juvenile Justice

In four decisions centering on juvenile court procedure following the landmark Gault ruling, the Supreme Court elaborated on the due process requirements that applied to juvenile court. *In re Winship* (1970) examined whether the adult standard of proof beyond a reasonable doubt applied to juveniles. *Breed v. Jones* (1975) considered whether the double jeopardy clause of the fifth amendment could prohibit a youth from being prosecuted in adult court following a delinquency finding in juvenile court. The *McKeiver v. Pennsylvania* (1971) ruling concerned the issue of whether juveniles have a constitutional right to a trial by jury. *Schall v. Martin* (1984) examined the issue of preventive detention, which is the practice of confining youths in detention facilities prior to their adjudication hearing in order to prevent situations where those juveniles might commit additional crimes.

The cases cited above resulted in the following requirements for juvenile court procedure:

1. Proof of delinquency must be established "beyond a reasonable doubt," rather than by the previous lower civil standards of proof *(In re Winship)*.
2. Youths cannot be prosecuted in adult court following a finding of delinquency in juvenile court. Such procedure would constitute double jeopardy and would violate the fifth amendment of the Constitution *(Breed v. Jones)*.
3. A jury is not a requirement in juvenile proceedings because the only requirement for "fundamental fairness" is that decisions are reached through "accurate fact-finding," that can be satisfied as well by a judge as by a jury *(McKeiver v. Pennsylvania)*. Although the McKeiver ruling denied the right of trial by jury to juveniles, it has not been viewed by legal scholars as inconsistent with other Supreme Court decisions that expanded due process rights in juvenile court. The McKeiver Court was concerned, most centrally, with retaining at least one important feature (the lack of a jury) of the intimate, informal hearings for which the juvenile court was ostensibly created. Writing for the majority in McKeiver, Justice Blackmun wrote:

> If the formalities of the criminal [adult] adjudicative process are to be superimposed upon the juvenile court system, there is little need for its separate existence. Perhaps that ultimate disillusionment will come one day, but for the moment we are disinclined to give impetus to it. (403 U.S. at 550–51)

Of course, informality is advantageous for the juvenile court only if (a) the informality actually does protect children, or (b) the court cannot find some way of thwarting the formal procedures, both of which are debatable assertions.

4. Unlike the decisions examined above, the U.S. Supreme Court's decision in the *Schall v. Martin* case was considered a blow for *parens patriae*. The Court concluded that the New York Family Court Act's preventive detention provision was constitutionally valid. The provision permitted the court to detain youths who were awaiting their adjudication hearings as long as there was a "serious risk" that they would commit additional crimes. The Court's decision hinged on the interests of protecting the due process rights of the accused juveniles, on one hand, against the dual interests of societal protection and protection of the juvenile offenders, themselves, from the consequences of their own criminal activity. The Court ruled that the youth in question had not been held for a punitive purpose, as a lower court had concluded, and that the court's interest in preventing crime was as legitimate as its interest in ensuring the youth's reappearance in court. The case provoked considerable controversy among observers who believed that the process was prejudicial to juveniles; however, language in the Court's opinion suggested that the rationale for upholding the preventive detention of juveniles could be applied to adults as well (Davis 1994). The case also engendered concern that overprediction of risk, which is typical in predicting dangerousness, would further fuel the unnecessary confinement of juveniles who had not yet been adjudicated delinquent or found guilty in a court proceeding.

Trying Youths as Adults

During the 1980s and into the 1990s, juvenile courts became more offense-oriented and less offender-oriented, and responding to the "needs" of the child was no longer the first priority. The courts began to rely on offense criteria in making decisions far more often than the philosophy of rehabilitation would suggest. The growing response of the juvenile court to the offense—rather than offender—was a consequence of the just deserts sentencing movement of the 1980s. As noted in the first chapter, many more youths found themselves in adult court due to three common mechanisms established in many states: expanded waiver provisions, concurrent jurisdiction, and offenses excluded by statute from juvenile court jurisdiction. It is important to note that while it is appropriate to try some youths as adults, these new procedures have contributed to the overcrowding of juvenile detention because most jurisdictions confine juveniles who are in adult court—

generally a far slower process than juvenile court—within juvenile detention facilities. In addition, as we discussed in the first chapter, the weight of research evidence suggests that juveniles in adult court generally do not receive dispositions any more severe than what is available in the juvenile system.

Expanded Waiver Provisions

The waiver mechanism requires a waiver hearing in the juvenile court, with evidence brought forth by both prosecutor and defense on the issue of waiving juvenile court jurisdiction. Compared to the concurrent jurisdiction approach, in which the prosecutor has full discretion to directly file a case in either court, or legislatively excluded offenses, the waiver mechanism maximizes the discretion of the juvenile court judge, who is authorized to decide, based on the evidence, when juvenile court jurisdiction should be retained, and when jurisdiction should be waived to the adult court. Unlike the other mechanisms, cases decided on the basis of a waiver hearing always originate in the juvenile court.

Procedural criteria contained in the U.S. Supreme Court's decision *Kent v. the United States* (1966) are intended to assure that only the most serious cases will be judicially waived to adult court—although compliance with that goal appears to be low in many states, as discussed in chapter 1. States' juvenile court procedures vary on a number of non-Kent criteria that relate to the issue of waiver. The first is the age jurisdiction of the juvenile court—up until what age must a youth be considered a "juvenile" in legal terms? Regardless of the offense, the maximum age of juvenile court jurisdiction in three states is sixteen (Connecticut, New York, North Carolina); in seven states it is age seventeen (Georgia, Illinois, Louisiana, Massachusetts, Missouri, South Carolina, Texas); and in the remaining majority of states, it is age eighteen (Davis 1994).

A second issue is what age and/or offense criteria are required before waiver can be considered. Most states require that the juvenile be over a certain age and be charged with a particularly serious offense before jurisdiction may be waived (Arkansas, Colorado, Connecticut, Louisiana, Massachusetts, Michigan, Missouri, Montana, Nevada, New Jersey, North Carolina, Ohio, Oregon, Texas, Utah, Vermont, and Virginia). A number of other states (Alabama, California,

Florida, Illinois, Iowa, Minnesota, and Mississippi) permit waiver of jurisdiction for youths above a certain age, regardless of the offense charged. A few states permit waiver on the basis of the seriousness of the charges alone, regardless of age (Maine, New Hampshire, and Oklahoma). A few others place no limitations on waiver, permitting waiver without regard to the age of the child or the nature of the offense (Alaska, Washington, and Wyoming). Finally, a number of jurisdictions permit waiver based on a combination of the above factors (Delaware, Washington, D.C., Georgia, Idaho, Indiana, Kansas, Kentucky, Maryland, North Dakota, Pennsylvania, Rhode Island, Tennessee, West Virginia, and Wisconsin). In a few states a juvenile may choose to be tried as an adult, in which case the court must transfer the case for adult prosecution (Davis 1994).

It is evident from the paragraph above that most states' juvenile codes permit waiver of jurisdiction under certain circumstances. A recent review of the statutes of the fifty states and the District of Columbia, conducted by juvenile law expert Samuel Davis (1994), found only three states that did not provide for a waiver of jurisdiction out of juvenile court—New York, Nebraska, and New Mexico. In New York, there are two procedural reasons why a waiver provision does not exist. First, juvenile court jurisdiction is limited only to youths who are aged fifteen and younger; all others are automatically considered adults. Moreover, New York established a "reverse waiver" provision in which thirteen- to fifteen-year-olds with specified serious offenses are charged in adult court, but the adult court then has discretion to transfer appropriate cases to juvenile court for adjudication and disposition.

In Nebraska, juvenile and adult courts have concurrent jurisdiction over the more serious offenses, so that the prosecutor can decide in which court (juvenile or adult) to file charges. Nebraska's reliance on prosecutorial discretion as the only means of establishing jurisdiction is unusual, however. Other states' concurrent jurisdiction provisions generally cover a minority of offenses, and waiver is available for the remainder. In New Mexico, all juvenile offenders are retained in juvenile court except for those aged sixteen or older who are charged with first degree murder. However, fifteen- to seventeen-year-old juveniles who are found delinquent by reason of a specified serious offense may receive an adult sentence if the prosecutor recommends one (Davis 1994).

Concurrent Jurisdiction

Some states allow prosecutors the authority to decide in which court (juvenile or adult) to initiate a case. Prosecutors have jurisdiction in both courts and can decide where cases can be filed, as long as the case meets the age and/or offense. Concurrent jurisdiction exists for specified offenses in Arkansas, Florida, Georgia, Louisiana, Nebraska, South Dakota, Utah, Wyoming, and the District of Columbia (Davis 1994).

The state of Florida, for example, has more mechanisms for trying youths as adults than any other state. It is therefore of no great surprise that over 6,000 cases are transferred per year, the majority of which are directly filed (that is, without a hearing) in adult court by the prosecutor, according to concurrent jurisdiction provisions. In addition to judicial waiver and grand jury indictment of certain juvenile offenders, the Florida Juvenile Justice Act (passed in 1979 and amended in 1981) permits the prosecutor to file a bill of information (similar to an indictment, only it is reviewed by a judge rather than by a grand jury) in criminal court on any child fourteen years of age or older who has previously been adjudicated delinquent for one of several violent felonies and who is currently charged with a subsequent such offense, and on any sixteen- or seventeen-year-old charged with any violation of Florida law "when in his judgment and discretion, the public interest requires that adult sanctions be considered or imposed" (Florida Statutes Annotated Chapter 39.04[2][e][4]). Perhaps because of the broad discretion permitted to prosecutors, the overwhelming majority of transfer cases are nonviolent offenses (Bishop, Frazier, and Henretta, 1989), which most observers agree is an inefficient and illogical use of the adult court.

Statutory Exclusion

Many states no longer allow juvenile courts the option of waiving their jurisdiction on a case-by-case basis for certain offenses. In particular, violent offenders have been recognized as the most critical test of individualized decision making and the rehabilitative correctional model (Coates 1981; Fagan and Hartstone 1984; Zimring 1981). Rather than allowing the possibility that the judge or prosecutor might retain serious cases within the juvenile court, the more serious offenders are automatically tried in adult court, based on the legal category of their offense and, perhaps, their prior offenses. "Statutory exclusion" automatically removes certain specified offenses from juvenile court jurisdiction by virtue of a statute enacted by the legislature. Such provisions empower lawmakers to set the policies, rather than allow discretion to juvenile court judges or prosecutors, although some states permit the originating adult courts to transfer cases down to the juvenile court level.

For example, the state of Oklahoma has an unusually long list of excluded offenses over which the adult court has original jurisdiction for any youth aged sixteen or over: murder; kidnapping; robbery with a dangerous weapon; rape in the first degree; rape by instrumentation; use of firearm or other offensive weapon while committing a felony; arson in the first degree; burglary with explosives; burglary in the first or second degree after three or more adjudications for burglary in the first or second degree; shooting with intent to kill; discharging a firearm, crossbow, or other weapon from a vehicle; intimidating a witness; manslaughter in the first degree; nonconsensual sodomy; or manufacturing, distributing, dispensing, or possessing with intent to manufacture, distribute, or dispense a controlled dangerous substance. However, the statute allows any such cases to be transferred, at the discretion of the judge, from adult court to juvenile court for adjudication (Davis 1994).

Not all states specifically exclude certain offenders from the jurisdiction of the juvenile court. In other states, such as California, Missouri, and Texas, even crimes of murder are not necessarily excluded by statute from juvenile court jurisdiction, but instead are considered for waiver by the court on a case-by-base basis. However, there may be a presumption that the youth is not appropriate for juvenile court based on the offense committed. For example, in California, if a youth aged sixteen or older is charged with one of twenty serious designated acts, then there is a presumption of non-amenability, or inability to be treated successfully within the juvenile system. This presumption can be overcome by evidence that the youth would be amenable to treatment in the programs available through the juvenile court. The court would consider five criteria in this regard: the degree of criminal sophistication; whether the minor can be rehabilitated prior to the expiration of juvenile court jurisdiction; the minor's previous delinquent history; the success of previous attempts by the juvenile court to rehabilitate the minor; and the circumstances and gravity of the offense alleged to have been committed by the minor.

Many state correctional agencies have opposed "statutory exclusion" provisions because they automatically remove serious offenders from the jurisdiction of the juvenile sector. Although the retention of juvenile murderers, rapists, and so on within the juvenile system may seem more like a liability than a benefit, it demonstrates confidence in the rehabilitative model for essentially all juvenile offenders, regardless of their offense. This has organizational advantages for the juvenile court and juvenile correctional agencies that have an interest in championing the rehabilitative model for youths. More importantly, the legal category of an offense is often misleading when used as the basis for automatic exclusion. An unarmed youth can be charged with "armed robbery" if they make the victim believe they are armed. "Aggravated assaults" vary widely in definition from one jurisdiction to another. Youths involved in group offenses can vary significantly in terms of their actual contributing behavior, yet they may all be charged with the same offense.

Many experts (e.g., Davis 1994) believe that automatic exclusion and concurrent jurisdiction are unjustified because neither provision allows for a hearing to first determine the facts. On the other hand, respected observers have gone so far as to recommend that the juvenile court be abolished, or its jurisdiction radically redefined to automatically exclude all serious, violent, or habitual juvenile offenders (Feld 1983; Wolfgang 1982). Meanwhile, there is evidence to suggest that juvenile court personnel have themselves grown more conservative. In a recent survey of three courts located in a large urban area, a suburban setting, and a rural area of a northeast state, more than three-fourths of the court personnel believed that the purpose of juvenile court had changed, primarily by using punishment as a dominant force (Sanborn 1991). However, not all states share this conservatism. In another study involving interviews with court personnel in Massachusetts juvenile courts, the author found overwhelming belief in the potential of rehabilitation (Laub 1985).

The Waiver Process in Massachusetts

Although excluded offense and concurrent jurisdiction provisions have increased since 1980, the waiver or transfer process is still a common mechanism for trying youths as adults in the United States. The waiver process in Massachusetts is examined as follows. Massachusetts courts handle serious juvenile offenders through a waiver statute that allows the juvenile court to waive its jurisdiction and transfer juveniles, aged fourteen to sixteen and charged with serious offenses, to the adult criminal court. It is the responsibility of the juvenile court judge to make individualized judgments concerning both the child's "amenability" to rehabilitation within the juvenile system and the child's dangerousness to public safety. Most of the states that permit waiver of jurisdiction require, within their statutes, a hearing on the waiver decision (Davis 1994). That requirement is based on the findings of the Supreme Court in *Kent v. United States* (383 U.S. 541, 1966), which examined due process of law in a District of Columbia waiver case.

The Massachusetts procedural law makes it somewhat difficult to waive juvenile court jurisdiction for most offenses because the burden is on the prosecutor to prove that youths are not amenable to treatment, as opposed to the youth needing to prove that he or she is amenable to treatment in the juvenile system. However, the statute governing the juvenile court's age jurisdiction in Massachusetts automatically excludes youths from the juvenile system who commit an offense on or beyond their seventeenth birthday. This is in contrast to most other states, which retain the majority of seventeen-year-olds within the juvenile system, and some states which retain eighteen-year-olds as well.

Massachusetts law outlines the conditions and requirements for waiving juvenile court jurisdiction (Massachusetts General Laws Ch. 119, Sec. 61). It states the following conditions must be met before a transfer to the adult jurisdiction is warranted:

(1) [If the child] who had been previously committed to the DYS as a delinquent child has committed an offense against a law of the Commonwealth, which if he were an adult, would be punishable by imprisonment in the state prison, or, has committed an offense involving the infliction or threat of serious bodily harm;
(2) If such alleged offense was committed while the child was between the fourteenth and seventeenth birthdays [that is, aged fourteen to sixteen];
(3) And if the court enters a written finding . . . that the child presents a significant danger to the public . . . and is not amenable to rehabilitation as a juvenile.

The criteria used to determine if a youth should be transferred to adult court are as follows:

1. The seriousness of the alleged offense;
2. School, family, and social history including any court and juvenile delinquency record;
3. Adequate protection of the public;
4. Nature of any past treatment efforts; and
5. The likelihood of rehabilitation.

Generally, all of these factors are considered, with the defense attorney attempting to weight factors two, four, and five more heavily, and the prosecutor emphasizing factors one and three.

The motion to waive juvenile court jurisdiction can be made by one of three participants: the judge, the assistant district attorney, or the police prosecutor. In some instances, the judge may file the motion *sua sponte* (on his own motion). The judge will rarely file the motion, though, because doing so would indicate that the judge is not impartial. In cases of exceptional seriousness, an assistant district attorney from Superior Court may be asked to handle the prosecution. Generally, however, depending on the court either an assistant district attorney or a police prosecutor will argue the motion to waive jurisdiction. A study of juvenile court processing in one Massachusetts county (Laub 1985) found that large variation exists in the involvement of assistant district attorneys in juvenile sessions of district courts, although police prosecutors tend to handle the bulk of juvenile cases.

The waiver hearing itself is bifurcated into the Part A and Part B hearings. Part A determines whether there is probable cause that the juvenile has committed the offense as charged. If the child is in custody, he or she has the right to a Part A hearing within fourteen days (versus ten for adults). If the child is not in custody there is no time limit, but the hearing is not usually put off longer than three weeks. The duration of the Part A hearing depends on how long it takes for the prosecutor to provide evidence in the case, which can range anywhere from fifteen minutes to four days, but typically takes one and one-half hours. During the Part A hearing, the burden is on the prosecutor to introduce some evidence on each element of the crime, either directly or by inference. Victims and witnesses are called to testify and all evidence is presented. For Part A, the prosecutor has a very low standard of evidence. He or she has to show "some evidence" that a crime was committed, and more likely than not that the youth was involved in it. If probable cause is not found, the case is dismissed and in some instances the record may be sealed. When probable cause is found, Part B of the waiver hearing is scheduled.

In Part B, the issue is whether or not it is in the public's interest to transfer the child. Part B involves a consideration of whether the child is both a significant danger to the public and is not amenable to rehabilitation in the juvenile system. For Part B, the prosecutor must show "clear and convincing" evidence that the child is not amenable to treatment. In deciding whether the youth should be transferred to adult court, the most important criterion is often the magnitude of the crime, and whether there was an infliction or threat of serious bodily harm. All of the defense witnesses are present to testify at the Part B hearing in order to demonstrate the youth's amenability to treatment, e.g., teachers, coaches, family members, DYS employees, members of the clergy. While there is no statutory definition of "amenability to treatment," it could be defined as follows: "Whether or not the child would respond to services and treatment to rehabilitate him, to cause the child to be a productive member of society." The Part B hearing is usually continued several times, often over a period of several months. According to research on court processing of violent offenders in six cities (Fagan et al. 1984), the average length of time in Boston from formal charging to disposition was 3.2 months, roughly eighteen days longer than the average time in the other cities studied (Denver, Memphis, Miami, Newark, and Phoenix).

The events that follow the waiver motion occur as follows. Probable cause is determined in Part A. If the youth is found to be not amenable to treatment in Part B, he or she will be arraigned in adult court on criminal charges. If the youth is found amenable to treatment, he or she will be retained in the juvenile court for disposition. Legislation passed in Massachusetts in 1990 and 1991 expanded the waiver provisions somewhat. The 1990 law specified that in cases of first or second degree murder, the burden would be placed on the youth, rather than the prosecutor, to provide evidence on the question of amenability during the waiver hearing. The 1991 legislation required mandatory waiver hearings (not mandatory waiver) for youths charged with first or second degree murder or manslaughter.

The Adjudication and Disposition Processes in Juvenile Court

Delinquency proceedings are analogous to an adult criminal trial, but are referred to as "hearings." The standard of proof is beyond reasonable doubt, as established in the *Winship* decision, but rules of evidence may or may not be equivalent to adult standards depending on the state (Davis 1994). The juvenile defendant has the right to testify on his or her behalf and to call witnesses. One difference between juvenile delinquency proceedings and adult criminal trials is that, in most states, the public is excluded from juvenile sessions; only persons who have a direct interest in the case are admitted. Another difference is the number of parties involved in each juvenile case. For instance, in addition to the usual participants in a criminal case (the prosecutors, defense counsel, victim, and defendant), in juvenile court there are parents, school officials, community resource persons, court clinic staff, and, at times, youth services personnel. The number of participants is compounded by the fact that juveniles generally commit crimes in groups and the co-defendants increase the number of parties even more (Laub 1985).

At the conclusion of the adjudication hearing in Massachusetts, the juvenile court judge has three alternatives in Massachusetts: (1) find the child not delinquent; (2) find the child delinquent; or (3) find sufficient facts for an adjudication of delinquency. Upon a finding of delinquency or a finding of sufficient facts, unless the offense is murder or manslaughter, the judge may then consider the various disposition alternatives, which include: (a) continuance without a finding, (b) filed with or without a finding, (c) probation, (d) suspended sentence to DYS, (e) fine or court costs, (f) restitution, (g) community services, and (h) commitment to DYS. The disposition options permitted by other state codes are similar to those in Massachusetts, although many other states allow judges to commit youths directly to a particular institution, camp, or other facility.

In Massachusetts, commitment to DYS is the fullest extent of the juvenile court's commitment power, and DYS is then empowered to determine placement, length of stay, and conditions of parole. Upon an adjudication of delinquency or upon the court's disposition, the juvenile has the right to appeal. Appeals are made before six-person jury sessions of the district court department and are determined in the same way as adult criminal appeals, except that the trial is closed to the public. In cases involving an adjudication for first-degree murder, legislation passed in 1991 mandates sentences of twenty years, with parole eligibility beginning after the fifteenth year. In cases involving second-degree murder, the sentence is for fifteen years, with parole eligibility beginning after the tenth year. Youths sentenced in this manner may be confined in DYS until age twenty-one, and then transferred to the custody of the adult correctional agency. In manslaughter cases, youths must be committed to DYS until age twenty-one, which is three years beyond the maximum age of DYS jurisdiction for other offenses.

Three states with unusual disposition schemes are Washington, Texas, and New York. Rather than allow prosecutorial and judicial discretion, the state of Washington uses a specific point system to determine sentencing ranges. The points measure the seriousness of the offense and prior offense history (a detailed description of the Washington sentencing model is provided in chapter 5). In Texas, juvenile court judges can sentence juveniles convicted for any offense in a list of enumerated offenses for a determinate period of up to forty years, part of which may be spent in the Texas Youth Commission (Davis 1994). In New York, the juvenile code mandates "restrictive placement" of juveniles convicted of a "designated felony" offense (N.Y. Laws 1976, c. 878; N.Y. Laws 1978, c. 481). Depending on the seriousness of the offense, they may be committed to the Division for Youth for an initial period of three or five years, the first portion of which must be spent in a secure facility (Davis 1994).

A matter frequently raised in studies of court processing is the use of plea bargaining. According to representatives of the court and public defenders' offices in Massachusetts, plea bargaining rarely occurs with juvenile offenders. This is because the Department of Youth Services, not the court, controls all placement decisions. There are no sentencing powers at the court level to guide or enforce length of stay or type of placement, so manipulating the youth's offense charges would have only vague and indirect consequences for the youth. There is a marked contrast in the use of plea bargaining in states where sentencing is an issue. For example, an Illinois law enacted in 1982 provides for the automatic transfer of older juveniles charged with serious offenses to the adult courts. In a study of the law's impact, although half of the offenders were charged with murder, 40 percent of the cases were plea bargained to lesser charges (Reed 1983).

Plea bargaining is also common in the state of Florida, where pros-ecutors have used a "direct file" mechanism for charging youths with offenses under adult court jurisdiction. Since 1979, prosecutors have had full discretion in deciding which court (juvenile or adult) should have jurisdiction over thousands of sixteen- and seventeen-year-olds charged with any felony, as well as sixteen- and seventeen-year-olds charged with a misdemeanor, if they have two prior adjudications of which at least one is a felony. Prosecutors in Florida use the threat of transfer to adult court as a means of extracting guilty pleas in juvenile court (Bishop et al. 1989).

Ten states' juvenile codes were studied in 1986 to compare them on key components (Governor's Anti-Crime Council 1986). The states were California, Florida, Kansas, Massachusetts, New Jersey, New York, Ohio, Pennsylvania, Washington, and Wisconsin. Variation among the ten states was found in nearly sixty distinct provisions, from purpose of the code to provisions for enforcing dispositional orders. Issues on which states lacked consensus, that were not dis-cussed in the sections above, include: minimum age of jurisdiction, use of quasi-judicial decision makers, duration of pretrial detention, conditions of release/bail from detention, public or closed hearings, and sealing or destruction of records.

The Effect of Race on the Juvenile Justice Process

It should surprise few observers that black and Latino youths are most disproportionately represented in the juvenile justice system. In fact, the numbers of youths placed in public juvenile facilities (deten-tion, correctional, and shelter programs) from 1985 to 1989 revealed a 30 percent increase in black youths, a 32 percent increase in Hispanic youths, and a 106 percent increase in Asian-American youths. Over the same time period, however, there was actually a 5 percent decrease in white youths. It is clear that the juvenile system has been used to disproportionately control minority youths (Krisberg and Austin 1993).

A review of forty-six studies that examined the role of race in the juvenile justice process was conducted by Carl Pope and William Feyerherm (1990). Most of the studies reviewed were multivariate, so that offense and social factors could be held constant to determine the independent effect of race on decision making in the juvenile system. Roughly two-thirds of the studies found evidence of disproportionate treatment of minorities, even after other factors were controlled for statistically. In more recent research, evidence was found in California of cumulative discrimination at each subsequent decision point in the juvenile process, from arrest to commitment to the California Youth Authority, regardless of offense (Krisberg and Austin 1993). In Georgia, although socioeconomic status had a greater effect than race on case processing decisions, race nonetheless had a direct effect on disposition, and also indirectly affected how youths were handled at law enforcement, intake, and adjudication decision points (Kurtz, Giddings, and Sutphen 1993).

Summary

It is essential that policymakers consider the political origins of the juvenile court when looking to the court as a solution to the problem of juvenile crime. History informs us that the juvenile court was molded to fit the Illinois Supreme Court's decision in the Daniel O'Connell case—so that it could incarcerate a uniquely broad spectrum of youths, including those whose main "offense" was poverty. In recent years, evidence has mounted that not only poverty, but race and, particularly in detaining nonserious offenders, gender affects decisions in juvenile court.

During the 1980s and early 1990s, the most specific provisions of juvenile court procedure became highly politicized. Individual elements within state juvenile codes were "toughened" to provide the perception of a "quick fix" by allowing for the removal of additional categories of youths out of the juvenile system. Statutes were amended repeatedly without first considering the burden of these new procedures on other stages of the court process, in particular pretrial detention overcrowding. None of the new mechanisms addressed questions about the substance of correctional programming, or racial or gender over-representation, or long-term public safety. Instead of endlessly debating points of waiver and other fairly arbitrary strategies for removing youths from juvenile court jurisdiction, some jurisdictions have worked toward developing intensive, high quality services and programs in which youths and families are willing to participate; allocating confinement in secure facilities according to a rational process that is most protective of public safety; and developing interagency strategies with social services, youth correctional agencies, and schools.

The juvenile court is not a solution to the problem of juvenile crime. It can be, however, the best vehicle for obtaining balanced dispositions for the vast majority of offenders. In order for the juvenile court to retain the control of the wide array of youths ranging from status offenders to violent offenders, the different qualities of individual youths within those groups must be addressed with creativity, flexibility, and accountability. Juvenile correctional strategies for managing such diverse clientele are compared in the remaining chapters.

5

Balanced Decision Making in Juvenile Corrections

Key Decisions in Juvenile Corrections

Decision management is the cornerstone of any organization, and is a particularly visible component of juvenile correctional agencies. Suppose a juvenile offender named Matthew is adjudicated delinquent for dealing cocaine in his neighborhood. He is known to the police as a drug dealer and gang member, and has a court record of previous adjudications for offenses including assault and battery and attempted breaking and entering. In most states, a case such as this would be handled within the juvenile system, rather than adult court. Following an adjudication of delinquency, what should happen to Matthew? Who should have the power to decide? What criteria should they use in making their decision? The answers to these questions vary a great deal by state.

In some states, the juvenile court judge has wide discretion to simply "file" or "continue" the case for disposition, which means that for the indefinite future, Matthew will continue on probation without anything further happening to him. Judges in some states might, instead, be obligated by statute to place Matthew into a specific institution. In certain states the judge must follow disposition guidelines set by the legislature, unless there are valid reasons not to. In others, the judge can sentence to a juvenile correctional agency, but the agency has the authority to decide where youths are placed and for how long. Under some administrative models, the juvenile correctional agency decides where to place youths, but the parole board determines the actual length of stay. To complicate these matters even further, some judges, correctional agencies and parole boards use objective classification methods for determining disposition and length of stay, and others do not.

There are numerous questions that can be asked to determine how case decisions are made within a juvenile court or correctional agency. The most important question concerns the decision structure for making disposition decisions, that is, for determining what program is suitable for each individual offender. There are three organizational models for making placement decisions. The first is the legislative model, in which guidelines are established by the legislature and merely followed by the court; the second is the judicial model, in which the court determines placement; and the third is the administrative model, in which placement decisions are made by the juvenile correctional agency, without direct interference from the legislature or court. If you wish to identify which of these three entities wields the most power in a state's juvenile justice system, you can do so by determining which one has control of placement decisions. In other words, that particular sector has been empowered by the state to calculate the severity of punishment. It is that sector that has the authority to decide how much weight should be given to treatment concerns, how much emphasis should be placed on retribution, whether to concern itself with incapacitating high risk offenders; in short, to determine the purpose, or purposes, of punishment.

Legislative Decision Making

The state of Washington illustrates the legislative model for meting out juvenile dispositions. The Washington State Juvenile Justice Act of 1977 overhauled the system of sentencing and placing juvenile offenders in that state (Schneider and Schram 1980). Among other significant changes was the introduction of "presumptive sentencing" in Washington's juvenile code. "Presumptive sentencing" means that there is an "expected" or "normal" sentence—usually with a very small amount of deviation—for each particular offense. In the case of Washington, the sentence is computed from the juvenile's current offense, age, and time and nature of prior offenses. Each offense is assigned a certain number of points proportionate to its calculated seriousness. A multiplication factor is derived from the other criteria and assigned. The total point score is then located on a sentencing grid. The sentencing schedule specifies the level and length of confinement and other sanctions, but does not go so far as to determine placement in particular institutions. That decision is made by the juvenile courts. The courts may also go outside of the presumptive range in order to avoid a "manifest injustice," although the finding of a manifest injustice must be supported by clear and convincing evidence.

During the late 1980s there was a federal push for other states to adopt the Washington model, but the Washington code was ultimately rejected as a national model. Among the criticisms of the code (Wentworth 1979) were substantial confusion in calculating points, common (45 percent) use of the override process, widespread use of plea bargaining, and the relocation—not elimination—of discretion from caseworkers to prosecutors. Furthermore, the number of secure beds in the state increased dramatically to accommodate the code between 1974 and 1984, from 48 beds to 96 or 293 beds, depending on how they are counted. In 1984, 96 beds were in locked facilities, and the remainder were in unlocked cottages surrounded by perimeter fencing (Guarino-Ghezzi and Kimball 1986).

As to the types of disposition, the Washington code permits only two: confinement and community supervision. Community supervision is generally reserved for minor or first-time offenders although, since 1994, judges have been permitted to suspend prosecution or defer sentences of more serious offenders for up to one year, while the youth is placed on probation. The code defines three categories of offenders: serious offenders, middle offenders, and minor or first offenders. A serious offender is a person aged fifteen or older who commits a class A felony or another of a specifically enumerated set of offenses. A middle offender is a juvenile who has committed an offense but is not a serious offender, a minor offender, nor first offender. A minor offender is a juvenile (aged seventeen or under) who falls entirely within one of the following categories: (1) four misdemeanors, or (2) three misdemeanors and/or gross misdemeanors.

Although Washington uses a specific point system to determine sentencing ranges, the point system is not a part of the text of the code. Instead, the points and corresponding sentencing ranges are established by a Juvenile Dispositions Standards Commission, which is composed of juvenile justice professionals appointed by the governor, and which meets at least once every six months. This approach leaves some flexibility in the system by allowing the sentencing calculus to be amended by commission, rather than requiring that it be put to a legislative vote. The code provides that in setting the actual disposition from the range of available alternatives (which includes going outside of the standard range to avoid instances of "manifest injustice"), the court should:

- consider information and arguments offered by parties and their counsel;
- consider any predisposition report;
- allow the youth to have a parent or guardian speak on behalf of the youth;
- allow the victim or an investigative law enforcement officer to speak; and
- consider mitigating and aggravating factors.

In considering mitigating factors, the court is required to confine itself to the following:

- the youth's conduct neither caused nor threatened serious injury;
- the youth acted under strong and immediate provocation;
- the youth was suffering from a mental or physical defect that significantly reduced his or her culpability;
- prior to his or her detection the youth made a good faith attempt to compensate the victim for injury or loss sustained; and
- that at least a year has expired between the youth's current offense and the most recent prior offense.
- In considering aggravating factors the court is to restrict itself to the following:
- that the youth, in the commission of or flight from the offense, inflicted or attempted to inflict serious bodily harm;
- that the victim or victims were particularly vulnerable;
- that the offense was committed in an especially heinous, cruel, or vicious manner;
- that the respondent had a recent criminal history or failed to comply with conditions of a recent disposition order or diversionary agreement;
- that the respondent was the leader of a criminal enterprise involving several persons; and
- that there are other complaints that have resulted in diversion or a finding or plea of guilty, but which are not included as part of the criminal history.

Judicial Decision Making

Unlike Washington, the state of Pennsylvania represents a "judicial model" of placement authority because there are no presumptive guidelines set by the legislature. Pennsylvania's code gives to the juvenile courts the authority to make specific placements. The code states that the courts may commit juvenile offenders to institutions, youth development centers, camps, or other facilities for delinquent children operated under the direction of the courts or of another public agency, most likely the Division for Youth and Families, and approved by the Department of Public Welfare. Thus, Pennsylvania's juvenile court has total sentencing and placement power over all types of offenders with the exception of youths charged with murder, who are excluded from juvenile court jurisdiction and tried automatically as adults. Pennsylvania's code states that disposition decisions are to be made so as to best suit a child's treatment, supervision, rehabilitation, and welfare. The full array of disposition options includes:

- making any order authorized for the disposition of dependent children;
- placing the child on probation (including out of state) under conditions and limitations as prescribed by the court;
- committing the child to an institution, youth development center, camp, or other facility operated under the supervision of the court or another public authority;
- committing the child to an institution operated by the Department of Public Welfare (if the child is twelve or older); and
- ordering payment of reasonable amounts of fines, costs, or restitution.

As far as sentence lengths, the code sets only the maximum sentence, which is three years or as long as the child could have been sentenced if he or she were an adult. Again, the code provides the courts with considerable discretion as far as ordering length of stay in a particular program. The code also provides for modifications or extensions if the court finds after a hearing that the extension or modification will "effectuate the original purpose for which the order was entered." The committing courts are to review each commitment every six months and hold a disposition review hearing at least once every nine months. This model maximizes the role of the court vis-à-vis the legislature as well as the youth correctional agency that runs or oversees most of the programs, the Division for Youths and Families (DYF). Although the DYF programs have responsibility for youths sent to them by the court, they lack the authority to decide which youths are appropriate for which programs, and how much time they should serve.

Administrative Decision Making

Unlike Washington and Pennsylvania, Massachusetts represents the prototypical "administrative decision model." In Massachusetts, the juvenile code bestows placement authority with the Department of Youth Services, and the courts have no statutory authority to make specific placements. Whereas Pennsylvania's judges and Washington's legislators need to be familiar with the range and quality of available placements, in Massachusetts the judges make only the decision to commit to DYS, and the legislators have even less involvement than that. Commitment to DYS is one of essentially three options available to the court; the others are to place the case on file, or to place the child on probation. As far as DYS's responsibilities to the court subsequent to commitment, the code itself is vague. It states that, as a means of correcting socially harmful tendencies DYS may do any of the following:

- require participation by the child in vocation, physical education, and correctional training and activities;
- require such modes of life or conduct as seem best adapted to fit the child for a return to full liberty without danger to the public; and
- provide such medical or psychiatric treatment as necessary.

While the code does not provide any other sections on commitment and rehabilitation, the section on rules and regulations does state that the purpose of rules, regulations, and by-laws established by the Commissioner of Youth Services and of all education, employment, discipline, recreation, and other activities carried on in the facilities shall be to restore and build up the self-respect and self-reliance of the children lodged in the facilities and to qualify them for good citizenship and honorable employment. Clearly, this kind of language gives the DYS a great deal of leeway in deciding among programs ranging from home placement to secure treatment facilities.

In states that have recently deinstitutionalized, institutions were previously the placements of choice for even nonserious offenders. In states where there are but two institutions and no other placement choices, the decision is simple: send the youth to the boy's institution, send the youth to the girl's institution. No further classification is needed, because no further placement options exist. This is still the case in states that are not planning to develop alternatives to their institutions. Other states are only slightly more gradated. In Mississippi, the juvenile correctional agency is empowered to make placement decisions, yet they use only two criteria in making placements: offender's sex and age. They do not need to evaluate or classify youths any further, because their facilities do not attempt to specialize in programming in any way. In states where different programs offer different levels of services, such as education, security, or counseling (programs for sex offenders, substance abusers, etc.), classification of offenders is a necessity in order to make a good match.

All states have relied on the institutional model of care for up to a full century, and the long tradition of institutions makes it difficult to adjust to the idea of diversity in placement options. The situation in the state of Alabama illustrates this point. In 1988, the Alabama juvenile justice system was termed "at a crossroads" as it deliberated over expanding institutional beds versus community level programs. The Department of Youth Services wrote the following in a special report on future projections:

> The future of the Alabama juvenile justice system and particularly the Department of Youth Services is at a crossroads. The state must either dramatically increase its institutional capabilities at the cost of $30,000 per bed, or Alabama can adopt a more realistic approach to its problem of juvenile crime. . . . Years of experience and national trends indicate that all troubled children do not need to be incarcerated. While at the same time, it has also been proven that adequate facilities and programs need to be available to those youth who cannot function in an open society. Youth Services does not need, nor can the state afford, to fall into the cycle of continuously building more institutions without first developing alternatives at the community level for youth who do not need incarceration. (*Projected State Services for Delinquent Youth: A Road Map to the Future,* State of Alabama, Department of Youth Services, January 1988, as quoted in DeMuro and Butts 1989)

Alabama has an administrative model in that juvenile court judges commit to the DYS, but DYS has disposition authority over placement. This authority is exercised by a central placement committee comprised of representatives of the education, social services, and psychology bureaus of the DYS. In the past, a commitment to DYS has meant an institutional placement more often than not, due to the disproportionate number of training school beds. In 1987, the state came under court order due to overcrowded conditions in the DYS facilities. Then, in 1990, a new law exacerbated this situation by requiring that committed youths who are awaiting placement in detention be placed within seven days, rather than the previous two weeks. The volume of youths moving through the system and the overcrowding problems led to a situation in which serious offenders were being released from custody too quickly.

Ironically, the bottleneck was created in large measure by the courts' commitment of youths whose crimes were not very serious to begin with. Nearly half of youths whom the courts were committing to DYS were not serious offenders. A study of all 653 commitments during 1988 (DeMuro and Butts 1989) revealed that only 8 percent were adjudicated for Felony A offenses, another 18 percent for Felony B offenses, and 26 percent for class C felonies. In other words, status offenses, violations of probation, and misdemeanors accounted for 48 percent of the commitments. Not only did the courts overcrowd institutions with youths who did not threaten public safety, but as a result of the overcrowding, serious offenders—who were a threat to the public—were released early.

Classification of Juvenile Offenders

As a result of the apparent over-institutionalization of youths in Alabama, in 1990 the DYS worked with judges to develop a risk/ needs classification system for determining level of placement. It should be noted that no specific national risk classification model exists, nor could one, because the risk factors that predict recidivism are weighted statistically according to the particular population on which they are based, which varies from state to state. On the other hand, classification instruments for determining offenders' needs are fairly universal, because statistical weighting is not necessary. Before describing the Alabama risk/needs system, we will introduce the concept of classification with a discussion of its history, its different types, and its uses.

History of Classification of Juvenile Offenders

If we stop and observe any group of people, we mentally begin to categorize the individual members of the group into certain categories. Gender, age, and race are three categories that we can usually spot without too much difficulty. Classification beyond obvious external characteristics requires that we know more about the individuals. In corrections, either juvenile or adult, the first crude attempts at classification were for the purpose of making institutional placements, and were based merely on gender: men were sent to institutions for men, women to institutions for women. While there was nothing sophisticated about this, it was extremely accurate. But as services and professional service providers became increasingly differentiated into psychology, psychiatry, and social work, it became increasingly necessary to refine the process of classifying offenders. Specialization in services for offenders required that offenders' needs be determined through classification for treatment. Most past attempts at classification were based exclusively on treatment models, rather than risk of recidivism, because they were developed at the same time that the "helping professions"—psychologists, psychiatrists, social workers—came into prominence. Christopher Baird, an authority on juvenile classification, writes that the "history of juvenile classification is one of high expectations and disappointing results" (Baird, Storrs, and Connelly 1984: 7). This is for two reasons. First, the early classification models were based on treatment needs, and treatment needs alone, to the exclusion of factors about the seriousness of the offense or the pattern of prior offenses. Second, early models were highly subjective, and were based on clinical interviews between psychologists and offenders. On the basis of only one meeting, psychologists would determine the reasons for the youth's behavior and the appropriate treatment. If the youth did not improve, the treatment would simply continue until he did.

The I-Level system is a well-known example of a classification model for determining the psychological treatment of juvenile offenders. It was developed for use in California's juvenile correctional agency, the California Youth Authority (CYA). Juvenile offenders in the CYA are classified according to their I-level, or level of ego development. There are seven I-levels, or stages of interpersonal development, each of which marks a new level of judgment, or the ability to weigh "right" and "wrong" in relating to other people. Each I-level has a crucial interpersonal problem that must be mastered. If not mastered, the person may remain fixated at that stage—essentially, becoming a physical adult with the developmental skills of a child.

The lowest level, I-1, is that of the infant. The infant, who begins life alone in the womb, must simply learn to distinguish herself from others. Without that minimal perspective, she cannot look at the world and understand how she relates to it. At the second level, the infant views reality as it relates to her own needs, without concern for others. She wants her juice and she wants it *now,* even if daddy must drop everything and run upstairs to give it to her. At the next stage, the I-3 level, the child develops a few rules to guide her behavior. Usually they are extremely rigid, without allowing "gray areas" of judgment, and she applies the rules not only to herself but to others. Youths who remain fixated at this stage end up over-conforming on just a few rules (of their own making) while ignoring other rules that are more important to their social audience. At the I-4 level, the child becomes aware of the expectations that others have for her and she begins to internalize the values of others. While this is considered progress, the child may become overly concerned with the opinions of others, and youths who remain fixated at this stage are neurotic and anxious. In the fifth, sixth, and seventh stages, the youth develops an increasingly differentiated, abstract view of the world. Able to understand a variety of different perspectives, the world is no longer merely black and white. The youth can make decisions and judgments on her own, according to the situation, and is neither under-conforming nor over-conforming to those around her.

Most experts on offender classification would consider the I-Level system to have major weaknesses. For one thing, it classifies according to psychological need alone, but there are many other treatment needs that juvenile offenders may have, including education, vocational training, substance abuse counseling, and so on. There are also many other dimensions beyond treatment—such as risk and offense seriousness—that merit consideration. Finally, the system relies on the input of one staff member to complete each checklist, and there tends to be low inter-rater reliability, which means that there is serious disagreement about how to score offenders when staff decisions are compared to one another.

Classification for risk is a more promising approach to classification, although it too has an unimpressive history. "Risk" refers to the risk of recidivism, which may mean the probability of future arrest, conviction, or incarceration. Given a crystal ball, jobs in the criminal justice system would be made easy—find the future repeaters, then vigorously prosecute and incapacitate them for as long as the law allows. Lacking a crystal ball, actors in the system often resort to their own rules of thumb. In an article that has become a classic to sociologists of law, David Sudnow (1965) describes how public defenders determine "risk" of recidivism based on characteristics of crimes and offenders that probably have very little to do with risk, but which seem to distinguish some offenders from others. Certainly, however, the most outrageous use of risk classification has been in the area of psychiatric predictions of dangerousness. Clinical predictions of dangerousness among the mentally ill have been widely attacked for their lack of theoretical grounding and their low accuracy rate, which is no better than flipping a coin (Glaser 1987; Pfohl 1978; Sechrest 1987).

Classification of Juvenile Offenders Today

Classification of juvenile offenders continues to play a major role in determining how they should be handled after they are adjudicated in court. Classification for treatment is still performed, but it is far less developmentally oriented than the I-Level system. For example, the San Bernardino probation department uses a one-page form to score fourteen needs areas, including employment, alcohol use, family relationships, and academic achievement (see Appendix 1). The total score indicates that overall need for treatment, while each category score suggests the level of treatment needed in each area. In many jurisdictions, decisions of how to handle offenders are now based not only on treatment needs, but also on an assessment of risk that is more objectively calculated than in the past. Today, risk assessment instruments ideally contain factors that are statistically predictive of recidivism, and the factors are weighted according to their actual weight in a statistical model. Although the forms vary somewhat from region to region, the factors are quite universal:

- age at first adjudication, with the lower age groups recidivating at higher rates;
- prior criminal behavior (usually a combined measure of the number and severity of prior arrests or adjudications);
- number of prior commitments to juvenile facilities;
- drug/chemical abuse;
- alcohol abuse;
- family relationships or parental control;
- school problems; and
- peer relationships.

In risk classification, the individual category scores are far less important than the total score. The total score gives the probation officer, parole officer, or the correctional caseworker a fairly objective indication of the average risk of recidivism for subgroups of youths matching various profiles. Depending on their total score, each youth falls into a particular subgroup, generally low-, medium-, or high-risk (for a more detailed explanation, see Clear 1988). That classification is used to determine the level of supervision needed (such as the number of weekly contacts with the offender), if a residential placement is required, or if an electronic monitoring device is called for.

Program classification is a related and necessary step in developing a comprehensive client management system. An administrator must examine carefully all of the existing programs to determine how much structure and treatment each one provides. This is the only way that youths' risks and needs can be accurately matched to corresponding placements. Examples of program structure are staff-to-youth ratio, security, and daily activities. Some highly structured programs are locked twenty-four hours a day and require that youths participate in a variety of activities (i.e., school, chores, study periods) throughout the day. Other programs offer moderate security (without locks on doors and bars on windows) with high staff-to-youth ratios or geographic remoteness, such as wilderness "Outward Bound" types of programs. Still others have a fairly low level of structure and allow residents relatively more mobility and freedom of choice.

Information on program structure and treatment services for each program in the system's array of placements is vital, not only for improving placements but also for program development, capacity planning, and program evaluation. Program development refers to the processes of determining what types of new programs are needed to meet the changing needs of the client population. Capacity planning involves projecting the numbers and types of clients who would be placed in various programs and factoring in placement practices, resident movement, and program lengths of stay to calculate how much space is needed. Program evaluation examines the operation and outcomes of programs compared to their objectives. Program objectives are based on the clients' risk level, clients' treatment needs, program structure, and services offered.

In addition to classification for treatment and risk, another type of classification is classification for control, which refers to the "control" risk, rather than the offense risk, that the offender poses. Classification for control is used to incapacitate offenders who are at risk of running away from nonsecure placements, who fail to report in regularly, or who are generally likely to show defiance of authority. Classification for control serves only the agency responsible for maintaining control over the offender. It does not increase public safety, as does classification for risk, nor does it enhance rehabilitation, as does classification for treatment. Various characteristics of juvenile offenders are used to classify according to risk, treatment, and control models, and some of these characteristics are relevant to more than one type of classification model. Typically, the sources for much of this information are diverse and may include the courts' pre-sentence investigation and probation records, school records, medical records, social service reports, police records, institutional records, and interviews with the youth and his/her family. Table 5.1 below summarizes how these characteristics might be used.

TABLE 5.1
An Overview of Possible Risk, Need, and Control Factors

Factor	Risk	Need	Control
Total Offense Record	X		
Recent Offense Record	X		
History of Assaultive Behavior	X	X	
Commitment History (if applicable)	X	X	
Family Relationships		X	
Intellectual Ability	X		
Learning Disability	X		
Employment	X	X	
Voc/Tech Skills		X	
Health and Hygiene		X	
Sexual Adjustment	X		
AWOL Record	X	X	
Behavior in Previous Programs			X
Public Perceptions of Offender			X
Age			X
Drug/Alcohol	X	X	
Educational Adjustment	X	X	X
Peer Relationships	X	X	X
Emotional Response/Attitude	X	X	X
Placement Record	X	X	
Parental Control	X	X	X

Source: Guarino-Ghezzi and Byrne 1989.

One final method for classification is a just-deserts, or offense-based model. Offense-based models require that offenses be rank-ordered in terms of seriousness, and that corresponding sentences by determined. The Washington State model is a combination of offense-based categories to reflect the seriousness of the instant adjudication, and additional points for prior offenses, which reflect the offender's risk of recidivism. Massachusetts' DYS uses a purely offense-based model for deciding the minimum lengths of stay of serious offenders.

Decision Models in Individual States

Although the purposes are often similar, the methods for making such important decisions as where and for how long to place offenders are different in each of the different states. Formal decision models in individual states are in varying stages of development. The experiences of several individual states are described below.

Alabama

The state of Alabama has recently implemented a risk/needs classification system (see Appendix 2). In their system, the main criteria for assessing an offender's risk of recidivism are the seriousness of the instant (most recent) adjudication, the most serious prior, the number of felony adjudications within two years, the age at first adjudication, prior out-of-home placements, gang involvement, and substance abuse involvement. The courts now perform the risk assessment following adjudication but prior to disposition. According to their policies, only those youths who score ten or above should be committed to the Alabama Department of Youth Services (DYS). Should a youth's score fall below ten, there must be a written explanation for the commitment to DYS. This policy is designed to help reduce overcrowding and inappropriate commitments by pressuring the courts to send only the riskiest offenders to DYS. A needs assessment is also conducted to evaluate the youth's educational adjustment, peer relationships, health/ mental health, and sexual adjustment. One reason why the courts might legitimately commit a low-risk youth to DYS is an extremely high needs score, indicating that the youth requires the structure of a DYS setting, rather than probation, to respond to his needs. Other overrides of the model might occur as a result of aggravating or mitigating offense factors that are not reflected in the offense score.

Maryland

The state of Maryland is at a crossroads over the issue of placement authority. Traditionally, the juvenile courts had the power to make decisions concerning placement, length of stay, and parole in juvenile corrections. However, the state's juvenile correctional agency, the Department of Juvenile Services, would like to have more control over those decisions. Although some of the judges simply commit to the Department and allow the Department to decide where and for how long youths should be placed, most judges exercise their statutory authority to make those decisions themselves. The way the law is stated, the court makes decisions around the type of placement (i.e., institution or group home, rather than the specific facility. However, since there is only one institution (the Hickey School), it is a moot issue for institutional placement. On the other hand, some judges go beyond their authority and place youths in the Glen Mills institution in the state of Pennsylvania. A representative of the DJS told us that

> Glen Mills is a privately operated, 600–700 bed facility, on an open campus. Some people [in Maryland] don't understand the concept of "range of services" and have decided that Glen Mills is a panacea. Despite its being out of state, the location is actually preferable for some youths from northern Maryland because it is closer to them than our other Maryland programs.

A task force attempted to develop guidelines for court commitments, as was done in the state of Alabama, but it has been a difficult process. The classification instrument began as the so-called "Wisconsin risk model" (Baird 1982; Baird, Storrs, and Connelly 1984; see Appendix 3), which puts no weight on the seriousness of the instant offense, but instead weights non-offense factors that are correlated with recidivism, including number of prior offenses, emotional maturity, school behavior, and number of out of home placements. The DJS official who was overseeing the project, however, had come from a long career in the adult system and was dissatisfied with the model because it lacked offense-based criteria. As a result, Maryland staff worked on their own to develop a combination of risk, needs, and offense-based criteria. Because the courts have the placement authority in Maryland, the DJS was unable to influence the placement after court commitment. In order to pressure judges against committing youths to institutions, the DJS began to use the instrument at the point of intake, prior to adjudication, and to make one of four disposition recommendations to the court: commit, commit for institutional care, commit for residential care, or probation. Unfortunately, the recommendations were apparently not respected by the judges, because they continued to commit to institutions against the DJS recommendations 40 percent of the time.

North Dakota

In North Dakota, the Division of Juvenile Services also struggled to increase its discretionary control of how youths are handled. The courts have the option of making a direct commitment to the state's institution, a decision over which the DJS has no control. In order to expand their role in relation to the court, the DJS followed a strategy similar to that in Maryland. They borrowed and revised the risk assessment model from the state of Colorado, which had earlier success in expanding community-based services for youths (see Appendix 4). As in Maryland, the assessment is conducted prior to disposition by the DJS. Generally, a score of four or below results in a home recommendation; five to nine means short-term institutional placement or residential group home; ten and over is an automatic institutional placement. The DJS worked vigorously to build consensus among the stakeholders by inviting representatives of the courts, schools, and human services to participate in the risk classification development. A DJS official reported to us that

> [c]hange is always uncomfortable for everybody. We had to work hard to sell programs to courts, legislature, human services, county sheriffs, police. A helpful hint is don't be afraid to tell people that some of these kids are going to fail. We spent a lot of time saying, "the adult system is not working, so you'd better give us a chance to start dealing with kids." This was persuasive with some people.

The classification system, it should be noted, has not been studied to determine how effectively it actually distinguishes low-risk from medium- and high-risk offenders based on actual recidivism. However, there has been an impact on the courts' decision process, particularly on the appropriateness of placements. Since the model was implemented, youths classified as low risk have been placed into therapeutic foster care, group homes, and other appropriate settings. In 1994, North Dakota's officials continued to closely watch classification in Colorado, where officials had recently implemented a combined risk/needs model to identify high-risk areas as indicators not only of risk, but of treatment needs. Since there are many factors that overlap both risk and treatment (see table 5.1), the new model prioritizes treatment for areas most associated with risk of recidivism.

New York

The New York Division for Youth (DFY) was one of the earliest states to develop a comprehensive classification system. The development of classification in the DFY is notable for two reasons. First, its early attention to client management in 1984 preceded other states by several years, and thus anticipated the growing interest in juvenile offender classification. Second, the DFY model emphasized "control," or offender management, far more than the systems discussed above. Whereas administrators in North Dakota, Maryland, Delaware, and Alabama have used risk classification results to justify fewer institutional placements and to better manage offenders in the community, the DFY developed its model for two primary purposes: (a) to control institutional management risk and (b) to control risk to the community (New York State Division for Youth, n.d.). Risk management was thereby defined as primarily institutional management (note: what we are calling "control") and, secondarily, community protection. A DFY report describes these dual purposes as follows:

> When designing the classification system, the agency accepted as a given the fact that the provision of rehabilitative services could only occur in an institutional environment that provides adequate control, and that beyond this, the agency had an obligation to protect the community from the potential harm that some clients may inflict if inadequately restricted. (DFY, n.d.: 3)

The assessment of risk to the community (what we have been calling "risk") was developed in a similar manner to the states discussed above. Assessment of risk *inside* of programs ("control") referred to the likelihood that an offender would be difficult to handle in a program, in particular that he or she would resist staff efforts or be assaultive or threatening to staff or other program residents. While acknowledging the difficulty of predicting such behavior, the model examines such indicators as detention behavior, substance abuse, and age at first offense.

It should be pointed out that an underlying assumption of the DFY model is that youths who are difficult to control in particular settings would benefit by more, not less, physical plant security, institutional surveillance, and staff custody activities. This assumption was made for all youths regardless of their risk of recidivism in the community. However, many critics would claim that youths who pose little or no risk to the community deserve the least restrictive alternative to institutions. In such cases, a least restrictive placement decision would not alter the risk to public safety, and it would relieve the pressure on program staff to control youths' behavior by relaxing the requirements of a highly structured environment. Furthermore, it would serve the interests of justice by matching the seriousness of *offense* (not in-program) behavior to the appropriate level of placement.

Delaware

The state of Delaware recently implemented changes in their decision criteria for handling juvenile offenders. The juvenile code currently permits the juvenile correctional agency, the Division of Youth Rehabilitative Services to have partial release authority, but not placement authority. If a youth is committed to the Ferris Institution, the judge gives an indeterminate sentence that allows the division to make the release decision unless the offense is murder, rape or kidnapping, or it is the second felony adjudication in a year. In those cases, the statute mandates a minimum six-month institutional sentence. The state of Delaware uses a variety of other placements besides the Ferris School, including privately contracted day and residential treatment programs, but, as described in chapter 2, the expansion of community-based programs is relatively recent, having been fueled by funding that began in 1988. Because of the growing diversity of programs in the state of Delaware, a law was passed in 1990 that directed the DYRS to construct guidelines for incarceration decisions.

Risk Reassessment

Reassessment of risk is a process that is conducted in a manner similar to initial risk assessment. An instrument is used to score each risk factor at some point following the initial placement to determine what, if any positive (or negative) changes might have occurred. Generally, reassessment is conducted at specific intervals (e.g., every three or six months after placement). Unscheduled risk assessment may be triggered by a new arrest, a serious violation of program rules, the identification of a new treatment need that cannot be addressed within the current placement, or by some other unforeseen change. If the client's new risk or needs score changes enough to move the client to another program level, then the downward (or upward) movement is initiated. Some observers have noted that risk reassessment at scheduled intervals makes it difficult to respond with an immediate message to reinforce positive behavioral changes (Guarino-Ghezzi and Byrne 1989). A behavior modification system of assessing and rewarding behavior that is based solely on the youth's behavior in the new program may be a more effective method for deciding questions like how long a youth should remain in a particular program, or whether the placement should be downgraded to a less structured level, than reassessment of risk and needs factors.

Handling the Authority to Make Decisions

One important fact of correctional organizations merits a more complete discussion. There are important distinctions between decision authority that is given to an agency, and decision authority that is given to an individual decision maker. Each level is somewhat independent of the other, and changes in one do not necessarily translate into changes in the other. For example, a state's juvenile code may provide that the juvenile correctional agency has complete statutory control over placement, length of stay, parole, and other important decisions, and the courts control only the decision of whether or not to commit to the juvenile correctional agency. This scenario maximizes the discretion of the agency. It does not necessarily, however, mean that each decision made by an agency staff person is without internal guidelines, regulations, or monitoring. In fact, "line" staff such as intake workers and caseworkers, the "front line" that actually conducts assessment and screening, could be just as regulated in this scenario as any other. On the other hand, if the agency does not promulgate guidelines, or does so but fails to monitor the compliance of line staff to the agency's guidelines, line staff may operate with unbridled discretionary power.

This point is important for several reasons. First of all, several states' juvenile correctional agencies are seeking to control the key placement decisions that have traditionally been made by the juvenile courts in those states. These agencies will undoubtedly need to demonstrate that they are well prepared to take on the task. One argument in the agencies' favor is that the personnel who work most closely with the youths make the most informed decisions about how youths should be handled. However, this does not give agencies carte blanche to carry out their own agendas, since they must also be responsive to each of the key stakeholders external to the agency. Building a decision management system that is responsive and accountable requires at least two additional components within the management structure. The first is a set of guidelines, or a classification model, which specifies what criteria are important in making decisions, and how strongly each criterion should be weighted. Second, the agency needs a monitoring capability to ensure that the decision makers are in compliance with the guidelines or model. This is the point where the system is the most vulnerable, in part because line staff may not believe in the guidelines.

Clearly, adhering to boundaries that restrict one's discretionary judgment is not a natural inclination. For example, a federal judge, anticipating federal sentencing guidelines, protested that he would quit his job if the guidelines were enacted because exercising discretion was the most enjoyable part of his job. Subjective decision making has been the tradition in the criminal justice system, and actors within the system tend to overly inflate the effectiveness and accuracy of subjective judgments. A review of the literature illustrates that this phenomenon existed prior to objective classification models for parole officers, but the subjectivities were partially obscured by an "everybody does it this way" type of attitude (McCleary 1978). Similarly, police officers conduct much of their law enforcement efforts through a combination of negotiation, hunch, and selective observation (Lipsky 1980; Skolnick 1966).

Despite the unattractiveness of subjective decisions, they remain popular among individual decision makers, even when objective classification methods are recommended or even mandated. Daniel Glaser, a correctional specialist who developed one of the early objective models for classifying parolees, describes the psychological process of subjective control:

> Reaching a difficult decision that may have important consequences is an anxiety-producing experience. There is usually much relief when the decision is made, especially if there is confidence that the correct choice was made. The gratification

from such anxiety reduction tends to reinforce overconfidence in the wisdom of one's past judgments by the process that Leon Festinger (1964) conceptualized as minimizing cognitive dissonance. He asserts that "the greater the conflict before the decision, the greater the dissonance afterward. Hence the more difficulty the person had in making the decision, the greater would be his tendency to justify that decision (reduce the dissonance) afterward. The decision can be justified by increasing the attractiveness of the chosen alternative and decreasing the attractiveness of the rejected alternative, and one would expect a post-decision cognitive process to occur that accomplishes this spread apart of the attractiveness of the alternatives." (Glaser 1987: 253)

Glaser (1987) has also identified the common mistakes that are made in the process of subjective decision making. One source of bias is "availability," or the tendency to attach too much importance to easily recalled information, such as the high visibility of a particular case. Another source of bias is "selective perception," which is the tendency to overlook information that does not correspond to a previously established opinion. In criminal justice, Glaser notes that excess conservatism may result over time because of receiving a preponderance of feedback about the cases that fail, and proportionately less information about cases that succeed. After being "burned," practitioners may learn to adopt safer practices, but in doing so they increase their rate of "false positives" and use resources unnecessarily. Experimental psychologists have found that the problem of subjectivity is complicated even further because decisions are often based not on the merits of two or more alternatives, but merely on how those alternatives are framed. For example, if given a choice about a failure, the majority of people would take a risk; if presented with a choice about a success, the majority would avoid taking a risk (Tversky and Kahneman 1981).

Decision guidelines, while they are necessary to establish an agency's accountability, contain an inherent flaw: they must be followed. This is true for all three correctional models that were discussed above—legislative, judicial, and administrative. Under any of these systems, unless the line staff are centrally involved in the development of the guidelines, appreciate their worth, receive rigorous training, and are consistently monitored, problems develop because the staff prefer to exercise discretion rather than adhere to grids. There are several forms that staff resistance can take. Corbett, Cochran, and Byrne (1987: 62) identified the following forms of resistance demonstrated by probation officers during the implementation of a carefully monitored intensive probation supervision (IPS) program in Massachusetts:

(1) ritualism (i.e., doing the paper, but not following the [recommendations of the] risk/needs [client] assessment;
(2) denial of ownership (i.e., rather than carve out a control-oriented role for supervision, the PO denies ownership in the program; e.g. "it's the Commissioner's idea, not mine, so don't blame me");
(3) rebellion (i.e., failure to fill out the risk/needs forms correctly for marginal IPS cases).

Summary

A well-structured and closely adhered to classification system is essential for a balanced system of juvenile corrections. The main purpose is to accurately identify individual characteristics which suggest appropriate strategies of correctional supervision and services. Classification systems must be fairly sophisticated in order to incorporate the diverse factors presented by youthful offenders in today's society. For those reasons, administrative models have some advantages over judicial and legislative models. First, procedures in administrative models can be adapted to changing characteristics of youthful offenders and correctional resources more easily than in other models since they do not require legislative approval. Second, administrative models more directly manage available resources in a rational manner because they do not rigorously mandate that certain offenders be placed in certain programs for designated periods of time. Finally, administrative models encourage program development through the communication between staff who design and operate programs and decision makers who place youths and allocate resources. In other words, maintaining placement authority within the organization that is directly responsible for carrying out punishment and treatment reduces the randomness and inconsistency that often characterizes the juvenile justice system, and improves the system's resiliency to adapt to changing societal needs.

6

Development of a Balanced Continuum of Correctional Programs

Defining the Balanced Correctional Continuum

Social workers have used the term "continuum of care" to describe a correctional system offering a range of programs for juvenile offenders. While "continuum of care" is a well-known term, it may be misleading to suggest that juvenile corrections simply means "care" for offenders who happen, through their offenses, to become eligible for services. In addition to providing care and services in the juvenile justice system, equal emphasis needs to be placed on punishment and controlling the behavior of offenders who pose a risk to public safety. Therefore, the term "balanced correctional continuum" is more appropriate to describe a system that contains a range of supervision levels, from secure placements to nonresidential services for offenders residing at home, as well as a range of treatment options which selectively meet the needs of different types of offenders, such as gang members, sex offenders, or substance abusers.

In describing a balanced correctional continuum, we turn to two jurisdictions—one state and one county—to discuss classification structures of the programs which operate in those locations.

Case Study: Developing a State Correctional Continuum in the Massachusetts Department of Youth Services

Massachusetts, Utah, and Missouri have been pointed to as the better state systems of juvenile corrections in the country (Krisberg et al. 1986). The Massachusetts model will be presented as an example of a system which many states have emulated, and which was found by the National Council on Crime and Delinquency (1991) to have lower re-arrest rates after twelve months than Pennsylvania, California, and Utah, lower reconviction rates after twelve months than Florida, Utah, and California, and lower re-incarceration rates after thirty-six months than Wisconsin, Texas, Illinois, and California. The model began to develop in 1972 in Massachusetts and is still functioning, but the system has been precariously overcrowded. Utah also digressed by passing a law creating categories of offenders who are sent to adult court, and in 1994 by opening large institutions. Missouri fended off an automatic waiver bill in 1994 and was still remaining true to a balanced model.

The Massachusetts Department of Youth Services enjoys a uniquely broad command of decision authority over committed youths. This is true for four reasons. First, the state's model is an administrative decision model. The courts in Massachusetts can commit a youth to DYS, but cannot specify placements or lengths of stay. All youths are committed until the age of majority, which is eighteen. Until that time, DYS determines whether secure placements are warranted and for how long, whether alternatives to secure placement, such as group homes, are appropriate and for how long, the type of aftercare the youth will receive, and whether to petition the court for an extension of commitment beyond the eighteenth birthday. As conceived by statute, the court has virtually no authority over placement decisions in Massachusetts. However, in practice, some courts have attempted to exercise greater control through a variety of sub-rosa mechanisms, including ordering nonserious offenders into pre-trial detention facilities by charging them with contempt of court.

Second, DYS's jurisdiction over serious offenders is maximized by the fact that the state of Massachusetts allows no automatic transfers to adult court. This has resulted in an exceedingly low number of youths who are transferred to the adult courts (roughly fifteen per year through the 1980s). However, two important caveats must be underscored. For one thing, the age of adult criminal jurisdiction in Massachusetts begins at seventeen; the majority of states begin at eighteen, so there is a built-in bias that reduces the number of youths who would be available for transfer. For another, although transfers to adult court are not automatic, two amendments to the transfer statute were passed in 1990 and 1991. The new laws required transfer hearings in juvenile court for eight categories of violent crimes, as well as mandatory minimum sentences of fifteen years for first degree murder, and ten years for second degree murder, for juveniles retained in the juvenile court and adjudicated for those offenses. The impact of these amendments on the numbers of violent offenders retained in the juvenile system is not yet known.

Third, the range of placements available within DYS is far more varied, and is far more dominated by community-based placements, than any other state. The fact that several different alternatives exist for most youths increases the complexity of the decision process, and the fact that most of the alternatives are in the community increases the stakes involved in making a bad decision.

Finally, the Massachusetts code provides for indeterminate commitments to DYS, meaning that youths committed for delinquency must be discharged at the latest at age eighteen, but may be discharged at an earlier age at the discretion of DYS. The Department may also apply for an extension of commitment up to age twenty-one. The default threshold of age eighteen as the point of discharge from DYS supervision overlaps, by one year, with the beginning of adult court jurisdiction, which is age seventeen. In Massachusetts, with the exception of youths adjudicated and committed for murder or manslaughter, youths are generally discharged from DYS on their eighteenth birthday. However, if they commit an offense as a seventeen-year-old, they are automatically considered adults from that point forward. The simultaneous jurisdiction of seventeen-year-olds in DYS by both DYS and the adult court is a transition management tool that acknowledges the gradual aspect of the transition between "juvenile" status and "adulthood."

Improving Secure Placement Decisions

In an organization such as DYS, the dilemma of discretionary judgment boils down to the tension between individualized decision making and centralized control. The past history of DYS favored the use of individualized decision making, particularly during the period in the 1970s immediately following deinstitutionalization, while the 1980s emphasized centralized control in making secure placement decisions, accompanied by a case management model for all youths. Prior to 1981, when a centralized, offense-based classification model was implemented, DYS was widely criticized for its handling of serious offenders who had been committed to the agency for armed robbery, kidnapping, aggravated assault, and even murder. Critics pointed to a lack of uniformity in DYS decision-making (e.g., variations by region, age, minority status, and resource availability); a lack of relationship between offense committed and placement provided (as measured by DYS placements and levels of restrictiveness); and concerns related to public safety and offender accountability (as indicated by use and availability of secure care.

The emphasis on factors other than offense seriousness in making placement decisions throughout this time period was unequivocally demonstrated by an outside task force's analysis of placement data. Non-standardized procedures in the decision-making processes were found at two levels: the juvenile court's commitment decision, and DYS's placement decision. At the court level, it was learned through interviews with twenty-nine juvenile court judges that the use of DYS commitment as a disposition option varied from judge to judge:

> For example, one judge indicated that he committed all multiple offenders to DYS. Another used a DYS commitment only after the third offense. Another stated that he preferred the use of probation, even for repeat offenders. Still another stated that if any juvenile committed a serious violent offense he would automatically seek a transfer hearing. For judge after judge, this was the pattern—no pattern. The current judicial handling of violent juvenile offenders appears not to be guided by a set of uniformly visible criteria. It is guided, instead, more by the varying judges involved. (JJAC 1981: 63)

An analysis of placement decisions found no statistical relationship between offenses committed and placements recommended (Rocheleau 1980). In effect, DYS was grossly underclassifying youths based on offense seriousness. In some of the DYS regions, factors such as race, age, and resource availability were driving the placement decisions; in other regions, there were no patterns whatsoever. Where correlates were found, black youths were disproportionately placed in their own homes rather than in group homes or foster homes due to a scarcity of residential programs specializing in the unique needs of minority offenders. The greatest gap in resources during this time period, however, was the lack of long-term secure facilities. The task force study found a considerable amount of frustration among DYS caseworkers concerning secure placements. This was in part because each region was allocated a certain quota of secure treatment slots. Caseworkers complained that, "We can't follow through on our treatment plans because there aren't enough beds or secure slots." "We need more secure facilities, specifically in (Region X) . . . . [We] have to barter and trade off slots with other regions to get a boy into secure confinement" (JJAC 1981: 66).

Data from the task force's three-year study of placement patterns also suggested that regional variations played a role in understanding the use of secure placement. It found that regional placement practice, rather than offense seriousness, accounted for variation in secure placements. It also appeared that the youths who *were* placed into secure treatment were far more likely to be control problems (e.g., AWOL risks) rather than youths with a serious offense history. This is not completely surprising, since it was chronic runaway youths and other technical violators who threatened the stability of the emerging private community-based programs (Guarino-Ghezzi 1988).

Despite the scathing criticism of DYS's handling of serious offenders in the late 1970s, at the height of the "get-tough" movement, a review team consisting of highly respected experts was optimistic. The review team included David Gilman, Executive Director of the New York Temporary Commission to Recodify the Family Court Act; Donald J. Newman, Dean of the School of Criminal Justice, SUNY-Albany, who had worked with the Wisconsin legislature to revise its delinquency code; and Paul Strasberg, who was Commissioner of the New York City Department of Juvenile Justice and former Associate Director of the Vera Institute of Justice. Rather than punish DYS with judicial or legislative control, they recommended to the Massachusetts governor that DYS be allowed to retain its full discretion in placement decisions. Their rationale cited the new offense-based secure classification system as a significant step toward greater accountability and uniformity of decisions:

> The DYS Commissioner and staff have developed a sophisticated classification system that will insure uniform placement of juveniles no matter from what court they enter the system. . . . Therefore, it is our opinion that proposals to allow judges to determine which juveniles receive secure placement and for how long, be opposed because of the ensuing disparity that would result and because DYS is much better equipped to make better informed placement decisions. (Gilman, Newman, and Strasburg 1982: 12, quoted in Guarino-Ghezzi 1988)

In 1981 the Secure Classification Panel was implemented with markedly different policies for serious offenders than the previous individualized approach. According to the manual for interpreting DYS classification policy for serious offenders, "The primary goal of the Classification and evaluation process is to give special attention to the violent and repetitive juvenile offenders committed to DYS, and to deal with them in the most consistent, effective and judicious manner possible" (Massachusetts Department of Youth Services 1982: 1). The Classification Panel was composed of three members, including a permanent chairperson appointed by the DYS Commissioner and two non-permanent members appointed by the Deputy Commissioner. The classification policy was developed by the chairperson with input from DYS Central Office administrators, regional personnel and legal advocacy groups. The Panel was responsible for reviewing all mandatory and optional referrals made by the Regional Directors, as well as cases of parole violation referred by the Parole Revocation Hearing Officer. Mandatory referrals, categorized as either A or B, were based on the instant offense (see figure 6.1).

Included in Category A offenses were attempted murder, voluntary manslaughter, involuntary manslaughter and vehicular homicide. (First and second degree murder offenses now receive mandatory minimum sentences of fifteen and ten years respectively, as mandated by statute.) Category B offenses included armed robbery, assault and battery (armed) causing serious bodily injury, sexual offenses involving a victim, arson of a dwelling house, kidnapping, and possession of a firearm. Optional referrals, a process initiated at the discretion of the region, included "any juvenile whose offense behavior presents a risk and danger to the community or who exhibits a persistent and escalating pattern of delinquency." The purpose of the classification hearing was to decide whether or not a youth required the supervision and control of a secure treatment program. The chief criterion for that decision was whether the youth presented a risk and danger to the community, based on a qualitative assessment of the youth's actual and potential capability to control and modify his or her behavior. Only the offenses listed in the left-hand column of figure 6.1 were referred to the Classification Panel; all other cases were placed in less secure programs. Among the cases that did reach the Panel, the instant offense was a primary consideration in weighing the need for security. In addition, the Panel considered aggravating and mitigating circumstances pursuant to the instant offense, as well as other behavioral characteristics: extensive property damage, serious bodily injury, or

FIGURE 6.1
Classification of Juvenile Offenders by Offense and Offense Behavior

Offense Category	Age Limit	Time Assignment
Mandatory Referrals: Category A		
Murder: First Degree* Murder: Second Degree* Attempted Murder† Voluntary Manslaughter Involuntary Manslaughter Homicide by Motor Vehicle	13-16 years	A minimum of 12 months to a maximum indeterminate stay. Length of time subject to period evaluation by treatment staff and legislation, mandating release at age 18 years unless extension is granted by the court.
Mandatory Referrals: Category B		
Armed Robbery and Battery with a Dangerous Weapon (causing serious bodily harm) Arson of a Dwelling Kidnapping Possession of a Firearm Sexual Offenses (involving victim)	13-16 years	A minimum of 6 months to a maximum of 14 months possible. The length of time will be based on an examination of the circumstances associated with individual case. Case conference can lead to early release or extension of maximum.
Optional Referrals:		
Any juvenile whose offense behavior presents a risk and danger to the community and/or to himself/herself or who exhibits a persistent and escalating pattern of delinquency.	14-16 years	A range of months between a minimum of 4 months to a maximum of 12 months. Case conference can lead to early release or extension of maximum.
Revocation Referrals:		
Any juvenile who has violated his/her Grant of Conditional Liberty as determined by a Revocation Hearing and referred by the Hearing Officer.	14-17 years	A range of months between a minimum of 4 months to a maximum of 12 months. Case conference can lead to early release or extension f maximum.

* As a result of legislation passed in 1992, youths committed for first or second degree murder now receive mandatory sentences of fifteen and ten years, respectively.
† As a result of legislation passed in 1992, youths committed for manslaughter are now committed to DYS until the age of 21.
Source: Secure Classification Manual, Massachusetts Department of Youth Services, 1986.

cruel and sadistic behavior; the degree to which the offender played an active role in the offense, whether involvement occurred under pressure or coercion, or was committed while out on bail; prior history of violent or chronic offenses and vulnerability of victims; community ties and family support; and prior DYS placement record.

During the hearing, youths' DYS caseworkers presented oral summaries of written reports that were read in advance by the Panel members. Along with identifying demographics and circumstances of the offense, the report included sections on family history, youth's education, medical history and current needs, psychiatric evaluation, psychological tests, court history, placement history, and the caseworker's evaluation and recommendation. In most cases, the psychiatric and/or psychological evaluation accompanied the report.

In order to relieve the secure classification panel of the decisions for optional and revocation cases, in 1991 DYS piloted a second review system to accompany the secure classification process. The new system, known as the Dispositional Review Panel, handled all of the optional and revocation referrals, as well as a new category of substance abuse offenders (called Mandatory D Drug Referrals), which included any youth who was adjudicated for a drug trafficking or distribution offense. The placement options available to this panel, compared to the secure classification panel, were significantly more varied. Boys may be placed in a twenty-eight-day outward-bound type of program; a forty-five- to sixty-day secure cottage; a sixty- to ninety-day secure residence; seventy-five to ninety days in detention; or three to five months in secure treatment. Girls' placements were more restricted: ninety days in detention, or three to five months in secure treatment. In all of the placement alternatives with the possible exception of secure treatment, the length of stay was less than it was under the old model. That suggested that DYS was looking for ways to more efficiently control the kinds of behavioral problems that did not present a physical danger to the community. Under DYS's administrative model, that type of organizational restructuring did not require a change in statute, but merely a change in departmental regulations. As in many other areas, the administrative model allowed DYS to experiment with new policies and programs with a minimum of bureaucratic resistance.

Expanding Community-Based Programs with a Case Management Model

The development of community-based programs was facilitated by two factors in Massachusetts and elsewhere: implementation of a case management model, and the involvement of the private sector in program development and management. A case management system can help to increase the effectiveness of decision making in an agency and can serve as a "revitalizing theme" for agencies undergoing transformation (Gilmore and Schall 1986). Case management, for agencies undergoing transformation, can be part of a comprehensive agenda that focuses on the relationship between care and custody in the agency's mission. By emphasizing case management, top administrators employ a tool of bureaucracy to place staff and youth in more meaningful contact. At the same time, case management can aid in the use of a community's resources for effectively reintegrating a youth back into his/her neighborhood. The essential elements of case management are: assessment of offenders' risks, needs, and strengths; service planning; service coordination; and monitoring and continuous evaluation of the offender, service delivery, and available resources (Barton, Streit, and Schwartz 1991; Weil and Karls 1985). Those objectives can best be reached by assigning to each youth a single case manager who is involved in all sequences of programming.

Advocacy is considered integral to the case management process so that the offender receives quality services and opportunities to reintegrate back to the community. Distinctive to a highly structured case management model is the shift away from disconnected and fragmented movement of offenders from court disposition to institution to parole or aftercare supervision and discharge, instead to a planned pathway through placements based on assessment and continued reassessment of progress or failure in successive placements. The transition from an institution to a nonsecure residential placement or home for high-risk offenders requires intensive aftercare (Altschuler and Armstrong 1991). Five basic programmatic principles that collectively establish a set of fundamental operational goals for high-risk offenders are (Altschuler and Armstrong 1991: 62): (1) preparing youths for progressively increased responsibility and freedom in the community; (2) facilitating youth-community interaction and involvement; (3) working with both the offender and targeted community support systems (e.g., families, peers, schools, employers) on qualities needed for constructive interaction and the youth's successful community adjustment; (4) developing new resources and support where needed; and (5) monitoring and testing the youths and community on their abilities to deal with each other productively.

A decentralized service delivery system, including the establishment of several regional offices within a state, facilitates the reintegration of youths back to the community, the ultimate goal of a balanced system of juvenile corrections. There are two guiding principles of a decentralized service delivery system. First, placement decisions for each youth are best made by the person in the system who is closest to the youths, who knows most about the youths (risks and treatment needs) and who is most familiar with the diverse array of programs and services in the community, the case manager. Second, an agency's money should follow the youths. Instead of the practice of placing youths in an available bed, each regional office should be allocated a budget to purchase the program and services dictated by individual treatment plans.

Developing Community-Based Programs Using the Private Sector

The private sector is a critical player in expanding placement options. In Massachusetts, over 60 percent of the total DYS budget is allocated to purchasing services from private vendors in the community. Forty-five private, nonprofit companies account for approximately ninety individual contracts. DYS also purchases services from approximately fifty noncontracted providers on an as-needed basis. Although private vendors predominate, the state is not excluded from operating programs as well, which provides another level of competition for the vendors. Approximately 65 percent of DYS commitments are placed into a nonsecure setting. The continuum of programs and services is defined as follows:

Secure treatment. Long-term residential programs for youths committed on serious charges that warrant placement in a physically secure (locked) facility. There are nine such prógrams in the state. Seven programs are operated by private vendors. Each program provides five hours of academic education each day, group and individual counseling, vocational training, and medical and recreational services, in additional to many other specialized services and program emphases that have developed to meet the changing needs of youths involved in serious offenses. All programs provide substance abuse treatment, and all but two programs offer specialized group therapy for sex offenders. All programs use a "level system" which is based on cognitive/behavioral theories to gradually instill, through approval as well as tangible rewards, the youths' adherence to relatively strict rules of conduct, including no fighting, no stealing, and no arguing with staff.

Secure detention. Short-term residential programs in a physically secure facility for youths awaiting trial on serious charges, awaiting classification, or preparing for a program opening. There are eight such programs in the state, two of which are operated by private vendors. Each program includes five hours of academic education per day, interim group counseling, vocational training, and medical and recreational services.

Shelter care. Short-term residential programs in staff-secure (twenty-four-hour staff supervision) facilities for youths awaiting trial on charges that do not warrant secure confinement. There are eight such programs in the state (all of which are run by private vendors), each providing five hours of academics daily, interim group counseling, vocational training, medical and recreational services.

Transitional management programs. Short-term evaluation programs for youths awaiting presentation to the classification panel for serious crimes or youths awaiting placement in community-based programs for nonviolent crimes. There are seventy secure transitional beds for serious offenders, and forty-six staff-secure transitional beds for youths awaiting community placement. All but one of these programs are operated by private vendors.

Group homes. The Office of Juvenile Justice and Delinquency Prevention (OJJDP) recommends that effective treatment can be facilitated by small programs, as opposed to large institutions (OJJDP 1993). Many excellent, small treatment programs operate around the nation and accept some of the most serious offenders in any given state system. In DYS, community-based residential homes are for youths who have committed nonviolent offenses and can be placed in a community setting without risk to the public. Youths receive academic and vocational training in-house or at schools in the community. The programs provide group and individual counseling, medical and recreational services. There are twelve private, contracted group homes, in addition to more than twenty private, noncontracted group homes that accept DYS youths on an as-needed basis.

An example of a group home for serious male offenders is a Massachusetts program called Alpha Omega, which is now two decades old. The program houses seventeen residents in a semi-rural area. The doors are unlocked and frequent passes out of the program are encouraged. Yet, the program is extremely structured, with activities including cleaning, school, and group therapy from 6:00 A.M. until 10:00 P.M. Alpha Omega's philosophy is that all residents are expected to do what they would do in a "normal" home.

Residents are primarily involved in schoolwork during the school year, but during the summer they are paid minimum wages, out of federal grants, to perform various "home improvement" projects around the house, which have included building a greenhouse, a classroom wing, and upgrading the kitchen. The money is deposited into a bank account, so each youth leaves the program with approximately $1200.00. Youths attend group therapy for ten hours per week, and in addition they attend family therapy either with their own parents, who are available in about half of the cases, or with surrogate parents, who allow youths an opportunity to discuss issues concerning parents. No physical restraints are ever used on youths, but the threat of local police—with whom the program maintains an excellent relationship—is compelling to residents. Aftercare and continued family therapy are provided for six months after release (the average length of stay is ten to twelve months), and Alpha Omega will accept a youth back who appears, in the judgment of his caseworker, to need to return to the program.

Homeward bound program. A short-term, state-run program for forty-five youths designed to build self-esteem through rigorous physical challenge in an outdoor setting. The program, based on the Outward Bound model, also serves as a transitional program for youths leaving long-term secure treatment and preparing to re-enter the community. Although the Homeward Bound model has been replicated and borrowed from in many jurisdictions, the Massachusetts program was the first in the nation.

Foster care/mentor model. Community-based residential care in private homes for first-time or low-risk offenders who would benefit from a supportive family environment, but cannot return to their own home for reason such as abuse or lack of supervision. DYS averages sixty-five youths in foster care on a given day. Approximately half of the youths placed into foster care receive more intensive services known as the mentor model. Under the mentor model, youths live in foster homes and caseworkers from a vendor agency provide additional intensive support and supervision for the youth and foster parents. The increased supervision expands foster care into a more controlled setting, which may be appropriate as a reintegration program or as an alternative to residential group care.

Outreach and tracking. This service was pioneered in 1972, and is designed to provide intensive supervision of newly committed or low-risk offenders in the community, or youths who are gradually being reintegrated into the community from long-term secure programs. Youths must report to their tracking worker on a daily basis; three times a week in person, and four times by telephone. The program requires that youths be in strict compliance with their conditions of liberty/parole. Tracking workers monitor school attendance, employment, counseling, AA or NA attendance, and assist in family counseling. DYS contracts over 250 Outreach and Tracking slots per year.

Tracking plus. A tracking program with a residential component, this program provides supervision to sixteen youths. Youths are first placed in a four-bed group home for an initial four to six week residential phase. In the second phase, after youths return home, they are intensively supervised by a tracker. If the youths violate rules set for them at home or elsewhere in the community, the tracker has the option to return them to a respite bed which is made available for that purpose in the residential program.

Family continuity program. Borrowing from the Homebuilders program that originated in Washington state to provide intensive services to families of troubled youths, the Family Continuity Program (FCP) provides in-home family therapy in DYS's Central Region. The program provides two therapists, one assigned to the family and one to the youth, who work as a team with the youth's caseworker. Families of DYS youths have traditionally resisted going out to attend family therapy sessions, but in this program, a master's level family therapist and bachelor's level counselor go into the home and provide family therapy on at least a weekly basis, dealing with such issues as disciplinary techniques, communications patterns, and reintegration of youths returning home from residential programs. Twelve families receive these services.

Health and other services. DYS offers a wide range of medical, clinical, and educational services that are made available through private providers and other state agencies. In some cases, for example, juvenile sex offender treatment is supplemented by the Department of Mental Health, while substance abuse treatment is supplemented by the Department of Public Health. In addition, DYS is affiliated with several hospitals, which provide mental health, diagnostic, and medical services. Other DYS services include dental care, AIDS-related education, employment training, 766-approved special education (cost-shared with local school districts), federally subsidized Chapter One supplemental education, art therapy, AA and NA meetings, and religious services.

Case Study: Los Angeles County's Correctional Continuum

The County of Los Angeles comprises an area of over 4,000 square miles and 88 cities. The county's population is larger than all but eight states and is one of the most culturally diverse jurisdictions in the United States, with 50.5 percent Hispanic/Latino, 27.4 percent white, 11.4 percent black, 10.0 percent Asian-American, and 0.7 percent other. The Los Angeles County Probation Department was formed in 1903 and is the largest probation department in the world. It operates three juvenile detention facilities, eighteen youth camps, one treatment center, and sixteen adult/juvenile investigation and supervision field offices throughout the county. As a result, courts in Los Angeles County have a variety of options for retaining youths in the county for services and supervision, rather than committing youths to the state California Youth Authority. As in Massachusetts, where the state entity—the Department of Youth Services—has control over youth placement and development of resources, the Los Angeles Probation Department retains youths under its control under probation orders, and has developed a continuum of county programs.

In 1990, the county expanded its program range with the implementation of two drug treatment boot camps for 105 youths each. Although boot camps are widespread, these are the first drug treatment boot camps in the United States, and are unique because of their intensive treatment and aftercare components. The drug treatment boot camps are residential treatment programs with lengths of stay ranging between eighteen and twenty weeks. Residents are male offenders aged sixteen to eighteen with documented histories of substance abuse. In keeping with the boot camp model, the program is rigidly structured. However, the structure includes not only chores and drills, but education and treatment.

Every other day residents attend an on-site school program which includes a full academic high school curriculum. On the alternate days, youths participate in job training followed by a paid contract work assignment doing cleanup, basic landscaping, graffiti removal, and other projects for the county or city of Los Angeles. Residents earn money to help pay court ordered fines and to reimburse victims through restitution compensation.

In addition, each resident attends a fifteen-week drug education program which is run on-site by a contracted provider agency. Program effectiveness is continually measured through pre- and post-tests of youths' understanding of health issues related to drug use. Simultaneously, agency staff provides a ten-week parenting course in the community for parents and guardians of substance abusing youths. The drug treatment youth camp incorporates an important element that is lacking in the ordinary "boot camp" approach. While boot camp supporters believe that discipline is the answer to juvenile delinquency, and that the military model is the best for imposing a disciplined regimen, research on boot camps reveals the following (Parent 1993b): There is no evidence that traditional military-style boot camps significantly affect graduates' recidivism rates, and boot camps do nothing to alleviate overcrowding in residential facilities and will, actually, increase incarcerations (unless more than 80 percent of those admitted to boot camps would have served prison terms if boot camps did not exist, a standard which is not being applied).

Upon successful completion of the camp phase of the program, residents are released to intensive aftercare supervision directed by county probation officers who work exclusively with drug treatment boot camp releasees. Probation officers are paired with a contracted drug counselor; together, they have caseloads of thirty-five to forty. The contracted provider offers drug counseling and education to the youth and his parents upon his return home. The provider also tests for drug use on a random basis. Probation officers have an average of four contacts per month with the youths on their caseload, including four face-to-face. While youths are still in the boot camp prior to their release, probation officers are required to meet with them on a monthly basis for the purpose of developing their aftercare plans. According to internal studies, drug treatment boot camps have substantially lower recidivism rates than regular youth camps, which lack the structure, drug treatment, and intensive aftercare of the drug treatment boot camps.

If youths fail to complete the program successfully, by either violating the terms of probation or failing to comply with the general rules of the program, they are returned to court by their probation officer with the recommendation that they be given a more rigid sentence, such as a term at the California Youth Authority. In addition to the camps, there are other programs in the county that are used to divert youths out of the camps. The Boyle Heights Project, for example, selects camp-bound violent offenders who are not hard-core gang members, but are referred to the project by court probation. Youths are interviewed and, if accepted, the probation officer recommends that the judge give a camp-stayed order and approve the placement. The program is nonresidential, and is a consortium of community-based agencies, which, together, provide a full array of social, employment, personal development, and recreational services, including a mentoring program and parenting classes for parents of the youths.

Another diversion program in Los Angeles County is "teen court," which is designed for first-time, minor offenses. Youths are referred by the probation department to a court of their peers rather than processed through the formal system. Teen courts are operating in at least a dozen states, including Texas, Indiana, Arizona, and Nevada (Gerlin 1994). In Los Angeles, peer juries of high school students determine not only the punishment, as in other states, but also the guilt or innocence of the accused. They are given latitude to devise an appropriate punishment, including various forms of community service and restitution, tailored to the specific offense. If a youth is found guilty by the teen court, she or he is diverted for six months. If the diversion period is completed satisfactorily, she or he will have no record and will be brought back to "teen court" at a later date to serve on the jury.

Model Programs for Supervision and Treatment
of Juvenile Offenders

A number of stand-alone programs, independent of a full continuum of services, offer specialized services to juvenile offenders and are notable because of their unusual focus, or the creative integration of services. A sampling of such programs follows.

Associated Marine Institutes (AMI)

AMI has been cited by Greenwood (1986), Krisberg and Austin (1993), and Lerner (1990) as an exciting vendor specializing in outdoor marine programs for juvenile offenders. AMI is a nonprofit corporation of twenty-four programs which are operated in eight states. Primarily a hands-on vocational program in navigation and boat repair, the program also offers instruction in fishing, scuba diving and power-boat handling. Recreational activities are used as rewards for good behavior and the program helps youths with school and job placements when they leave. Academic education is a strong component of the program, and each instructor has only seven students. Academic instruction is made more exciting by the hands-on marine component; math is connected with navigation, biology with marine life, and so forth. It is not unusual for students to move up one to four grade levels during their six-month stay in the program. In addition, approximately half of the students eligible earn high school equivalency diplomas (Lerner 1990). Comparative research conducted by the Florida Department of Health and Rehabilitative Services on the programs used for juvenile offenders suggests that AMI graduates have recidivism rates as good or better than most, at far less cost than institutional settings (Tollett 1987).

Sex Offender Treatment

Treatment of juvenile sex offenders is a relatively young field in juvenile corrections. Early treatment programs were developed during the 1970s in such locations as the Adolescent Clinic of the University of Washington's School of Medicine and the University of Minnesota's Program in Human Sexuality. At that time, many of the clients were identified in the course of child protection work with incest cases, and treatment approaches relied heavily on a family-systems model. Because there were no scientifically based theories or model programs to guide their development, most of the early programs were designed through trial and error. As the similarities were shared among the various programs, the basis of many current treatment programs began to evolve.

Perhaps because treatment models for adolescent sex offenders are still in an early stage of development, most programs have adopted an eclectic approach, making replication and evaluation difficult (Knopp and Stevenson 1989). However, clinical evidence suggests that treatment of juveniles, and particularly juveniles in correctional settings, is more achievable than older categories of sex offenders. For instance, many juveniles do not perceive that sexually abusive behavior is actually illegal, nor do they anticipate the public embarrassment and intrusion associated with formal system processing. Theoretically, these circumstances should increase the youths' amenability to treatment. Clinical experience suggests that the most successful treatment models use peers to confront and support one another, since adolescents are less resistant when challenged by their peers than in similar interactions with adults (Heinz, Ryan, and Bengis 1991).

The concept of the sexual abuse cycle was developed in 1978 at the Closed Adolescent Treatment Center (CATC) of the Division of Youth Services in Colorado (Lane and Zamora 1984). The cycle provides a theoretical framework to help juveniles and staff objectively and comprehensively examine sexually abusive behaviors and develop intervention strategies to prevent recurrence. Juveniles are taught to recognize the mental and emotional stages that precede their decision to rape so that they can stop the cycle before it reaches that point. The cycle is believed to begin with an event or perceived event that produces an emotional response which, for that youth, is intolerable, leading to compensating feelings of control, anger, or rage. These stages are followed by a decision to rape, refinement of a rape plan, selection of who, when, and where to rape (which may be either opportunistic or premeditated), and culminate in the actual rape or sexual assault (Lane and Zamora 1984). Although the concept of the sexual abuse cycle has not been empirically validated in total, early research in the field has begun to confirm various elements of the concept.

Homebuilders

In many cases where family problems appear too complex to address, the response is to remove the child from the home. While it is true that for some youths removal is the best option, as in cases where physical or sexual abuse is occurring, most youths want to grow up with their real families and most parents want to keep their children even when they are having serious difficulties. This realization has led to many programs developed through the philosophy of family preservation known as "intensive family preservation services" (IFPS).

One of the first and most successful IFPS programs is a program called Homebuilders which was founded in 1974 in Washington state. Not coincidentally, this was the year in which the Juvenile Justice and Delinquency Prevention Act was passed which deinstitutionalized status offenders. Washington, like other states, was at a loss to provide assistance to troubled youths and turned to Homebuilders to treat some of those youths who were at risk for out-of-home placement. In order to be accepted by Homebuilders, at least one child in the family must be in imminent danger of being placed out of the home, and at least one person in the family must be willing to work with a Homebuilders counselor.

Homebuilders counselors are assigned to families for four weeks, although some families continue for up to eight weeks. Counselors provide intensive face-to-face counseling and referral services and are available to families twenty-four hours per day. Counselors spend eight to ten hours per week in face-to-face contact with family members. Each family is given the counselor's home phone number as well as a team-shared beeper. Because so much time and intensity is spent with one family, counselors in some locations carry only two cases at a time. Homebuilders provides not only crisis intervention but concrete services as well, such as shopping, house cleaning, or transportation. These ancillary services build trust between Homebuilders and clients and allow family members to concentrate on their immediate family problems. Evaluations of the Homebuilders program indicate that the programs are highly effective for up to one year (Pecora et al. 1992). Beyond that, additional intervention may be required. The annual cost for one worker to supervise one family is $4,000, with each worker responsible for four to five families.

The Choice Middle Schools Program

The Choice Middle Schools Program is a highly intensive casework program that supervises delinquents, status offenders, and at-risk youths referred from various agencies in Baltimore, Maryland. The program is designed to improve academic performance and behavior among students in grades six, seven, and eight. Caseworkers are recent college graduates with caseloads of only ten youths. They are required to work seventy hours per week and have multiple daily contacts with youths, their families, and school staff. Their responsibilities include: monitoring daily school attendance and nightly curfews; providing informal counseling and crisis intervention; and imposing gradual and certain sanctions for misbehavior, which may include removing the youth to a "suspension school." Supervision periods range from three to six months. The program operates out of the University of Maryland-Baltimore Campus' Shriver Center.

Conflict Resolution Training

Several states have provided funding for local schools to develop training programs in conflict resolution. For example, the Massachusetts Attorney General's office funds a program called SCORE (Student Conflict Resolution Experts) which trains student mediators to resolve violent and potentially violent conflict among their peers. The Attorney General's office provides grants of $15,000–$20,000 per school to community mediation programs, on the condition that matching funds be raised by those programs. The funds pay for a full-time coordinator who works in a targeted school to develop and run a mediation program staffed by trained students and teachers. Typical mediations involve fights, threats, harassment, and rumors among students who know one another. Many of the disputes concern sensitive racial issues with large groups of students on each side. Trained student mediators hear each side and help the parties to work out an agreement. Based on over 1000 disputes mediated by SCORE mediators, 98 percent resulted in an agreement and less than 5 percent of the agreements were broken (Massachusetts Office of the Attorney General, n.d.).

Mentors

Some local schools assign a teaching assistant or college students to work with youths who are beginning to fail in school. Mentors serve as adult companions, helping children with homework and supervising them during after school hours. The annual cost of one mentor working with four youngsters is $8,500. Wherever possible, public schools servicing high-risk youths should employ students from local colleges or citizens in the community as part-time mentors. President Clinton's national service plan to develop community service among college students is consistent with this approach.

Restitution/Community Service

The goal of restitution/community service is to establish a plan whereby youths are assigned a community service or job to reimburse their victims, as well as serve justice and instill a sense of accountability in the offenders. Restitution programs also introduce young offenders to the world of work, and they have been cited among the most successful programs for court-involved youths (Bazemore 1991; Hughes and Schneider 1990). Gordon Bazemore (1991) has described a new model of intensive aftercare which combines work experience with restitution, which he calls a "productive engagement" model of supervision. Employment is found for youths not primarily as a rehabilitation tool, but instead as a "tool to accomplish the primary goal of intensive supervision—public protection through 'incapacitation in the community'" (Bazemore 1991: 124). Productive engagement is designed to appeal to traditional community "work ethic" values by requiring that offenders make themselves accountable to victims by providing restitution payments, which they earn through carefully supervised work. There are several methods for creating programs, including subsidized individual placements, which use public funds to pay for work in public or private nonprofit agencies; private sector job banks, which are based on arrangements with local small businesses to reserve job slots for restitution clients; project-supervised work crews, which pay groups of offenders through contracts with government agencies; a "youth enterprise" approach in which offenders form a business to produce goods or deliver services to earn money for restitution.

Developmental Curricula for Preschools and Elementary Schools

It is beginning to be recognized by child development experts that many inner-city children, having been exposed to violent trauma in their communities, are suffering from post-traumatic stress disorders, which reduce their concentration in the classroom and make learning difficult. However, the school is a relatively safe environment for most young children and naturally resilient children learn to use relationships with teachers and the activities of learning to help stabilize their lives. Garbarino and his colleagues (1992) have developed a curriculum that is based on developmental theory and is designed to enhance all young at-risk children's resiliency and coping abilities. Children are taught in small, permanent subgroups to increase their attachment to teachers and fellow students. They learn as a group by mastering daily challenges, and self-expression through the arts is used as a chance for children to "escape" from trauma and stress.

Rites of Passage

The Rites of Passage program is designed to provide African-American male offenders with important developmental milestones that are otherwise lacking in their lives. Its aim is to reduce the delinquency rate among African-American males by leading them away from high-risk situations. For example in Iowa, where the project won an award for excellence from the Office of Juvenile Justice and Delinquency Prevention in 1992, the project includes tutoring, mentoring, crisis intervention, individual and family counseling, and recreational activities. The project emphasizes the development of self-esteem and personal responsibility in a supportive atmosphere.

Balanced Correctional Policy: What are the Goals?

Most states continue to operate large institutions as their primary response to juvenile crime. But many are now examining the community-based approach as an alternative, for reasons of cost as well as rehabilitation. The shift in focus from reactive punishment to prevention that underlies such changes is essential if we are to help those children most likely to become serious delinquents. Organizational structures that enhance the confidence, quality, and dedication of staff in their contact with youths need to be developed, along with participation from community sectors. We believe that the organizational models discussed in this chapter provide those critical aspects.

Federal and state governments continue to face daunting fiscal challenges in the 1990s, with little certainty of relief. As state purchase power diminishes, legislative and executive branches will be placed under increasing pressure to justify expenditures across many government agencies. When juvenile correctional agencies are placed under scrutiny, policymakers can find significant opportunities to improve the efficiency and effectiveness of youth corrections. This is particularly true when they are given information and ideas about restructuring correctional systems (Schwartz and Loughran, n.d.).

As we approach the year 2000, the following goals are underscored as critical in establishing and maintaining correctional agencies that are best designed to meet the growing challenges of crime, social problems, and government.

Goal 1. Offender Accountability/Punishment

It is generally understood that the disposition of punishment a youth receives should be proportionate to the harm done. However, the historical and present practices of juvenile justice show otherwise. Detention and incarceration of juveniles in youth facilities are often based on "control" criteria having nothing to do with public safety (such as gender and unavailability of alternative resources) leading to irrational release and placement decisions throughout state systems. For any correctional agency, youth or adult, to run successfully—that is, by protecting the constitutional rights of offenders, controlling resources to avoid overcrowded facilities, protecting public safety by gradually increasing offenders' freedom in the community, and responding quickly to new arrests and violations in the community—there must be an array of programs to absorb offenders at every level of needed supervision. The Office of Juvenile Justice and Delinquency Prevention (OJJDP) recommends that intervention must be immediate and that agency sanctions must include a range of intermediate sanctions (OJJDP 1993). Immediate response to violations and offenders can be made more certain by raising the staff-to-youth ratio of aftercare workers, and by retraining community police officers to respond to juvenile offenders in a clear and constructive manner (Guarino-Ghezzi 1994;

OJJDP 1993). Examples of intermediate sanctions with juvenile offenders include the following (OJJDP 1993): short-term placement in
community confinement; day treatment; outreach and tracking; drug
testing; weekend detention; and inpatient substance abuse treatment.
*Policymakers and juvenile justice professionals should design levels
of programs and implement rational disposition schemes for juveniles
based on criteria that provide rationally escalating consequences for
behavior and certainty of enforcement.*

Goal 2. Public Safety Protection/Risk Control

No one can predict which youths will continue to commit delinquent acts—including those adjudicated for violent crimes. Despite
this, the risk of future offending and concern for public safety are key
issues. Given these concerns, decisions must be made regarding the
type and intensity of supervision various youths should receive. As we
discussed in the chapter on decision making, research suggests that
current offense, prior offense history, age at first adjudication, school
adjustment, substance abuse, peer relationships, and the ability of parents to provide adequate control and supervision are important factors
to take into account. Public safety protection is best provided by an
administrative model of decision making in which the correctional
agency's placement decisions, rather than the court's, benefit from
their increased knowledge of the offense and the offender. *Caseworkers who manage small caseloads, who control placement decisions,
and who monitor youths' progress in programs are an integral part of
risk control.*

Goal 3. Competency Development

Youth correctional agencies must be designed to equip young people
with the skills and resources needed to both survive and thrive in an
increasingly technologically advanced society. Youth corrections agencies must be able to carefully and comprehensively assess the needs of
youths under their control. They must also have a broad array of
options available to meet the needs of every individual youth. This
includes providing educational opportunities at all levels—special education, high school curricula, GED training, and post-high school
courses for youths who qualify. Courses in marketable trades and

technical training should be made available, as well as work experience. Other programs must meet the varied psychological needs of youths, including drug and alcohol counseling, family counseling, sex offender treatment, and sexual abuse counseling. *Services and rewards are essential for building offenders' self-control and sense of self-worth.*

Goal 4. Develop Public/Private Partnerships

Unlike state bureaucracy, private providers are better positioned to involve the community as full partners in youth rehabilitation. Boards of directors overseeing privately contracted programs are chosen from business, religious, academic and political leaders who have a stake in the programs' performance. In effect, the programs' staff and residents must constantly demonstrate to the larger community that they are good neighbors.

The providers for their part have a right to look to the state for clear and reasonable expectations for program performance, general guidelines in which to operate, and adequate funding and support to fulfill their contractual obligations. The state, in turn, has a right to expect a reasonable return on its investment. The return will be measured by the degree of law-abiding behavior produced in the youths as well as the academic achievements and marketable skills they acquire in private programs. *The private sector is a valuable political ally in extending programs into the community, so that offenders can experience the benefits of reintegrative programming.*

Goal 5. Maintain a System that is Both Constitutional and Humane

Each state's correctional system, from intake to discharge, must incorporate the elements of due process in the handling of youth, must provide program components that insure growth opportunities for the youths and, above all, must be free from abuse in any form. Abusive settings are generally marked by large, unwieldy populations and underfunding. Openness and standards of excellence can be promoted by: keeping program size small and staff-to-youth ratio high; monitoring programs; allowing complete access to programs and not allowing isolation to develop; and refusing to tolerate either abusive or mediocre practices. Rebidding of contracted programs every three years keeps a competitive edge alive among vendor agencies. *Correctional models that are overly punitive, or that provide inadequate treatment, are extremely vulnerable to allegations from legal advocates for youths, and thereby contain the costly seeds of their own destruction.*

Goal 6. Build Consensus among the Principals of the Juvenile Justice System: The Executive, Legislative, Judicial, and Law Enforcement Branches

Public credibility in a juvenile correctional agency exists when professionals in other parts of the system respect its decisions. Policy debates about delinquency should take place in a public arena with the involvement of the agencies which are needed to support policies and programs in juvenile corrections. Management information systems are critical in tracking client characteristics and agency decisions so that aggregate trends in clients, and agency processes are anticipated, noted, and reported by the correctional agency, and other sectors of the system can be made aware quickly of changing trends and their impact. A cost-share approach is used in some locations for serving youths who are covered by the jurisdiction of more than one agency. For example, social service and correctional agencies may jointly pay for specialized, nonresidential counseling for a youth who has been a victim of sexual abuse. The history of juvenile justice has produced a disproportionate amount of energy on debating issues which may be unresolvable, rather than devoting energy toward areas of consensus. *Research has reinforced the value of the following components, which should provide the basis for mutually supportive juvenile justice policies: clear and consistent rules and consequences, including the use of rewards; immediate response to rule/law violation; reintegrative programs in the community; programs to increase offenders' skills; specialized treatment to fit individualized needs; emphasis on promoting resiliency so that offenders can resist destructive environmental influences.*

7

The Possibility of a Balanced
Juvenile Justice System

Resolving the Dilemma of Juvenile Justice

The ultimate dilemma of juvenile justice is not how to avoid the complex problems, but how to devise balanced policies that fulfill the competing segments of its mission, to protect the community, provide rehabilitative education to youths, reintegrate youths back to their communities, punish youths, and hold them accountable for their behavior. States must create balanced systems of juvenile corrections that do not contain the seeds of their own destruction. Agencies must put policies in place that allow them to take measured, defensible risks with youths in the community, permitting youths to "test reality" while still within reach of vigilant supervision and counseling to help them maintain resiliency. Simultaneously, agencies must have programs in place that ensure safety and treatment for youths who are held in confined settings. In short, it is a relatively simple thing to provide treatment in the community when risk is not a factor, and it is a relatively simply thing to control risk through incarceration, when rehabilitation and public safety are not goals. Unfortunately, neither strategy is realistic, because all objectives must be included in any model that stands the test of time.

Just like good families, effective juvenile justice systems manage to achieve complex goals by developing multidimensional programs and policies that adhere to basic, unwavering principles. While it is important that juvenile offenders "pay" for their crimes, it is equally urgent that they do not fall victim to mistakes of parents, politicians, juvenile justice officials, and other overseeing adults, well-intentioned or otherwise. Adult actions of neglect, of abuse, of oversimplifying problems, of rescinding needed resources, of stigmatizing youths, of sending mixed messages, of manipulating the crime problem to gain votes, and so on, will ensure that crime and criminal justice are our nation's most distinguishing features.

Signs of Imbalance

Juvenile correctional systems that are out of balance are those which fail to acknowledge the heterogeneity of youthful offenders and, accordingly, fail to develop a diversity of programs. The first sign of imbalance is a system that lacks an objective mechanism for identifying youths' characteristics, including their risk to the public, service needs, offense seriousness, and strengths/sources of resiliency, as well as a conjoining classification of programs and services. The second sign of imbalance is the failure to provide program diversity, for example, by overly relying on one or two levels of security, or one or two types of vocational training. Youths need to be handled in relatively homogeneous subgroups so that they do not resist programming efforts because they "don't belong with those kids." Trends in youth characteristics need to be identified and resource adjustments made so that programming can be acutely responsive to youths' behavior and life circumstances.

The third sign of imbalance is the failure to control overcrowding in programs. Overcrowded programs are not programs that are in demand because of their programmatic advantages; rather, they are programs where youths are dumped because other viable alternatives do not exist or are in short supply. Program overcrowding produces assaultive and other disruptive behavior, and prevents youths from receiving appropriate services (Parent et al. 1994). In many states, imbalance is created by a lack of resources due to fiscal constraints on spending. Ironically, one source of budget reductions for juvenile offenders is the overcrowded adult correctional system, which siphons monies away from juvenile offenders to pay for the unprecedented building of prisons and jails for adults. If the juvenile system suffers while adult correctional budgets are expanding, we are replacing long-term investment with short-term fixes.

The fourth area in which imbalance is revealed involves staffing patterns: shortages, turnover, disciplinary problems, lack of qualifications, below average time allocated to direct interaction with youths, low commitment to their work. Systems that are out of balance do not invest in staff, and do not reward or demand excellence. Juvenile justice, fundamentally, is a human service endeavor; implementation of goals depends on the connections that staff develop with youths. In an important demonstration of that "implementation factor," a national study tested a reintegration model for violent juvenile offenders. An implementation model, based on theories of juvenile crime, specified frequent interactions between case managers and youths, along with improved resources, advance case planning, regular information sharing between case managers and program staff, and consistent enforcement of rules. A random assignment design determined if youths were handled under the experimental model, or in the traditional manner, in four cities: Boston, Detroit, Memphis, and Newark. In the two program sites, Boston and Memphis, where the program design was well implemented, significantly lower recidivism rates (compared to controls) were detected for violent crimes, other serious crimes, and total crimes (Fagan, Forst, and Vivona 1988).

Strategies for Reform

The environment surrounding criminal justice policy is inevitably composed of divisive elements. The stakeholders are many, and they often work at cross-purposes. Persons or organizations with a stake in the juvenile justice system include judges, prosecutors, defense attorneys, victims, victim advocacy groups, offenders, offender and child advocacy groups, legislators, governors, and youth correctional agencies. Opposition to change can come from unlikely sources. For example, Jerome Miller, the former Commission of the Massachusetts Division of Youth Services who dramatically closed the institutions for juveniles in the early 1970s, cited as his biggest obstacle his own institutional staff who undermined and sabotaged earlier attempts at reform. Other foes of Miller's included the House Ways and Means Chairman, who threatened to cut his budget if he closed programs (Behn 1976; Guarino-Ghezzi 1988). Oklahoma's director of youth services was troubled in 1990 by the loss of jobs that institutional closure would mean for his employees, most of whom resided in the same small town.

Successful strategies for reform emphasize coalition building and negotiation. Generally, youth correctional agencies themselves are the most enthusiastic supporters of institutional closure as well as downsizing, although many publicly understate their support because they fear political repercussions from opposing stakeholders. A variety of states have found it helpful for outside experts to testify to the state legislature on the feasibility of community-based programs for middle-range juvenile offenders and on the over-incarceration of low and medium risk offenders in institutional settings. The Center for the Study of Youth Policy at the University of Michigan, which offered research services to assist states in classifying offenders according to risk during the early 1990s, had considerable success in identifying low and medium risk offenders who were needlessly institutionalized in several states. Most states' correctional officials were receptive to their findings, in part because the definition of "low risk" and "medium risk" was based on a consensus model of offender classification, meaning that legislators, judges, police, child advocates, and so on, provided input into the classification process.

Studies of several states by the Center for the Study of Youth Policy seem to reveal patterns of over-institutionalization. In particular, a study of all 653 youths committed to the Alabama Department of Youth Services on 3 October 1988 was undertaken to determine risk. In addition to calculating the seriousness of the instant offense, points were added for prior offenses, early involvement in delinquency, gang involvement, pattern of violence against women, substance abuse involvement, and prior out-of-home placements. The actual scores ranged from zero to nineteen, with higher scores indicating greater risk. A total of 345 offenders were identified as low-risk because they scored less than seven points on the risk instrument. Of these 345, 218 (63 percent) had been placed in Alabama training schools (DeMuro and Butts 1989). Using similar methodology in New Hampshire, actual risk scores ranged from one to eighteen for youths who were committed to the Division for Children and Youth Services on 10 May 1989. One hundred youths were in the state's institution on that date; of those, 23 percent were scored low risk (under seven points) (Butts and DeMuro 1989). In a third similar study, risk data on Nebraska youths who were placed in the Kearney institution for boys and the Geneva institution for girls in 1989 suggested that 35 percent of the Kearney boys were low risk (under seven points), as were 64 percent of the

Geneva girls (Van Vleet and Butts 1990). The disproportionate pattern of over-institutionalizing low-risk girls was found in other states as well. In some states, the findings of such studies were successful in mobilizing alternatives to incarceration (Butts 1990).

Other strategies for achieving deinstitutionalization include the co-optation of opposing stakeholders, which generally means finding the common ground on which to negotiate. Although juvenile court judges are responsible for protecting public safety, they are also philosophically invested in the continuation of a separate system of justice for juveniles that emphasizes rehabilitation. Reform efforts, therefore, need to cultivate judicial support. Legislators tend to be more oppositional to reform because they view the issue of institutional downsizing or closure as political high stakes. However, some legislators (for example, in Utah) have championed reforms as vital to children's rights and protection, particularly when institutions are overcrowded. Legislators as well as other public officials can be persuaded by the efficiency of a risk control model that uses institutions primarily for high-risk offenders. Fiscal benefits are undoubtedly factored in, and the fiscal consequences of institutional reductions are generally predicted to be favorable by legislators and governors. A surprising source of support from a child advocacy perspective is the local media, which was a key player in the Massachusetts' closures and has supported deinstitutionalization advocates in states such as Florida and Georgia.

A pattern that we detected is that in their initial planning stages, reform strategies tend to include accessing an informal network of shared technologies that travel from one state to the next. Edward Loughran, the former director of the Massachusetts Department of Youth Services, for example, provided technical assistance to downsize institutions and develop a continuum of care approach in such states as Oregon and Utah. It is a fairly common occurrence for the commissioner of one state's youth services agency to call on a neighboring state that might be somewhat more advanced in a particular area of community corrections, such as risk prediction, offender classification, or case management. The sharing of experiences, both positive and negative, and the provision of technical assistance, however laudable, is nonetheless a time-consuming and repetitive effort. In addition, the states that are considering adopting certain policies are understandably concerned about the "transplantability" of one state's policies into their own state's laws, organizations, demographic and offense profiles, and unique histories.

Juvenile Justice Reform and the Private Sector

Prior to the development of the juvenile court at the turn of the century, wayward children were often controlled by public and private child-care organizations. When the juvenile court first emerged, many of the private agencies attempted to remain autonomous and relatively isolated from government regulations and inspections. However, the juvenile court was in a superior position in relation to the established private agencies because it possessed legal power to affect the structure and operations of private, child welfare agencies. The histories of the New York Juvenile Asylum and the Pennsylvania Society for the Prevention of Cruelty Toward Children reveal those patterns (Block and Hale 1991).

The historical subordinance of private agencies suggests that government agencies did not necessarily lose control by utilizing private correctional resources, and may indeed have gained control in addition to other key advantages. For example, government agencies are held in such low regard that private companies' ability to outperform them is grossly distorted in many peoples' minds. Private corrections therefore has political appeal, if only on a superficial level. More importantly, public corrections agencies often labor under an institutional inertia that severely limits their ability to respond to changing needs. According to one view, contracting, by eliminating the need to make long-term commitments, can overcome this inertia and provide much greater flexibility. The contract between the government and the provider will be renegotiated at mutually agreed upon intervals. As long as government retains the upper hand over its private operators, it can reserve the right to adjust contracts or cancel them outright. Adjustments are far easier to make in the private sector, and government can take advantage of private flexibility and lack of internal bureaucracy. Private companies, for example, are able to hire and fire employees much more easily than government agencies that have to contend with civil service requirements, public employee unions, and political patronage considerations. Moreover, the private sector is generally acknowledged to be considerably more efficient at adjusting program and service levels, planning and modifying purchasing agreements and otherwise adapting to changing circumstances. Given these advantages, private programs appear to offer a flexible alternative to public operations.

Indeed, the rigidity of long-established cultures may well be an argument for privatization. Just as constructive work cultures are difficult to establish, unconstructive ones are difficult to correct. It is sometimes easier to create an entirely new culture than to fix the one at hand. These opportunities, whatever their implications for a specific privatization decision, are unlikely to emerge in the cost-oriented analyses that typically accompany public policy deliberations—although the political process is often quite responsive to such opportunities (O'Hare, Leone, and Zegans 1990).

A case in point is the reform of the Massachusetts Department of Youth Services initiated by Commissioner Jerome Miller in 1971-72. When Miller took over the management of the department in 1969 there was a pressing need for innovation in the delivery of youth services, but the existing culture was an overwhelming obstacle to change. As long as youth services were provided in state-run institutions, a network of conventions, habits, and expectations made it almost impossible to make innovations in care delivery. The buildings themselves seemed to impose an obligation not to waste resources by housing offenders outside them. The communications links between institutional supervisors and legislators did not carry information about care delivery, nor did they provide authorization to experiment. The civil service system gave implicit instructions, backed by law, to perform tasks according to written job descriptions that embodied the traditional way of delivering youth care. After disappointing attempts to fix the existing system, Miller sought to create an entirely new one by eliminating institutions and privatizing services in the community (O'Hare, Leone, and Zegans 1990).

One observer who witnessed the closing of the Lyman School in 1972 described the scene as follows:

> Jerome Miller hops off the first of several school buses that have just pulled through the gate. Like a commissar bent on dismantling one of the dreaded symbols of the "ancient regime," Miller strides into the administration building unannounced, determined to create history. "You can have the buildings," he tells the motley collection of political hangers-on who pass for the staff of the school, "but I'm taking the kids." (Quoted in Loughran 1988)

The majority of the programs that were needed to replace institutions did not exist when Miller closed the institutions. Initially, DYS turned to traditional child welfare agencies for assistance in handling youths in the community, such as the New England Home for Little Wanderers and Catholic Charities. Before long, the market demand created an array of private alternatives to incarceration. For example, DYS cultivated the interest of a group of young professionals who had worked for the short-lived presidential campaign of Robert F. Kennedy. Still grieving over his loss, the group often gathered to comfort one another and discuss how best to memorialize Kennedy. They transformed their anger and sadness into political action and created an organization to take care of children in trouble. The nonprofit Robert F. Kennedy Action Corps (RFKAC) was thus born (Loughran 1988).

RFKAC began contracting with various state agencies in the early 1970s to care for neglected and abused children in Massachusetts. By 1988, the RFK Action Corps ran DYS secure treatment units and four additional programs for the Commonwealth's social service agency. It had more than 300 employees and an operating budget of $5 million. Around the time that the RFK Action Corps became established, the Community Aftercare Program Inc. (CAP) entered the market. Now called the KEY program, CAP consisted of two brothers, Scott and Bill Wolfe. The Wolfes, one at Harvard, the other at Clark University, formed CAP with a novel idea. Both brothers had volunteered at institutions soon after Jerome Miller became DYS commissioner. Aware that DYS institutions were closing, the Wolfes believed they could supervise many of the youths at home and do it more cheaply and effectively than the state. Their program model allowed nonviolent juveniles to remain at home, albeit under intense supervision. The supervision was provided by young, energetic college graduates with small, manageable caseloads. CAP workers oversaw seven youths at a time, supervising, tutoring, and assisting in job placement. The worker was responsible for making personal contact with each youth and his family at least three times a week, as well as phoning school officials and employers to ensure attendance. The intensive supervision came to be known at Outreach and Tracking and represents the most successful model of diversity and innovation in Massachusetts' era of deinstitutionalization (Loughran 1988).

Jerome Miller's decision to privatize programs for juvenile offenders produced three critical results. First, it became obligatory for care providers to be innovative and specialize. Only by distinguishing themselves from other providers competing for state contracts could they stay in business, and DYS made it clear that it was looking for new kinds of care, not just marginal cost reductions. The environment of care providers and potential providers changed from one that rewarded innovation with indifference or punishment to one that gave an inventor resources with which to demonstrate and refine innovation. Second, privatization resulted in different patterns of information flow. In the days of state institutions, every administrative problem in community relations, food service, physical plant, and so on had an easy route to the commissioner's office, both directly and through the legislature. Each of these areas was important to care delivery, but all of them together prevented a focus on new kinds of care because they absorbed the attention of the commission and the staff. Contracting, in contrast, filtered these "micromanagerial" issues out of the commissioner's in-box. In addition, information began to flow between providers and the larger world of psychologists, educators, and social workers through the less focused network for professional associations and relationships. By removing the formal division between providers and the rest of the world, privatization opened up opportunities for new ideas to circulate informally and at relatively low risk (O'Hare, Leone, and Zegans 1990).

The final contribution of the private sector was that written contracts helped clarify DYS's aims and the means to achieve them. With privatization, programs were required to describe the care being provided beyond the most rudimentary elements of nutrition, beds, and escape prevention. Under the old system, institutions could be in the youth care business for years without having to explain exactly what was being done for youths. Providers and administrators alike now had to confront a written contract, a promise of actions and responsibilities that forced them to think about what the youths really needed and what services might provide it (O'Hare, Leone, and Zegans 1990). DYS's contractual control was not in place initially, however. Typically, contracts with new providers were based on trust, and handshakes rather than formal contractual agreements were the order of the day. Given the abruptness of deinstitutionalization in Massachusetts, in the immediate aftermath, little thought was given to bureaucratic requirements or expectations on either side of the bargaining table. Once a youth entered a vendor's program it was not even clear who had ultimate decision-making responsibility—DYS or the vendor. Soon, DYS realized that such an informal purchase of service systems involving millions of dollars was not sound policy fiscally or programmatically. New programs were springing up overnight, and DYS felt pressure to place as many youths as possible in them (Loughran 1988).

As the Massachusetts experience with privatization at the DYS indicates, the many differences in operating conventions between the public and private sectors make the boundary important. In addition to differences in personnel policy, there are differences in procurement systems and contracting arrangements and even differences in accounting practices. All are likely to be quite significant in any individual privatization decision. Other things being equal, there are positive opportunities afforded by privatization to free corrections from some of the most troubling rigidities and irrationalities of public managerial conventions (O'Hare, Leone, and Zegans 1990).

There are several important "turf" boundaries that separate the power of the private sector in relation to governmental control in the area of juvenile corrections. These boundaries are important in determining which sector, public or private, has control of operational decisions. Most observers agree that it is critical for the public sector to maximize its control over private programs, without stifling the benefits of private flexibility and initiative.

Privately operated community-based programs, such as group homes and specialized schools, have historically had the right to refuse to accept offenders according to their own admissions criteria. This is both good and bad. The good side is that community-based program operators assume risks with offenders, and they are in the best position to evaluate the offenders with whom they can work. Particularly with small programs that hold perhaps a dozen youths, the idea that one "inappropriate" youth (private operators often refer to fire setters in this context) could be forced into the program without its consent could seriously disrupt operations. The majority of providers would refuse a contract without the stipulation that they decide on admissions. However, that should not stop state agencies from requiring clear admissions criteria and selection procedures that are not made up arbitrarily. Also, state agencies can monitor the admissions by keeping statistics on characteristics of offenders who are accepted, rejected, terminated early, and so on, in order to hold providers to their objectives. For example, if Rainbow House contracts with the state on the basis of its expertise in handling minority youths with drug problems, they should be willing to accept most of the minority youths who are referred with drug problems.

The problematic side about private selection procedures is that they cause delays and they leave behind a layer of undesirable youths. For example, Joe Smith has run away from a group home in the past. He also attempted to assault a program staff person. The state placed Joe in a locked facility for a "cooling off" period, and is now reattempting to place him in the community. He is not a violent offender, but indeed has a problem with his temper. While he is escorted from one private program to the next for admission interviews, and then rejected, months go by. He spends this time in a locked detention facility, which is difficult because he presumes that it is only temporary. It is also very expensive for the state to hold him there, and it absorbs considerable state employee time and effort to try to place him elsewhere. Ultimately, if no one accepts Joe he is sent home from detention, which probably means that he is going from one unstable environment to another, without benefit of treatment in a structured community residence.

Massachusetts DYS has an unusual arrangement with its privately contracted secure treatment programs. Although more than half of DYS's twelve- to fifteen-bed, physically secured programs are run by private providers, such as the Robert F. Kennedy Action Corps, the contracts prevent the secure treatment programs from rejecting youths. The decisions are made by DYS's Secure Classification Panel, and are guided by the programs' geographical location, their programming emphasis (if any), and waiting list considerations. In general, it has been feared that privately run programs would "cream" the best offenders and leave the most difficult offenders for the state to work with. However, it is perhaps indicative of these private programs' desire to work with difficult youths that there are no differences in seriousness of offenses between private and public programs, and that in fact, a private program made the decision to specialize in the treatment of violent sex offenders (Urban Institute 1989).

One of the private sector's key features that distinguishes it from the public sector is competition. Whether one is referring to automobile manufacturing, fashion design, or juvenile corrections, a main advantage of private enterprise is competition, because it raises quality and lowers costs to the public. Indeed, private entrepreneurs in corrections emphasize their ability to provide higher quality programs, and lower costs, than the public sector, in part because they have less "red tape" to consume their time and energy, and in part because competition with other companies providing similar services will ensure high quality and low costs. While this may be true, there is a long-term tendency in the private sector toward "oligopoly," which means the concentration of business down to a small, noncompetitive handful (e.g., the oil industry). States need to be extremely cautious to ensure that providers continue to compete with one another, and they should protect themselves against declining competition. One way of buying protection is to run public programs that are similar to the private programs, thereby forcing the private sector to "compete" with the state.

Massachusetts' DYS, which has by far the oldest private network in juvenile corrections in the nation, illustrates this technique. Historically in Massachusetts, while there has been a multitude of different private operators running community-based programs, there have been only two main providers in the area of secure treatment programs. Justice Resource Institute runs two secure treatment programs and the Robert F. Kennedy Action Corps operates five. These two primary providers tend to operate in different parts of the state, each respecting the others' "territory" in responding to RFPs (Request for Proposals). Unlike the community-based arena, where numerous small providers compete for contracts, the secure care process is virtually noncompetitive. In order to combat this problem, DYS retains five publicly operated secure treatment programs, in some senses to "compete" with the private providers. This way the state does not have to rely exclusively on the private sector, and can legitimately point to its own worthwhile programming initiatives in order to stimulate quality in the private programs.

True cost comparisons of private versus public corrections are extremely rare. That is because correctional programs have traditionally been divided into community-based programs, which are usually run by private providers, and secure programs, which are almost always state-run. This has made cost comparisons of similar programs extremely difficult. Without research, many observers have assumed that private operations would hold down costs by paying less in salaries, retirement pensions, sick leave, and other benefits, although benefits have been increased recently in an effort to attract workers at a lower pay scale (Patrick 1986). Some have taken the opposite view, predicting that low wages would cause turnover, inefficiencies, and eventual salary increases (Allen and Simonsen 1986). Added to the program operational costs are the costs, borne by the state, of monitoring each program, which tend to offset savings (Henig 1985).

Even if costs are equivalent, the private sector is certainly more efficient. Government program construction is burdened by layers of red tape, bid requirements, planning requirements, and other regulations. Furnishing and staffing a government-run program can take months. To hire government employees, new positions must be approved, job descriptions must be posted for several weeks, interviews must be conducted by committee, and so forth. The private sector, although indirectly spending the taxpayers' money, is far less regulated and can theoretically open a program in a week.

Because the private sector is in a position to operate more freely and is guided by a profit motive, some observers fear that economics may lead to lower quality. Planning, design, construction, and staffing might be rushed or fall victim to cost-cutting measures, and the result might be a program of barest minimal standards (Johnson and Ross 1990). This fear may be unrealistic, given the political nature of crime and the traditional support for spending on crime control. For example, the private programs that have replaced the institutions in Massachusetts are not necessarily less costly than their counterparts elsewhere. Unlike the state bureaucracy, the private boards of directors— chosen from among business, religious, academic, and political leaders—have a stake in the program's performance, as an issue separate from costs. It is naive to view deinstitutionalization and privatization solely in terms of money spent. Quality programs, whether they exist in institutions or in the community, will be expensive if they are adequately staffed and have adequate resources. Cost savings should be viewed as a by-product of a continuum of care model, in which a range of services is provided that avoids over-spending on youths who require something less costly than maximum security.

In empirical research that compared public and private corrections, the Urban Institute conducted a study of private-public differences in correctional programming in four Massachusetts DYS programs and two Kentucky adult prisons in 1987 and 1988. Their study focused on secure treatment programs in DYS. Four programs were selected out of DYS's thirteen secure treatment programs, two public and two private, and they were matched on offender characteristics as closely as possible. The study's primary objective was to assess and identify any differences in cost, service quality, and effectiveness between private and publicly operated institutions. A secondary objective was to identify reasons for any differences that were found. In DYS, the publicly operated facility cost was approximately 1 percent lower than that of privately operated facilities. In Kentucky, the private facility unit-cost was 10 percent high than the public facility, but the private figure included construction costs, and the public facility held 50 percent more inmates, which meant that the fixed costs of the facility were spread over a larger number of inmates, yielding a lower unit cost (Urban Institute 1989).

In terms of cost comparison, the greatest operating cost is staff salaries. In Massachusetts, the Urban Institute found that salaries and fringe benefits were somewhat higher for public than for private employees. However, private programs were more likely to hire credentialed employees, particularly in the area of clinical psychology, and they relied less on overtime and on the DYS on-call team, which fills in for sick or vacationing employees. Service quality and effectiveness were also examined. The Urban Institute looked at a number of dimensions of service quality, including programs' physical conditions, escape rates, security and control ratings, assessments of physical and mental health of residents, adequacy of the program components (e.g., education, counseling, training, recreation), and re-incarceration. Overall, the private programs had at least a small advantage, in Kentucky as well as in Massachusetts. "By and large, both staff and inmates gave better ratings to the services and programs at the privately-operated facilities; escape rates were lower; there were fewer disturbances by inmates; and in general, staff and offenders felt more comfortable at the privately-operated facilities" (Urban Institute 1989: ES-7).

The differences between public and private programs were not dramatic, but tended to favor private programs slightly. For example, the researchers found the staff in privately operated DYS facilities to be younger and more enthusiastic about their work, although this is obviously a highly subjective measure. If indeed they were more motivated than public employees, this may have been a function of slightly more turnover in private programs, whereas state employees tend to become more entrenched. However, although the turnover rate was higher among private staff, the difference was not statistically significant, and the job satisfaction ratings were higher among staff in the private programs. Staff of private programs reported that their work environments were more flexible and less regimented, and they were subject to less stringent controls than their public counterparts. This was found despite the fact that privately operated programs are required to follow the same basic rules as the publicly operated facilities.

An obvious question to consider is whether private programs really differ from public programs in terms of their focus. Private operators claim that they can deliver higher quality, due to their freedom from rigid requirements that allows them to be innovative and experimental. The Urban Institute studied such differences in DYS and identified two areas in which public and private programs differed. The first had to do with the program models, namely, that the private programs tended to have more clinically oriented program models. In private programs, more of the professional staff (who had advanced degrees) provided counseling than line staff (with bachelor's degrees), resulting in more formal counseling for residents. One of the private programs was experimenting with a sophisticated psychodynamic model of treatment. In contrast, the public programs that were studied were not as psychologically oriented. Instead, they emphasized behavior modification systems, with most of the responsibility for counseling youths residing with line staff acting as "lay" counselors.

The second difference identified in the Urban Institute study was program integration of the various components, particularly education. The study reported that private programs tended to be better integrated because all of the staff of private programs are homogeneously private employees. In public programs, on the other hand, there is a sometimes confusing mixture of public and private sector staff. For example, the line staff and management staff are state employees, but the educational services, as well as some of the clinical services, are contracted out to private service providers. This results in a bifurcation of staff into various levels, with differences in salary and lines of authority. Although program integration is difficult even in private programs, the supplementary contracts and added organizational complexity of public programs seem to create deeper problems of integrating the key components. The line staff at public programs view the clinical and educational staff through a "we-them dichotomy in which the 'we' were viewed as nonprofessionals and the 'them' were viewed as professionals. This distinction may generate a self-perpetuating system in which staff functions grow further apart" (Urban Institute 1989: 184). Compounding the internal staff issues is the difficulty of managing the various private and public players from the perspective of the program director. The study's clear implication is that an all-private staff is superior to a public/private mixture, particularly where the public/private distinctions correspond to levels of professional training. On the other hand, there may be advantages to a mixture of public and private staff. For example, if the state is unhappy with the services provided by a private vendor, it is much easier to terminate a particular service rather than an entire facility. Transferring the operations of an entire facility can be costly and disruptive, and should lead agencies to carefully consider the risks in completely turning over a facility to a private operator (National Institute of Justice 1985).

By the same token, there is no magic wand that the private sector uses to transform a bad public program into a good one. For example, in 1982, the state of Florida turned over the Okeechobee School for Boys, one of four juvenile training schools, to the Jack and Ruth Eckerd Foundation, which is financed by the fortunes of the Eckerd drugstore chain. The foundation had been running "wilderness-experience" programs for troubled children but had never been involved with hard-core delinquents. The Eckerd Foundation is a private, non-profit enterprise, and officials of the organizations say they took on the project as a public service. With about 400 residents, the Okeechobee School is the biggest privately run institution for juvenile offenders (Krajick 1984).

Unfortunately, the Eckerd Foundation inherited tremendous problems. A year after its takeover, the Okeechobee school was sued, along with the other state training schools, by the American Civil Liberties Union and a coalition of other public-interest groups for "cruel and abusive conditions of confinement" (*Bobby M. v. Martinez*, 1983, the so-called "Bobby M. case"). The class-action lawsuit included a list of allegations: overcrowding, unsanitary conditions, inadequate feeding and clothing of residents, poor security, which resulted in frequent beatings and sexual assaults among residents, grossly inadequate medical care, lack of psychological counseling, and a general "atmosphere of fear and violence." The Eckerd Foundation was not named in the lawsuit, but has brought in additional private resources to address the longstanding problems in Okeechobee. For example, the foundation donated $280,000 to raise salaries in hopes of attracting more qualified staff and purchased computers for residents. They were also successful in persuading a grocery store chain to donate equipment for a bakery where residents receive training (Krajick, 1984).

However, it must be emphasized that private resources are not a substitute for effective state management. Overlaying a private operator on an outmoded model of care is not the answer. The management of juvenile corrections must include carefully planned systems of assessing offenders' risks and needs, matching those risks and needs to placements within a range of settings, managing cases throughout the duration of their commitment, and monitoring program placements. For that reason, the Bobby M. case has influenced the Florida juvenile correctional system toward a continuum of more specialized programs in which private vendors can play an important role. In most regions of the United States, the programs and needs presented by today's young offenders are somewhat different from those presented by delinquents of twenty years ago. Increases in the numbers of juvenile sex offenders, emotionally disturbed delinquents, violent offenders, youths who have been victimized or abused, and drug- and alcohol-dependent youths all require specialized responses. Purchase of service accounts permit the state to redirect funding to new programs rather than trying to alter already existing programs in the state bureaucracy.

The state or county's role in monitoring privately contracted services is becoming more and more crucial, as an increasing number of states are purchasing private services in many fields, including juvenile corrections. It is the responsibility of the government to see that private programs live up to their contracts, and to negotiate favorable contracts in the first place. The government is in a far better position to negotiate contracts if private businesses are truly competitive with one another. Once businesses organize, fix prices, and refuse to compete, the government's position is greatly weakened. Government must supervise programs for many of the same reasons that programs supervise youthful offenders. The message must be sent that the public sector has the upper hand because it has the staff and technical expertise to conduct regular monitoring, and it will then use information on programs to maintain standards, expand contracts, or, if necessary, terminate contracts. If government fails to establish strong linkages to its programs, then it loses control over its youthful offenders as well.

Although monitoring is a difficult task, it is far from impossible. There are many strategic methods that an agency can establish in order to enhance its position in relation to the private sector. Massachusetts' DYS has been cited as a national model for program monitoring

(Hackett et al. 1987). During the mid-1970s, a contract unit was established within DYS's Central Administrative Office. The contract unit executed each contract under general purchasing guidelines established by the state. Needs assessments of the youths to be served were conducted annually and helped determine both the retention of existing programs and the development of new ones. Procedures were developed to encourage private sector initiative.

For example, the Massachusetts DYS routinely disseminated Requests for Proposals (RFP) inviting responses from interested vendors. A contract review committee, composed of a contract officer and field staff, assembled for each review. Their task was to evaluate written proposals, hear oral presentations, negotiate mutual obligations and cost agreements, and finally to make a recommendation. Contracts were rebid on a three-year basis, subject to DYS's annual budget allocation. By regularly rebidding contracts, a competitive spirit was maintained that ensured the development of new and varied approaches to combating juvenile crime. Forty-five private agencies accounted for seventy individual contracts, including secure treatment facilities, group homes, alternatives schools, outreach and tracking programs, psychological assessments, and health services (Loughran 1988).

Achieving Political Balance in Juvenile Corrections

A balanced continuum in juvenile justice means that "balance" must be achieved organizationally. Organizational balance requires that community-based programs be made attractive politically. Too often, communities are unwilling to accept the creation of community-based programming in their jurisdictions. The Not in My Backyard ("NIMBY") mentality creates insurmountable obstacles to planning and innovation, although communities, by avoiding knowledge of offenders who emerge out of those environments and then return, are not contributing to a solution.

Several principles can be drawn from our analysis of state and county management of community-based programs. First, youth correctional agencies need to have the authority to manage their own resources. That is, the authority to make placement decisions—where to place and for how long—as well as parole decisions, should reside within the youth correctional agency, rather than with juvenile courts or a separate parole agency. Not allowing correctional agencies to make these decisions creates turf battles with courts and parole boards and wastes energy on activities that do not directly benefit youths' needs or community protection. Second, youth correctional agencies must have standardized criteria for making decisions concerning youths, particularly serious offenders, so that their decisions are open and accountable. Third, states need to carefully examine the changing characteristics of youths in their care so that programs can be tailored to meet their needs.

The impetus for the reform "movements" seems to be coming from several directions. Changes in bureaucratic or institutional interests have produced organizational reasons for reform in some states. These changes have been forced on juvenile justice organizations from various system "stakeholders" such as the courts, the media, the legislature, and the governor's office. In some jurisdictions, juvenile agencies have been placed under federal court order to address institutional conditions that are constitutionally unacceptable to the courts. In other areas, media pressures have forced correctional administrators to respond to charges of mismanagement. Other sites have experienced legislative pressure to adhere to organizational mandates. Still others have been forced to respond to campaign pressure, usually from a gubernatorial candidate running for re-election, to align the correctional agency with the interests of the executive branch of government.

On a more philosophical level, the ongoing crisis in adult corrections—namely, prison overcrowding accompanied by high crime rates—may provide renewed support to a continuum philosophy for juveniles, and may be one explanation for the more balanced approach that some jurisdictions are now quietly embracing. Another explanation may be the "get-tough" spate of legislation of the 1980s that resulted in more juvenile offenders being held for longer periods awaiting adult trial in juvenile detention facilities, leading to overcrowding of not only those facilities, but logjamming entire systems.

State and local fiscal crises also help explain changes in public sector management and have been linked in the past with deinstitutionalization of mental hospitals, adult prisons, and juvenile institutions (Scull 1984). In our analysis of the present-day reforms, the need for fiscal austerity seems to have influenced the direction of reforms, although budget problems certainly do not explain the entire story. Evidence of this is the fact that some states with serious budget deficits are maintaining, if not expanding, costly incarceration models for youths.

Strategies for developing a correctional continuum can be quite varied. In general, institutional downsizing and concurrent expansion of community-based alternatives have originated from interests outside of the juvenile correctional agencies. Successful reform efforts have been preceded by strategic planning that includes all of the jurisdiction's key stakeholders in juvenile corrections. In addition to political strategizing, the planning phases have addressed some substantive administrative concerns, such as employee relations or program monitoring, although to a lesser extent. It is important to note because some states have not fully prepared themselves for the substantive management problems that will inevitably surface following reform, as we have seen in several states where reforms have already been implemented.

Policymakers must continue to sort out substantive contributions from the confusing cross-section of political ideas, and have confidence in the correctional continuum approach. Neither under-incarceration nor over-incarceration is progressive. Instead, in systems where reforms have been maintained, resources have been provided on all levels of supervision, and for a range of programs that incorporate a balance of goals.

Appendix 1
San Bernardino

Juvenile Division   County of San Bernardino
              (Rev. 5-80) Probation Department
                   Juvenile
            Assessment of Client Needs

Name_____ DOB_____ Court Number____
      Last   *First*   *Middle Initial*

Probation Officer_____ Phone Number_____

Date of Evaluation_____
          Month Day Year

Select the appropriate answer and enter the associated weight in the score column. Total all scores to arrive at the needs assessment score.

			Score	Reclass-ification
Employment	0	Part-time, full-time, not relative		
	1	Needs employment	_____	_____
Alcohol Use	0	None		
	1	Prior use		
	2	Current use		
	3	Chronic use	_____	_____
Illegal Drug Use	0	None		
	1	Prior use		
	2	Current use		
	3	Chronic use	_____	_____
Family Relationships	0	No conflict		
	1	Sibling conflict		
	2	Parent(s), guardian conflict or parent/parent conflict		
	3	Sibling and parent(s), guardian conflict	_____	_____
School	0	Attending, graduated, G.E.D., equivalence		
	1	Problems handled at school level		
	2	Severe truancy or behavioral problems		
	3	Not attending/expelled	_____	_____

Academic Achievement	0	At or above grade level	
	1	Below grade level	____ ____
Emotional Instability	0	No symptoms of instability	
	1	Limited symptoms but do not prohibit adequate functioning	
	2	Symptoms prohibit adequate functioning	____ ____
Family Finances	0	No current difficulties	
	1	Minor difficulties	
	2	Severe difficulties	____ ____
Peers	0	Good support and influence	
	1	Negative association influence or loner	____ ____
Opposite Sex Peer	0	Has appropriate sex peer relationship or not relevant (age)	
	1	General disinterest or no opposite sex peer	
	2	Inappropriate sex peer	____ ____
Recreation/Hobby		If no constructive leisure time activities or hobbies or no regular physical exercise, enter 1	____ ____
Organization		If juvenile does not belong to any positive extracurricular clubs (i.e., church, school, social, athletics), enter 1	____ ____
Learning Disability	0	No/Unknown	
	1	Yes	____ ____
Health	0	Sound physical health	
(Physical appearance)	1	Handicap or illness interferes with functioning	
	2	Serious handicap or chronic illness	____ ____

Appendix 2
Alabama Risk Assessment Instrument

Youth _____   Date _____

Instant Offense _____   County _____

Most Serious Prior Offense _____

Scoring Sheet

Circle the appropriate number in each column:

	Point Value	
	Most Serious Instant Adjudication	**Most Serious Prior Adjudication**
Class A Felony	10	7
Class B Felony	7	5
Class C Felony (involving violence to people)	5	3
All Other Class C Felonies	4	2
Class A Misdemeanors	2	1
Technical Violations of Probation/Parole	1	0
Status Offenders who non-criminally violate a Court Order (e.g., don't go to school, run from foster care, etc.)	1	0

Other Scoring Factors	Point Value
Three Adjudications for a Felony Within prior 2 Years (or two Felonies and an adjudication for a misdemeanor involving violence to people)	5
First Delinquency Adjudication 12 Years Old or Younger	1
Prior Out-of-Home Placement as a Result of a Delinquency Adjudication	1

185

	None	Some	High
Gang Involvement with Instant Offense	0	1	2

Substance Abuse Involvement with Instant
Offense:

	None	Some	High
a) Alcohol, Marijuana, Inhalants	0	1	2
OR			
b) Crack, Cocaine, Heroine	0	2	3

Scorer_____   Total_____

Alabama Needs Assessment Instrument

For each item below, select the single appropriate answer and enter the associated number in the adjacent blank. Where appropriate, concretely describe the present situation/need.

Drug/Chemical Abuse
0 No interference with functioning

1 Occasional abuse, some disruption of functioning, unwilling to

2 Frequent abuse, serious disruption, needs immediate treatment participate in treatment program   ____

Specify:

Alcohol Abuse
0 No known use

1 Occasional abuse, some disruption of function, unwilling to participate in treatment program

2 Frequent abuse, serious disruption, needs immediate treatment   ____

Specify:

Primary Family Relationships
0 Relatively stable relaships or not applicable

1 Some disorganization or stress but potential for improvement

2 Major disorganization or stress   ____

Specify:

Alternative Family Relationships ("Significant" adult relationships)
0 Relatively stable relaships or not applicable

1 Some disorganization or stress but potential for improvement

2 Major disorganization or stress   ____

Specify:

Emotional Stability
0 Appropriate adolescent responses

1 Exaggerated periodic or sporadic responses, e.g., aggressive acting

2 Excessive responses; prohibits or limits adequate functioning   ____

Specify:

Intellectual Ability
0 Able to function independently

1 Some need for assistance, potential for adequate adjustment; mild retardation

2 Deficiencies severely limit independent functioning, moderate retardation   ____

Specify:

Learning Disability
0 None   1 Mild disability, able to function   2 Serious disability, interferes   ____
                      in a classroom   with social functioning
Specify:

Employment (where applicable)
0 Not needed or currently 1 Currently employed but poor   2 Needs employment   ____
employed   work habits

SPECIFY:

Vocational/Technical Skills
0 Currently developing   1 Needs to develop marketable skill   ____
                          marketable skill

SPECIFY:
If appropriate, enter the value 1 for each characteristic which applies to this case.

Educational Adjustment Not working to potential .... ____
                            Poor attendance .... ____
                            Program not appropriate for needs, age and/or ability .... ____
                            Disruptive school behavior .... ____
                                                                                            Total ____

Peer Relationships   Socially inept .... ____
                            Loner behavior .... ____
                            Receives basically negative influence from peers .... ____
                            Dependent upon others .... ____
                            Exploits and/or victimizes others (especially in placement) .... ____
                                                                                            Total ____

Health, Mental Health   Medical or dental referral needed .... ____
and Hygiene   Needs health or hygiene education .... ____
                            Handicap or illness limits functioning .... ____
                            Need for mental health intervention (Specify) .... ____
                                                                                            Total ____

Sexual Adjustment   Lacks knowledge (sex education) .... ____
                            Avoidance of the opposite sex .... ____
                            Promiscuity (not prostitution) .... ____
                            Sexual deviant (not prostitution) .... ____
                            Unwed parent .... ____
                            Prostitution .... ____
                                                                                            Total ____

Range: Low (0-12); Medium (13-23); High (24-36)   **Total Needs Score**____

Appendix 3[*]
Juvenile Probation and Aftercare
Assessment of Risk

Select the highest point total applicable for each category

AGE AT FIRST ADJUDICATION   _____
0   =   16 or 17
3   =   14 or 15
5   =   13 or younger

PRIOR CRIMINAL BEHAVIOR   _____
0   =   No prior arrests
2   =   Prior arrest record, no formal sanctions
3   =   Prior delinquency petitions sustained;
           no offenses classified as assaultive
5   =   Prior delinquency petitions sustained;
           at least one assaultive offense recorded

INSTITUTIONAL COMMITMENTS OR PLACEMENTS OF 30 DAYS OR MORE   _____
0   =   None
2   =   One
4   =   Two or more

DRUG/CHEMICAL ABUSE   _____
0   =   No known use or no interference with functioning
2   =   Some disruption in functioning
5   =   Chronic abuse or dependency

ALCOHOL ABUSE   _____
0   =   No known use or no interference with functioning
1   =   Occasional abuse, some disruption of functioning
3   =   Chronic abuse, serious disruption of functioning

PARENTAL CONTROL   _____
0   =   Generally effective
2   =   Inconsistent and/or ineffective
4   =   Little or none

*Taken from Baird, Storrs, and Connelly 1984.

189

SCHOOL DISCIPLINARY PROBLEMS   ‾‾‾‾‾‾

0   =   Attended, graduated, GED equivalence
1   =   Problems handled at school level
3   =   Severe truancy or behavioral problems
5   =   Not attending, expelled

PEER RELATIONSHIPS   ‾‾‾‾‾‾
0   =   Good support and influence
2   =   Negative influence, companions involved
        in delinquent behavior
4   =   Gang member

        Total   ‾‾‾‾‾‾

Arthur D. Little, Inc.

Appendix 4
North Dakota

NAME: _____ DOB: _____
Last First MI

Score

1. <u>Severity of Current Offense</u> (adjudications/informals) _____
   [Raters refer to a list of offenses and severity scores; for example,
   Murder is 10, Manslaughter 5, Burglary 5, Criminal Trespass 3,
   Prostitution 1. In general, Class A Felonies are 10, Class B Felonies
   are 5, Class C Felonies are 3, Misdemeanors are 1, and Status
   Offenses are 0.]

2. <u>Severity of Prior Adjudications</u> (adjudications/informals) _____
   [Raters refer to a list similar to the current offense list, but with
   reduced scores. For example, Murder is 5, Manslaughter 3,
   Burglary 3, Criminal Trespass is 2, Prostitution is 1.]

3. <u>Number of Prior Adjudications and/or Informals</u> _____
   2 or more felonies   (5)
   Less than 2   (0)

4. <u>Age at First Adjudication</u> _____
   1–13 years old   (2)
   14+ years old   (0)
5. <u>Prior Runaway Behavior While Under Supervision</u> _____
   Secure facility   (2)
   Community placement   (1)
   Parents' home   (0)

Placement Scale:
   10 and above: Consider for Secure Placement
   5–9   Short-term placement
   0–4   Community placement/services

Mitigating/Aggravating Factors — Review for Placement: Yes ____ No ____

References

Abbott, Jack. 1981. *In the Belly of the Beast.* New York: Random House.

Allen, H. E., and C. E. Simonsen. 1986. *Corrections in America: An Introduction.* New York: MacMillan.

Allen-Hagan, Barbara. 1991. "Public Juvenile Facilities: Children in Custody 1989," *OJJDP Update on Statistics,* 1–10. Washington, D.C.: U.S. Department of Justice, Office of Juvenile Justice and Delinquency Prevention (January).

Altschuler, David M., and Troy L. Armstrong. 1991. "Intensive Aftercare for the High-Risk Juvenile Parolee: Issues and Approaches in Reintegration and Community Supervision." In *Intensive Interventions with High-Risk Youths: Promising Approaches in Juvenile Probation and Parole,* edited by T. Armstrong, 45–84. Monsey, NY: Criminal Justice Press.

American Bar Association. 1986. Section of Criminal Justice Report to the House of Delegates, February.

Arkansas Advocates for Children and Families. 1983. *Due Process Rights and Legal Procedures in Arkansas' Juvenile Courts.* Little Rock: Arkansas Advocates for Children and Families.

Armstrong, Troy L., ed. 1991. *Intensive Intervention with High-Risk Youths: Promising Approaches in Juvenile Probation and Parole.* Monsey, NY: Criminal Justice Press.

Baird, S. Christopher. 1982. "Probation and Parole Classification: the Wisconsin Model." In *Classification as a Management Tool: Theories and Models for Decision Makers,* edited by L. Fowler. College Park, MD: American Correctional Association.

Baird, S. Christopher, Gregory M. Storrs, and Helen Connelly. 1984. Washington, DC: Arthur D. Little, a report to the U.S. Department of Justice, Office of Juvenile Justice and Delinquency Prevention (July).

Bandura, Albert. 1973. *Aggression: A Social Learning Analysis.* Englewood Cliffs, NJ: Prentice-Hall.

Bartollas, Clemens, Stuart J. Miller, and Simon Dinitz. 1976. *Juvenile Victimization: The Institutional Paradox.* New York: Wiley.

Barton, William H. 1976. "Discretionary Decision-Making in Juvenile Justice." *Crime and Delinquency* 22: 470–80.

_____. 1994a. "New Hampshire Juvenile Dispositional Guidelines Evaluation." Paper presented at the *46th Annual Meeting of the American Society of Criminology,* Miami, 9–12 November.

___. 1994b. "Implementing Detention Policy changes." In *Juvenile Detention: No More Hidden Closets,* edited by I. M. Schwartz and W. H. Barton. Columbus: Ohio State University Press.

Barton, W. H., S. M. Streit, and I. M. Schwartz. 1991. *A Blueprint for Youth Corrections.* Ann Arbor: University of Michigan, Center for the Study of Youth Policy.

Bazemore, Gordon. 1991. "Work Experience and Employment Programming for Serious Juvenile Offenders: Prospects for a 'Productive Engagement' Model of Intensive Supervision." In *Intensive Interventions with High-Risk Youths,* edited by Troy L. Armstrong, 123–52. Monsey, NY: Criminal Justice Press.

Behn, R. D. 1976. "Closing the Massachusetts Public Training Schools." *Policy Sciences* 7, no. 2: 151–72.

Bell, Carl. 1991. "Traumatic Stress and Children in Danger." *Journal of Health Care for the Poor and Underserved* 2: 175–88.

Berke, Richard L. 1993. "Politicians Feel a Crime-Induced Chill in the Air." *The New York Times Week in Review* (24 October): 1.

Berman, Sidney. 1984. "The Relationship of Aggressive Behavior and Violence to Psychic Reorganization in Adolescence." In *The Aggressive Adolescent,* edited by Charles R. Keith, 3–16. New York: Free Press.

Bernard, Thomas J. 1992. *The Cycle of Juvenile Justice.* New York: Oxford University Press.

Bishop, Donna M., and Charles E. Frazier. 1991. "Transfer of Juveniles to Criminal Court: A Case Study and Analysis of Prosecutorial Waiver." *Notre Dame Journal of Law, Ethics and Public Policy* 5, no. 2: 281–302.

Bishop, Donna M., Charles E. Frazier, and John C. Henretta. 1989. "Prosecutorial Waiver: Case Study of a Questionable Reform." *Crime and Delinquency* 35, no. 2: 179–201.

Black, Donald J. 1980. *The Manners and Customs of Police.* New York: Academic Press.

Block, Kathleen J., and Donna C. Hale. 1991. "Turf Wars in Progressive Era Juvenile Justice: The Relationship of Private and Public Child Care Agencies." *Crime and Delinquency* 37, no. 2: 225–41.

Bortner, M. A. 1986. "Remand of Juveniles to Adult Court." *Crime and Delinquency* 32: 53–73.

Boston Police Department Management Review Committee. 1992. *Report of the Boston Police Department Management Review Committee.* Boston.

Bowker, Lee H. 1991. "The Victimization of Prisoners by Staff Members." In *The Dilemmas of Corrections,* edited by Haas and Alpert, 121–44.

Braithwaite, John. 1989. *Crime, Shame and Reintegration.* Cambridge: Cambridge University Press.

Brandau, Timothy. 1992. "An Alternative to Incarceration for Juvenile Delinquents: The Delaware Bay Marine Institute." Unpublished dissertation, University of Delaware.

Braswell, Michael, Steven Dillingham, and Reid Montgomery, Jr. 1985. *Prison Violence in America.* Cincinnati: Anderson.

Brazelton, T. Berry. 1990. "Why is America Failing Its Children?" *The New York Times* (9 September): 50.

Brown, Gerald L., and Frederick K. Goodwin. 1984. "Aggression, adolescence, and psychobiology." In Keith, *The Aggressive Adolescent,* 63–95.

Bureau of Justice Statistics. 1982. *Jail Inmates.* Washington, DC: U.S. Department of Justice.

___. 1984. *Jail Inmates.* Washington, DC: U.S. Department of Justice.

Butts, Jeffrey A. 1988. "Youth Corrections in Maryland: The Dawning of a New Era." In Jeffrey A. Butts and Samuel M. Streit, *Youth Correction Reform: The Maryland and Florida Experience,* 1–31. Ann Arbor, MI: Center for the Study of Youth Policy.

___. 1990. *Juvenile Corrections Risk Assessment: Recent State-Based Studies.* Ann Arbor, MI: Center for the Study of Youth Policy (draft; February).

Butts, Jeffrey A., and Paul DeMuro. 1989. *Risk Assessment of Adjudicated Delinquents; Division for Children and Youth Services, Department of Health and Human Services, State of New Hampshire.* Ann Arbor, MI: Center for the Study of Youth Policy (December).

Bynum, Tim S., Gary Cordner, and Jack Greene. 1982. "Victim and Offense Characteristics." *Criminology* 30: 301–18.

Carter, Percy. 1989. "The New-Look Police Club." In *Preventing Juvenile Crime,* edited by Julia Vernon and Sandra McKillop. Canberra: Australian Institute of Criminology.

Cashmore, Ellis, and Eugene McLaughlin. 1991. "Out of Order?" In *Out of Order,* edited by Cashmore and McLaughlin, 10–41. London: Routledge, Chapman and Hall.

Champion, Dean. 1989. "Teenage Felons and Waiver Hearings: Some Recent Trends, 1980–1988." *Crime and Delinquency* 35, no. 4: 577–85.

Chase, Naomi F. 1976. *A Child is Being Beaten.* New York: McGraw-Hill.

Chesney-Lind, M., and R. G. Shelden. 1992. *Girls: Delinquency and Juvenile Justice.* Pacific Grove, CA: Brooks/Cole.

Clear, Todd R. 1988. "Statistical Predictions in Corrections." *Research in Corrections* 1: 1–40.

Cloward, Richard, and Lloyd Ohlin. 1960. *Delinquency and Opportunity: A Theory of Delinquent Gangs.* New York: Free Press.

Coates, Robert B. 1981. "Deinstitutionalization and the Serious Juvenile Offender." *Crime and Delinquency* 27, no. 4: 477–86.

Coffey, Alan R. 1975. *Juvenile Corrections.* Englewood Cliffs, NJ: Prentice-Hall.

Cohen, Albert. 1955. *Delinquent Boys.* Glencoe, IL: The Free Press.

Cohen, Albert K., and James F. Short, Jr. 1958. "Research in Delinquent Subcultures." *Journal of Social Issues* 14, no. 3.

Commonwealth of Massachusetts Legislative Research Council. 1986. *Report Relative to Prisons for Profit,* House No. 6225 (31 July).

Corbett, Ronald P., Donald Cochran, and James Byrne. 1987. "Managing Change in Probation: Principles and Practice in the Implementation of an Intensive Probation Supervision Program." In *Intermediate Punishments: Intensive Supervision, Home Confinement and Electronic Surveillance,* edited Belinda R. McCarthy. Monsey, NY: Willow Tree Press.

Cornwall, Thomas P., Virginia Ritchie, Marie E. McCann, Douglas M. Conrad, Elliot M. Silverstein, R. Reid Whiteside, Judy H. Marx, Mary Catherine Bass, and Patrick J. Koehne. 1984. "A Neuropsychiatric Perspective of Aggressive Adolescents." In Keith, *The Aggressive Adolescent,* 96–125.

Curran, Daniel J. 1988. "Destructuring, Privatization, and the Promise of Juvenile Diversion: Compromising Community-Based Corrections." *Crime and Delinquency* 34, no. 4: 363–78.

Davis, Samuel M. 1994. *Rights of Juveniles; The Juvenile Justice System.* New York: Clark Boardman.

DeMuro, Paul, and Jeffrey A. Butts. 1989. *At the Crossroads: A Population Profile of Youths Committed to the Alabama Department of Youth Services.* Prepared for the Alabama Department of Youth Services (February).

DiIulio, John J., Jr. 1988. "Private Prisons." U.S. Department of Justice, National Institute of Justice, Crime File Study Guide.

Edelman, Marian Wright. 1992. *The Measure of Our Success.* Boston: Beacon Press.

Ehrensaft, Kenneth, and Irving Spergel. 1993. *Police Model.* Arlington, VA: National Youth Gang Information Center.

Fagan, Jeffrey, and Deschenes, Elizabeth Piper. 1990. "Determinants of Judicial Waiver Decisions for Violent Juvenile Offenders." *Journal of Criminal Law and Criminology* 81, no. 2: 314–47.

Fagan, Jeffrey, Martin Forst, and T. Scott Vivona. 1988. *Treatment and Reintegration of Violent Juvenile Offenders: Experimental Results.* San Francisco, CA: URSA Institution. Prepared for the U.S. Department of Justice, Office of Juvenile Justice and Delinquency Prevention.

Fagan, Jeffrey, and Eliot Hartstone. 1984. "Strategic Planning in Juvenile Justice_Defining the Toughest Kids." In *Violent Juvenile Offenders,* edited by Robert A. Mathias, Paul DeMuro, and Richard Allinson. San Francisco: National Council on Crime and Delinquency.

Fagan, Jeffrey, E. Hartstone, C. Rudman, and K. Hansen. 1984. "System Processing of Violent Juvenile Offenders: An Empirical Assessment." In *Violent Juvenile Offenders,* edited by Robert A. Mathias, Paul DeMuro, and Richard Allinson. San Francisco: National Council on Crime and Delinquency.

Fagan, J., M. Schiff, E. Brisben, and D. Orden. 1991. *The Comparative Impacts of Juvenile and Criminal Court Sanctions on Adolescent Felony Offenders.* Washington, DC: National Institute of Justice, U.S. Department of Justice.

Farber, E. 1984. "Violence in the Families of Adolescent Runaways." *Child Abuse and Neglect* 8: 295–99.

Feld, Barry C. 1983. "Delinquent Careers and Criminal Policy: Just Deserts and the Waiver Decision." *Criminology* 21, no. 2: 195–212.

___. 1984. "Criminalizing Juvenile Justice: Rules of Procedure for the Juvenile Court." *Minnesota Law Review* 69, no. 2: 141–276.

___. 1987. "Juvenile Court Meets the Principle of Offense: Legislative Changes in Juvenile Waiver Statutes." *Journal of Criminal Law and Criminology* 78: 471–533.

___. 1988. "*In re Gault* Revisited: A Cross-State Comparison of the Right to Counsel in Juvenile Court." *Crime and Delinquency* 34, no. 4: 393–424.

___. 1989. "Bad Law Makes Hard Cases: Reflections on Teenaged Murderers, Judicial Activism, and Legislative Default." *Law and Inequality: A Journal of Theory and Practice* 8, no. 1: 1–101.

___. 1991. "Justice by Geography: Urban, Suburban, and Rural Variations in Juvenile Justice Administration." *The Journal of Criminal Law and Criminology* 82, no. 1: 156–210.

Festinger, Leon. 1964. *Conflict, Decision and Dissonance.* Stanford, CA: Stanford University Press.

Finckenauer, James O. 1982. *Scared Straight! and the Panacea Phenomenon.* Englewood Cliffs, NJ: Prentice-Hall.

___. 1984. *Juvenile Delinquency and Corrections.* Orlando: Academic Press Inc.

Florida Advisory Council on Intergovernmental Relations. 1994. *Community Corrections Partnership Act Report.* Tallahassee, FL: Advisory Council on Intergovernmental Relations (February 23).

Forst, Martin L., and Martha-Elin Blomquist. 1991. *Missing Children: Rhetoric and Reality.* New York: Lexington Books.

Friedman, Lawrence, 1993. *Crime and Punishment in American History*. New York, Basic Books.

Gadpaille, Warren J. 1984. "Adolescent Aggression from the Perspective of Cultural Anthropology." In Keith, *The Aggressive Adolescent*, 432–54.

Garbarino, James, Nancy Dubrow, Kathleen Kostelny, and Carole Pardo. 1992. *Children in Danger: Coping with the Consequences of Community Violence*. San Francisco: Jossey-Bass.

Gendreau, Paul, and Robert R. Ross. 1991. "Correctional Treatment: Some Recommendations for Effective Intervention." In *The Dilemmas of Corrections*, 2d ed., edited by K. Haas and G. Alpert, 316–29. Prospect Heights, IL: Waveland Press.

Gerlin, Andrea. 1994. "Teenage Defendants Get Juries of Their Peers." *Wall Street Journal* (3 June 1994): B1.

Giari, Maygene. 1991. "In Oklahoma, Building More Prisons has Solved No Problems." In *The Dilemmas of Corrections*, edited by Haas and Alpert, 399–412.

Gilman, D., D. Newman, and P. Strasburg. 1982. *Recommendations for Legislative Change in Massachusetts*. Washington, DC (March).

Gilmore, T. N., and E. Schall. 1986. "Case Management as a Revitalizing Theme." *Public Administration Review*. Washington, DC: Society for Public Administration.

Glaser, Daniel. 1987. "Classification for Risk." *Prediction and Classification; Criminal Justice Decision Making*, edited by Don M. Gottfredson and Michael Tonry, 249–92. Crime and Justice Vol. 9. Chicago: University of Chicago Press.

Goldmeier, John, and Robert Dean. 1973. "The Runaway: Person, Problem or Situation." In *Crime and Delinquency* 19, no. 4 (October): 539–44.

Gottfredson, Don M., and Michael Tonry, eds. 1987. *Prediction and Classification; Criminal Justice Decision Making*. Chicago: University of Chicago Press.

Governor's Anti-Crime Council. 1986. *Comparative Analysis of the Juvenile Codes of Ten States*. Commonwealth of Massachusetts: Governor's Anti-Crime Council (monograph).

Governor's Juvenile Justice Advisory Committee. 1981. *The Violent Juvenile Offender in Massachusetts; A Policy Analysis*. Commonwealth of Massachusetts.

Governor's Juvenile Justice and Delinquency Prevention Advisory Committee. 1992. *Profile of Delinquency Cases at Various Stages of the Florida Juvenile Justice System 1982–83 through 1991–92*. Florida Department of Health and Rehabilitative Services, Delinquency Services Program Office (November).

Grant, Traci. 1992. "Police Plan to Sue Boston Rappers." *Boston Globe* (5 August): 43.

Greenwood, Peter W. 1986. "Promising Approaches for the Rehabilitation or Prevention of Chronic Juvenile Offenders." In *Intervention Strategies for Chronic Juvenile Offenders*, edited by Peter W. Greenwood, 207–34. New York: Greenwood Press.

Greer, William C. 1991. "Aftercare: Community Integration Following Institutional Treatment." *Juvenile Sexual Offending*, edited by Gail D. Ryan and Sandy L. Lane, 377–91. Lexington, MA: D.C. Heath.

Grissom, Grant R., and William L. Dubnov. 1989. *Without Locks and Bars*. New York: Praeger.

Guarino-Ghezzi, Susan. 1988. "Initiating Change in Massachusetts' Juvenile Correctional System: A Retrospective Analysis."*Criminal Justice Review* 13, no. 1: 1–12.

___. 1993. "Project Reinforcement: Program Description and Findings." Boston (mimeo).

___. 1994. "Reintegrative Police Surveillance of Juvenile Offenders: Forging an Urban Model." *Crime and Delinquency* 40, no. 2: 131–53.

Guarino-Ghezzi, Susan, and James Byrne. 1989. "Developing a Model of Structured Decision Making in Juvenile Corrections: The Massachusetts Experience." In *Crime and Delinquency* 35, no. 2: 270–302.

Guarino-Ghezzi, Susan, and Lee Kimball. 1986. "Reforming Justice by Geography; Organizational Responses to the Problem of Juvenile Crime." *Law and Policy* 8, no. 4: 419–36.

Haas, Kenneth C., and Geoffrey P. Alpert. 1991. *The Dilemmas of Corrections.* Prospect Heights, IL: Waveland.

Hackler, James C. 1978. "The Need to do Something." *Juvenile Delinquency: A Justice Perspective,* 2d ed. (1990), edited by Ralph A. Weisheit and Robert G. Culberston. Prospect Heights, IL: Waveland Press.

Hackett, Judith C., Harry P. Hatry, Robert B. Levinson, Joan Allen, Keon Chi, and Edward D. Feigenbaum. 1987. *Issues in Contracting for the Private Operation of Prisons and Jails.* Washington, DC: Council for State Governments and the Urban Institute, chapter 6.

Hagedorn, John M. 1988. *People and Folks.* Chicago: Lake View Press.

Hamparian, D., L. Estep, S. Muntean, R. Priestino, R. Swisher, P. Wallace, and J. White. 1982. *Youth in Adult Courts: Between Two Worlds.* U.S. Department of Justice. Columbus, Ohio: Academy for Contemporary Problems.

Hamparian, D., R. Schuster, S. Dinitz, and J. Conrad. 1978. *The Violent Few.* Lexington, MA: D.C. Health.

Heinz, J., G. Ryan, and S. Bengis. 1991. "The System's Response to Juvenile Sex Offenders." In *Juvenile Sexual Offending,* edited by G. Ryan and S. Lane. Lexington, MA: D.C. Heath.

Henig, J. 1985. "Privatization and Decentralization: Should Governments Shrink?" *Public Policy and Federalism* 12: 26–53.

Hirschi, Travis. 1969. *Causes of Delinquency.* Berkeley: University of California Press.

Huff, C. Ronald. 1986. "Home Detention as a Policy Alternative for Ohio's Juvenile Courts: A Final Report to the Governor's Office of Criminal Justice Services." Columbus, OH: Program for the Study of Crime and Delinquency, Ohio State University.

Hughes, Stella P., and Anne L. Schneider. 1990. *Victim-Offender Mediation in the Juvenile Justice System.* Washington, DC: Office of Juvenile Justice and Delinquency Prevention (September).

Hummel, Ralph. 1977. *The Bureaucratic Experience.* New York: St. Martin's Press.

Immarigeon, Russ, and Meda Chesney-Lind. 1992. *Women's Prisons: Overcrowded and Overused.* San Francisco: National Council on Crime and Delinquency.

Institute of Judicial Administration—American Bar Association. 1980. *Juvenile Justice Standards. Standards Relating to Interim Status: The Release, Control and Detention of Accused Juvenile Offenders Between Arrest and Disposition.* Cambridge, MA: Ballinger.

Irwin, John. 1980. *Prisons in Turmoil.* Boston: Little, Brown.

Jamieson, Katherine M., and Timothy Flanagan, eds. 1987. *Sourcebook of Criminal Justice Statistics—1986.* Washington, DC: U.S. Department of Justice.

Jankowski, Martin Sanchez. 1991. *Islands in the Street.* Berkeley: University of California Press.

John Howard Association. 1974. *Illinois Youth Centers at St. Charles and Geneva.* Chicago: John Howard Association.

Johnson, Byron R., and Paul P. Ross. 1990. "The Privatization of Correctional Management: A Review." *Journal of Criminal Justice* 18: 351–58.

Juvenile Justice Advisory Committee. 1981. *The Violent Juvenile Offender in Massachusetts.* Boston, MA: Juvenile Justice Advisory Committee (June).

Keith, Charles R. 1984. *The Aggressive Adolescent.* New York: Free Press.

Kelling, George L. 1987. "Juveniles and Police: The End of the Nightstick." In *From Children to Citizens, Volume II, The Role of the Juvenile Court,* edited by F. Hartmann, 203–18. New York: Springer-Verlag.

Kinder, George, and Caesar Speight. 1994. "Community Intensive Supervision Project; 1993 Review." Allegheny County Juvenile Court (mimeo) (February).

Klein, Andrew R. 1988. *Alternative Sentencing.* Cincinnati: Anderson.

Knitzer, J., and M. Sobie. 1984. *Law Guardians in New York State: A Study of the Legal Representation of Children.* New York: New York State Bar Association.

Knopp, F. H., and W. Stevenson. 1989. *Nationwide Survey of Juvenile and Adult Sex Offender Treatment Programs and Models: 1988.* Orwell, Vermont: Safer Society Press.

Kohlberg, Lawrence. 1976. "Moral Stages and Moralization: The Cognitive-Developmental Approach." In *Moral Development and Behavior,* edited by T. Lickona. New York: Holt, Rinehart and Winston.

Kohlberg, L., and D. Freundlich. 1973. "Moral Judgement in Youthful Offenders." In *Moralization, the Cognitive Development Approach,* edited by L. Kohlberg and E. Turiel. New York: Holt, Rinehart and Winston.

Krajick, Kevin. 1984. "Punishment for Profit." *Across the Board* 221, no. 3: 20–27.

Krisberg, Barry, and James F. Austin. 1993. *Reinventing Juvenile Justice.* Newbury Park, CA: Sage Publications.

Krisberg, Barry, Paul Litsky, and Ira M. Schwartz. 1984. "Youth in Confinement: Justice by Geography." *Journal of Research in Crime and Delinquency* 22, no. 2: 153–81.

Krisberg, Barry, Ira M. Schwartz, Paul Litsky, and James Austin. 1986. "The Watershed of Juvenile Justice Reform." *Crime and Delinquency* 32, no. 1: 5–38.

Kurtz, David P., Martha M. Giddings, and Richard Sutphen. 1993. "A Prospective Investigation of Racial Disparity in the Juvenile Justice System." *Juvenile and Family Court Journal* 44, no. 3: 43–59.

Lacayo, Richard. 1994. "When Kids Go Bad." *Time Magazine,* September 19.

Lane, S., and P. Zamora. 1984. "A Method for Treating the Adolescent Sex Offender." In *Violent Juvenile Offenders,* edited by R. Mathias, P. DeMuro, and R. Allinson. San Francisco: National Council on Crime and Delinquency.

Laub, John H. 1985. "The Role of the District Attorney in Juvenile Court." Boston (mimeo).

Leaf, James G. 1988. *A History of the Internal Organization of the State Reform School for Boys at Westborough, Massachusetts (1846–1974).* Unpublished doctoral thesis, Harvard University.

LeClair, Daniel P., and Susan Guarino-Ghezzi. 1991. "Does Incapacitation Guarantee Public Safety? Lessons from the Massachusetts Furlough and Prerelease Programs." *Justice Quarterly* 8, no. 1: 9–36.

Lemert, Edwin M. 1972. *Human Deviance, Social Problems and Social Control,* 2d ed. Englewood Cliffs, NJ: Prentice-Hall.

Lerner, Steve. 1990. *The Good News About Juvenile Justice.* San Francisco: Commonweal Research Institute.

Lipsky, Martin. 1980. *Street Level Bureaucracy.* New York: Russell Sage.

Lockwood, Daniel. 1980. *Prison Sexual Violence.* New York: Elsevior.

___. 1985. "Issues in Prison Sexual Violence." In (eds.) *Prison Violence in America,* edited by Braswell et al., 89–96.

___. 1991. "Target Violence." In *The Dilemmas of Corrections*, edited by K. Haas and G. Alpert, 87–104. Prospect Heights, IL: Waveland.

Loffredo, Susan. 1993. "Clash Over Sex Ed." *The Newton Graphic* (8 April): 1 ff.

Loughran, Edward J. 1988. "Privatization in Juvenile Services." *Corrections Today* 50, no. 6: 78–83.

McCune, Shirley D. 1965. *Judges Look at Themselves: Profile of the Nation's Juvenile Court Judges*. George Washington University Center for the Behavioral Sciences (monograph).

McDermott, M. Joan, and John H. Laub. 1986. "Adolescence and Juvenile Justice Policy." *Criminal Justice Policy Review* 1, no. 4: 438–55.

McDonald, Douglas C., ed. 1990. *Private Prisons and the Public Interest*. New Brunswick, NJ: Rutgers University Press.

McDonald, Robin. 1994. "The Successor: DEA Official Gives Up Chicago Promotion." *The Atlanta Journal/Constitution* (3 September): C2.

McGarrell, Edmund F. 1988. *Juvenile Correctional Reform; Two Decades of Policy and Procedural Change*. New York: State University of New York Press.

McGarrell, Edmund F., and Timothy J. Flanagan, eds. 1985. *Sourcebook of Criminal Justice Statistics—1984*. Washington, DC: U.S. Department of Justice.

Mack, Julian. 1909. "The Juvenile Court." *Harvard Law Review* 23: 104.

McLeary, Richard. 1978. *Dangerous Men: The Sociology of Parole*. Beverly Hills, CA: Sage.

McShane, Marilyn, and Frank Williams. 1989. "The Prison Adjustment of Juvenile Offenders." *Crime and Delinquency* 35, no. 2: 254–69.

Martinson, Robert. 1974. "What Works?—Questions and Answers About Prison Reform." *The Public Interest* 35: 22–54.

Maryland Department of Juvenile Services. 1990. Ten Year Master Facility Plan. Maryland Department of Juvenile Services (mimeo) (January).

Massachusetts Advocacy Center. 1980. *Delinquent Justice: Juvenile Detention Practice in Massachusetts*. Boston.

Massachusetts Department of Youth Services. 1977. *Annual report, 1977*. Boston.

___. 1982. "Classification Policy: Guidelines for Governing Entrance into Secure Treatment Facilities." Boston: Massachusetts Department of Youth Services.

___. 1984. "The Classification Policies and Procedures." Boston: Massachusetts Department of Youth Services (February).

___. 1986. "Secure Classification Manual." Boston: Massachusetts Department of Youth Services.

___. 1987. *Interim Report: Pretrial Detention; A Comparative Study*. Boston: Massachusetts Department of Youth Services (July).

Massachusetts Office of the Attorney General (n.d.). SCORE: Student Conflict Resolution Experts. Boston (mimeo).

Massachusetts Taxpayers Foundation. 1980. *Purchase of Services: Can State Government Gain Control?* Boston.

Merton, Robert K. 1968. *Social Theory and Social Structure*. New York: Free Press.

Miller, Walter B. 1958. "Lower Class Culture as a Generating Milieu of Gang Delinquency." *Journal of Social Issues* 14, no. 3.

___. 1976. "Youth Gangs in the Urban Crisis Era." In *Delinquency, Crime and Society*, edited by J. F. Short, 91–122. Chicago: University of Chicago Press.

Moore, Joan. 1978. *Homeboys*. Philadelphia: Temple University Press.

Morris, Norval, and Michael Tonry. 1990. *Between Prison and Probation; Intermediate Punishments in a Rational Sentencing System*. New York: Oxford University Press.

Murphy, Sean P., and John Ellement. 1992. "Internal Police Probe Discounts Most Allegations of Misconduct." *Boston Globe* (20 August): 1.

Natalucci-Persichetti, Geno. 1991. "Speak Out—Ohio's Struggle to Improve Juvenile Justice." *Corrections Today* 53, no. 1: 18–26.

National Association of Social Workers. 1991. *National Survey of Shelters for Runaway and Homeless Youth.* Washington, DC: National Association of Social Workers.

National Council of Juvenile and Family Court Judges. 1990. "A New Approach to Runaway, Truant, Substance Abusing and Beyond Control Children." *Juvenile and Family Court Journal* 41 (3B): 1–49.

National Council on Crime and Delinquency. 1991. *Unlocking Juvenile Corrections.* San Francisco: National Council on Crime and Delinquency.

National Institute of Justice, United States Department of Justice. 1985. *The Privatization of Corrections.* Washington, DC: U.S. Department of Justice (February).

Needle, Jerome A., and William Vaughan Stapleton. 1983. *Police Handling of Youth Gangs.* Washington, DC: U.S. Department of Justice Office of Juvenile Justice and Delinquency Prevention.

New York State Division for Youth (n.d.). "DFY Classification System: An Overview." Albany: New York State Division for Youth (mimeo).

Norman, Sherwood. 1960. *Detention Practice.* New York: National Probation and Parole Association.

Office of Juvenile Justice and Delinquency Prevention. 1988. *Runaway Children and the Juvenile Justice and Delinquency Prevention Act: What is Its Impact?* Washington, DC: U.S. Department of Justice, Office of Juvenile Justice and Delinquency Prevention.

___. 1991. *Juveniles Taken into Custody: Fiscal Year 1990 Report.* Washington, DC: U.S. Department of Justice (September).

___. 1993. *A Comprehensive Strategy for Serious, Violent and Chronic Juvenile Offenders.* Washington, DC: U.S. Department of Justice (December).

___. 1994. "How Juveniles Get to Criminal Court." *OJJDP Bulletin* (May).

O'Hare, Michael, Robert Leone, and Marc Zegans. 1990. "The Privatization of Imprisonment: A Managerial Perspective." In *Private Prisons and the Public Interest,* edited by Douglas C. McDonald.

Ohio Department of Youth Services. 1993. *Reclaim Ohio.* Ohio Department of Youth Services (mimeo) (2 February).

Parent, Dale. 1993a. "Conditions of Confinement." *Juvenile Justice* 1, no. 1: 2–23 (U.S. Office of Juvenile Justice and Delinquency Prevention, Washington, DC).

___. 1993b. "Boot Camps Failing to Achieve Goals." *Overcrowded Times* 4, no. 4: 1–15.

Parent, Dale, Valerie Leiter, Stephen Kennedy, Lisa Livens, Daniel Wentworth, and Sarah Wilcox. 1994. *Conditions of Confinement: Juvenile Detention and Corrections Facilities.* Washington, DC: Office of Juvenile Justice and Delinquency Prevention (February).

Patrick, A. L. 1986. "Private Sector—Profit Motive vs. Quality." *Corrections Today* 48: 68–74.

Pecora, P., M. W. Fraser, and D. Haapala. 1992. "Intensive Home-Based Family Preservation Services: An Update from the FIT Project." *Child Welfare* 71: 177–88.

Pfohl, Stephen. 1978. *Predicting Dangerousness: The Social Construction of Psychiatric Reality.* Lexington, MA: D.C. Heath.

Phillips, Charles D., and Simon Dinitz. 1982. "Labelling and Juvenile Court Dispositions: Official Responses to a Cohort of Violent Juveniles." *Sociological Quarterly* 23, no. 2 (Spring): 267–79.

Piaget, Jean. 1948. *The Moral Judgment of the Child.* New York: Free Press.

Platt, Anthony. 1977. *The Child Savers: The Invention of Delinquency,* 2d ed. Chicago: University of Chicago Press.

Polier, Justine Wise. 1989. *Juvenile Justice in Double Jeopardy: The Distanced Community and Vengeful Retribution.* Hillsdale, NJ: Lawrence Erlbaum.

Pope, Carl E., and William H. Feyerherm. 1990. "Minority Status and Juvenile Justice Processing" (Part I). *Criminal Justice Abstracts* 22, no. 2: 327–35.

President's Commission on Law Enforcement and Administration of Justice. 1967. *The Challenge of Crime in a Free Society.* Washington, DC: U.S. Government Printing Office.

Reckless, Walter C. 1962. "A Non-Causal Explanation: Containment Theory." *Excerpta Criminologica* 1, no. 2 (March-April).

Reed, David. 1983. *Needed: Serious Solutions for Serious Juvenile Crime.* Chicago: Chicago Law Enforcement Study Group.

Reich, Robert B. 1992. *The Work of Nations.* New York: Vintage Books.

Reuss-Ianni, Elizabeth. 1984. *Two Cultures of Policing: Street Cops and Management.* New Brunswick, NJ: Transaction Publishers.

Rocheleau, Ann Marie. 1981. "Placing Youths in the Massachusetts Department of Youth Services." Unpublished master's thesis, Boston College.

Roysher, M., and P. Edelman. 1981. "Treating Juveniles as Adults in New York: What Does it Mean and How is it Working?" In *Major Issues in Juvenile Justice Information and Training: Readings in Public Policy.* Columbus, OH: Academy for Social Problems.

Rubin, H. Ted. 1976. "The Eye of the Juvenile Court Judge: A One-Step-Up View of the Juvenile Justice System." *The Juvenile Justice System,* edited by Malcolm W. Klein, 133–60. Beverly Hills: Sage Publications.

Rudman, C., E. Hartstone, J. Fagan, and M. Moore. 1986. "Violent Youth in Adult Court: Process and Punishment." *Crime and Delinquency* 32: 75–96.

Sagarin, Edward. 1976. "Prison Homosexuality and Its Effect on Post-Prison Sexual Behavior." *Psychiatry* 39: 245–57.

Sanborn, Joseph B. 1991. "The Juvenile, the Court or the Community: Whose Best Interests are Currently Being Promoted in Juvenile Court." Paper presented at the 41st Annual American Society of Criminology Conference, San Francisco.

Sarri, Rosemary. 1974. *Under Lock and Key: Juveniles in Jails and Detention.* Ann Arbor: University of Michigan National Assessment of Juvenile Corrections.

Schinitsky, Charles. 1961. "Observations with Respect to Children's Court." *Domestic Relations Court Committee Memorandum Report.* New York: The Association of the Bar (mimeograph) (May).

Schneider, Anne L., and Donna D. Schram. 1980. "A Proposal to Assess the Implementation and Impact of Washington's Juvenile Justice Legislation." Seattle (mimeo) (December).

Schwartz, Ira M. 1989. *(In)Justice for Juveniles.* Lexington, MA: D.C. Heath.

Schwartz, Ira M., William H. Barton, and Frank Orlando. 1991. "Keeping Kids Out of Secure Detention." *Public Welfare* (Spring): 20–26.

Schwartz, Ira M., M. Jackson-Beeck, and R. Anderson. 1984. "The Hidden System of Juvenile Control." *Crime & Delinquency* 30, no. 3: 371–85.

Schwartz, Ira M., and Edward J. Loughran (n.d.). "Restructuring Youth Corrections Systems: A Guide for Policymakers" (mimeo).

Schwartz, Ira M., Martha W. Steketee, and Jeffrey A. Butts. 1991. "Business as Usual: Juvenile Justice During the 1980s." *Notre Dame Journal of Law, Ethics and Public Policy* 5, no. 2: 377–96.

Schwartz, Ira M., Martha W. Steketee, and Victoria W. Schneider. 1990. "Federal Juvenile Justice Policy and the Incarceration of Girls." *Crime and Delinquency* 36, no. 4: 503–20.

Schwartzkopff, Frances. 1994. "Tests, Evaluators Said Rapist Should Be Released." *Atlanta Journal/Constitution* (16 September): F1.

Scull, Andrew. 1984. *Decarceration; Community Treatment and the Deviant,* 2d ed. New Brunswick, NJ: Rutgers University Press.

Sechrest, Lee. 1987. "Classification for Treatment." *Prediction and Classification; Criminal Justice Decision Making, Vol.9 Crime and Justice,* edited by Don M. Gottfredson and Michael Tonry, 293–322. Chicago: University of Chicago Press.

Shireman, Charles H., and Frederic G. Reamer. 1986. *Rehabilitating Juvenile Justice.* New York: Columbia University Press.

Sickmund, Melissa. 1994. "How Juveniles Get to Criminal Court." Washington, DC: U.S. Department of Justice, Office of Juvenile Justice and Delinquency Prevention (October).

Skolnick, Jerome. 1966. *Justice without Trial: Law Enforcement in Democratic Society.* New York: John Wiley.

Skolnick, Jerome H., and David H. Bayley. 1986. *The New Blue Line.* New York: Free Press.

Snyder, Howard N. 1990. "Growth in Minority Detentions Attributed to Drug Law Violators." *OJJDP Update on Statistics.* U.S. Department of Justice (March).

___. 1993. *Juvenile Court Statistics: 1990.* Washington, DC: Office of Juvenile Justice and Delinquency Prevention.

Snyder, Howard N., T. A. Finnegan, E. H. Nimick, M. H. Sickmund, D. P. Sullivan, and N. J. Tierney. 1990. *Juvenile Court Statistics 1988.* Pittsburgh: National Center for Juvenile Justice.

Sobie, Merril. 1981. "The Juvenile Offender Act: Effectiveness and Impact on the New York Juvenile Justice System." *New York Law School Review* 26: 677–722.

Sparrow, Malcolm, Mark Moore, and David Kennedy. 1990. *Beyond 911; A New Era for Policing.* New York: Basic Books.

Spergel, Irving. 1990. "Youth Gangs: Continuity and Change." In *Crime and Justice; A Review of Research,* vol. 12, edited by M. Tonry and N. Morris, 171–276. Chicago: University of Chicago Press.

Spergel, Irving, Ron Chance, Kenneth Ehrensaft, Thomas Regulus, Candice Kane, Robert Laseter, Alba Alexander, and Sandra Oh. 1993. *National Youth Gang Suppression and Intervention Program—Program Models.* Arlington, VA: National Youth Gang Information Center.

State of Alabama, Department of Youth Services. 1986. "Projected State Services for Delinquent Youth: A Road Map to the Future" (mimeo).

State of Georgia. 1991. "Remarks by Governor Zell Miller, Joint Study Committee on Children and Youth, Friday, September 27, 1991." Atlanta, GA: Office of the Governor (mimeo).

Streit, Samuel M. 1988. "Juvenile Justice Reform in Florida; Testimony to the Tennessee Legislature, February 5, 1988." In Jeffrey A. Butts and Samuel M. Streit, *Youth Correction Reform: The Maryland and Florida Experience,* 33–42. Ann Arbor, MI: Center for the Study of Youth Policy.

Streit, Samuel M., and William H. Barton. 1990. *Youth Services in the 1990s: A Blueprint for Policymakers* (draft). University of Michigan: Center for the Study of Youth Policy.

Sudnow, David. 1965. "Normal Crimes: Sociological Features of the Penal Code in a Public Defender's Office." *Social Problems* 12: 255–76.

Sutherland, Edwin H., and Donald R. Cressey. 1966. *Principles of Criminology,* 7th ed. Philadelphia: J.B. Lippincott.

Sykes, Gresham. 1958. "The Corruption of Authority and Rehabilitation." *Social Forces* 34 (March): 257–62.

Sykes, Gresham M., and David Matza. 1957. "Techniques of Neutralization: A Theory of Delinquency." *American Sociological Review* 22 (December).

Thrasher, Frederick. 1963. *The Gang* (abridged ed.; orig. 1927). Chicago: University of Chicago Press.

Tollett, T. 1987. *A Comparative Study of Florida Delinquency Commitment Programs.* Tallahassee, FL: Department of Health and Rehabilitative Services.

Treaster, Joseph. 1993. "Two Federal Judges, in Protest, Refuse to Accept Drug Cases." *The New York Times* (17 April): 1 ff.

Tversky, Amos, and Daniel Kahneman. 1981. "The Framing of Decisions and the Psychology of Choice." *Science* 211: 453–58.

U.S. Advisory Commission on Intergovernmental Relations. 1993. *The Role of General Government Elected Officials in Criminal Justice.* Washington, DC: U.S. Advisory Commission on Intergovernmental Relations.

U.S. Attorney General's Advisory Board on Missing Children. 1986. *America's Missing and Exploited Children.* Washington, DC: U.S. Department of Justice, Office of Juvenile Justice and Delinquency Prevention.

U.S. Congress, Senate, Committee on the Judiciary, Subcommittee to Investigate Juvenile Delinquency. 1973. "The Detention and Jailing of Juveniles." 93d Congress, 1st Session.

U.S. Department of Justice. 1972–1992a. *Uniform Crime Reports for the United States.* Washington, DC: U.S. Department of Justice, Federal Bureau of Investigation.

U.S. Department of Justice. 1992b. *On the Front Lines: Case Studies of Policing in America's Cities.* Washington, DC: National Institute of Justice, The United States Conference of Mayors.

U.S. Department of Justice. 1993. *A Comprehensive Strategy for Serious, Violent and Chronic Juvenile Offenders.* Washington, DC: U.S. Department of Justice, Office of Juvenile Justice and Delinquency Prevention.

Urban Institute. 1989. *Comparison of Privately and Publicly Operated Corrections Facilities in Kentucky and Massachusetts.* Washington, DC: The Urban Institute (August).

Van Vleet, Russell, and Jeffrey A. Butts. 1990. *Risk Assessment of Committed Delinquents; Nebraska Youth Development Center.* University of Michigan: Center for the Study of Youth Policy (draft; February).

Waas, Murray. 1986. "Al Regnery's Secret Life; The Pathetic Career of Reagan's Juvenile Justice Chief." *The New Republic* 194 (23 June): 16–19.

Washington Crime News Service (Springfield, VA). 1986. "DOJ Caves in to Senate: Will Release FY '86 Grant Funds, Including OJJDP's $60,797,000." *Juvenile Justice Digest* 14, no. 8 (21 April): 1–8.

___. 1986. "OJJDP Funds: Senator Specter Holds Hearing on the Freeze; Controversial Grant Awarded." *Juvenile Justice Digest* 14, no. 5 (10 March): 1–9.

___. 1986. "Missing Kids: Bill Treanor Analyzes the Program and Finds Serious Flaws." *Juvenile Justice Digest* 14, no. 16 (25 August): 7–10.

___. 1992a "Youth Prison to be Built." *Juvenile Justice Digest* 20, no. 23 (2 December): 7.

___. 1992b. "Hickey School Director Says School has Improved, More Must be Done." *Juvenile Justice Digest* 20, no. 20 (21 October): 1 ff.

___. 1992c. "Maryland Terminates Contract with Hickey School Vendor." *Juvenile Justice Digest* 20, no. 23 (2 December): 1 ff.

Weil, M., and J. M. Karls. 1985. *Case Management in Human Service Practice.* San Francisco: Jossey-Bass.

Wentworth, C. K. 1979. "Washington State Juvenile Reform: Preventive Intervention and Social Control." Seattle, (December).

Wheeler, Stanton, and Leonard S. Cottrell. 1965. *Juvenile Delinquency—Its Prevention and Control.* New York: Russell Sage Foundation.

Willey, Robert J. 1985. "The History of Juvenile Law Reform in Ohio Since Gault." *Ohio Northern University Law Review* 12: 469–590.

Wilson, James Q. 1975. *Thinking About Crime.* New York: Basic Books.

Wilson, James Q., and Richard J. Herrnstein. 1985. *Crime and Human Nature.* New York: Simon and Schuster.

Wilson, John J. 1994. "Statement Concerning the Treatment of Juveniles in the Criminal Justice System." *Juvenile Justice Digest* 22, no. 15 (August 3).

Wolfgang, Marvin. 1982. "Abolish the Juvenile Court System." *California Lawyer* 2, no. 10.

Zatz, Marjorie S. 1987. "Chicano Youth Gangs and Crime: The Creation of a Moral Panic." *Contemporary Crises* 11: 129–58.

Zimring, Franklin E. 1981. *The Changing Legal World of Adolescence.* New York: Viking Press.

Zimring, Franklin E., and Gordon Hawkins. 1991. *The Scale of Imprisonment.* Chicago: University of Chicago Press.

Legal Cases:

People v. Turner 55 Ill. 280 (1870)
In re Gault. 387 U.S. 1 (1967)
In re Winship 397 U.S. 358 (1970)
McKeiver v. Pennsylvania 403 U.S. 528 (1971)
Schall v. Martin 467 U.S. 253 (1984)
Breed v. Jones 421 U.S. 519 (1975)
Kent v. United States 282 U.S. 541 (1966)
Miranda v. Arizona 384 U.S. 436 (1966)
Lewis v. State 259 Ind. 431 (1972)

Index

Abbott, Jack, 29
Accountability:
  agency, 135, 141;
  offender, 14, 26, 31, 37, 114, 140, 157, 159
Administrative decision making, 120–22, 138
Adult criminal justice system, 3, 5, 11–12, 15–16, 18, 20, 22, 27–29, 36–37, 41, 52, 56, 60, 68–69, 111, 123, 129–30, 164, 175, 181
Aftercare, 55, 76, 81–82, 138, 145, 148, 151–52, 157, 159, 170
Age of juvenile offenders:
  as mitigating circumstance, 16, 18, 27;
  at commitment, 10, 55, 63, 97, 116, 121–22, 140, 184;
  at first offense, 125, 128, 131, 160, 189, 191;
  boundaries of juvenile court and, 2, 17, 45, 90, 93, 102–4, 107, 111–12, 138–39;
  police response and, 78
Alabama Department of Youth Services, 48–49, 121–22, 128, 131, 166, 185–86, 187–88
Allegheny County Juvenile Court, 74–76
Allen, H.E., 174
Allen-Hagan, Barbara, 29
Alternatives to incarceration, 10, 35, 43, 57, 66, 121, 164, 167, 182;
  for status offenders, 12, 21, 22;
  in Alabama, 48, 121;
  in Allegheny County, 74–76;
  in Delaware, 53–54;

in detention, 71–72, 74;
in Florida, 51, 53;
in Georgia, 40, 46;
in Maryland, 56;
in Massachusetts, 70, 138–39, 144;
in North Dakota, 62;
in Ohio, 44;
in Virginia, 61;
privatized, 170
Altschuler, David, 81, 145
American Bar Association, 68
American Civil Liberties Union, 54, 178
American Correctional Association, 49
American Youth Work Center, 25
Annie E. Casey Foundation, 39
Armstrong, Troy, 67, 81, 145
Associated Marine Institutes, 153
Austin, James, 112, 113, 153

Baird, Christopher, 123, 129
Bandura, Albert, 83
Bartollas, Clemens, 29
Barton, William, 35, 60, 64, 71, 73, 145
Bayley, David, 81
Bazemore, Gordon, 157
Behn, R.D., 165
Bell, Carl, 83
Bengis, Steven, 154
Berke, Richard, 83
Bernard, Thomas, 70, 88, 90, 91
Biden, Senator Joseph, 22
Bishop, Donna,19, 52, 104, 112
Black, Donald, 78
Block, Kathleen, 168
Blomquist, Martha-Elin, 21, 24

207